A BRIEF COMMENTARY
ON THE
GOSPEL OF MARK

by
John J. Kilgallen, S.J.

PAULIST PRESS
New York/Mahwah

Library of Congress Cataloging-in-Publication Data

Kilgallen, John J.
    A brief commentary on the Gospel of Mark / by John J. Kilgallen.
        p.   cm.
    Bibliography: p.
    ISBN 0–8091–3059–9 : $9.95 (est.)
    1. Bible.   N.T. Mark—Commentaries.   I. Title.
    BS2585.3.K55   1989
226'.307—dc19   89–31027
                                                                          CIP

Published by Paulist Press
997 Macarthur Blvd.
Mahwah, N.J. 07430

Printed and bound in the United States of America

Contents

Foreword 1

Introduction 3

Chapter 1 17

Chapter 2 49

Chapter 3 63

Chapter 4 77

Chapter 5 92

Chapter 6 105

Chapter 7 125

Chapter 8 141

Chapter 9 165

Chapter 10 182

Contents

Chapter 11 203

Chapter 12 220

Chapter 13 241

Chapter 14 255

Chapter 15 277

Chapter 16 297

Conclusion 312

Suggested Further Reading 319

Foreword

At the foot of his cross, Jesus' taunters expressed a logic which is difficult to deny: "If you saved others, you can save yourself; if God loves you, he will save you." Now, Jesus neither saved himself, nor did God save him. So one should conclude, when all is said and done, that Jesus was powerless and unloved by God—certainly not God's Son. And really it is silly to assume that God's own saving plan included such an abrupt, painful, humiliating and total termination; where is divine power and wisdom in all this? It turns out to be safer and easier to explain Jesus as misguided and wrong, though at times powerful and wise, than to believe he was from God while being terminated so quickly, so painfully, so easily and so thoroughly.

Mark's gospel, traditionally the second of the four great gospels, wants a chance to explain why Jesus is credible as God's Son—no matter what was done to him or how weak and shameful he ultimately appeared. Indeed, he will show that Jesus never did or said anything wrong, never anything which merited crucifixion. But Mark goes much, much further. He realized that the key to Jesus' being from God was not finally a power which heals or a wisdom which guides, but obedience to God and love of all others. Thus, the life of Jesus was sometimes a life of power and wisdom, but always a life of love and obedience. It was this love and

obedience which brought Jesus through death to live forever. Indeed, Mark knows this to be what God most wanted
to convey through his Son. Let us turn now to see how Mark
says all this, as he replays for us in his own way the life of
Jesus.

Introduction

WHO WAS MARK?

The "second" gospel has always been called the gospel of Mark, meaning that Mark was its author. The gospel writer, very early tradition said, was equivalent to a secretary for St. Peter; in this role, Mark wrote down systematically, not randomly or haphazardly, the essential elements of speeches Peter would give either to prospective converts or to those already Christian. Moreover, Peter's secretary, many scholars hold, is to be identified as that John Mark who was a companion of St. Paul and St. Barnabas (John Mark's cousin) for a short period which included preaching in Cyprus and the beginnings of the Christian mission in what is now Turkey (Acts 12:25–13:13). It is this John Mark whose family had a house in Jerusalem, a house to which Peter went after an angel released him from prison (Acts 12:1–19; particularly v 12). From his associations with great apostles one can understand why, though Mark was not a companion with and eye-witness to Jesus himself, Mark's account has always enjoyed great trust and confidence.

WHERE DID MARK WRITE HIS GOSPEL?

Though, as just noted, Mark had a rather stable family in Jerusalem, the unswerving tradition of Christianity is that Mark wrote his gospel where Peter had done much of his

3

preaching: in Rome. A less trustworthy tradition has it that Mark wrote his gospel on the slope of the Capitoline Hill, now adjacent to the modern Piazza Venezia, near the spot where a church, St. Mark's, was built to commemorate the gospel writing.

FOR WHOM DID MARK WRITE?

It has always been the solid tradition that, as the writing was done in Rome, so the audience was Roman and/or those living in the vicinity of the city. Though the gospel does "argue" to make clear and defend many aspects of Christian belief, scholars agree that the audience is Christian rather than non-Christian. At times the gospel so treats of Jewish matters that one must conclude that a good part of Mark's audience was not Jewish; Mark 7:2–4, which takes time to explain Jewish customs, is one sure indication that Mark's readers were, by and large, people unfamiliar with Jewish mores. Thus, Mark's immediate audience is considered to be Roman, Christian, non-Jewish.

WHEN DID MARK WRITE HIS GOSPEL?

Centuries ago, it was thought that Mark's gospel, like so many other pieces of the New Testament, was written not long after the completion of Jesus' earthly life. Now, almost all scholars agree that Mark wrote his gospel about 65 A.D. There are three observations which, more than others, help determine this dating. The first is a rather erudite claim that one "senses" that the stage of development of the Christian ideas represented in Mark's gospel demands at least a thirty year period between Jesus' death (about 28 A.D.) and Mark's writing. The second puts a cap on that thirty year period, limiting it to a time before the destruction of Jerusalem in 70 A.D. That is to say, when one compares Mark's account of the predicted destruction of Jerusalem (13:14–42) with the similar predictions in Matthew (24:15–24) and Luke (21:20–24), it seems likely that the more detailed descriptions of Matthew and Luke are different from Mark's less precise description because Matthew and Luke wrote after the destruction of Jerusalem and Mark wrote before it—thus before 70 A.D. The third observation is this: there is so much about Mark's gospel which seems aimed at supporting Christians in trouble that it appears likely that Mark's Christians are undergoing (or about to undergo) the persecution of Nero, dated to the middle 60's A.D. For these three reasons, then, most scholars think Mark's gospel was written about 65 A.D.

WHY DID MARK WRITE HIS GOSPEL?

Many scholars believe that Mark wrote his gospel in order to support and console Christians who were either undergoing or about to undergo persecution at the hands of Nero. With this state of persecution in mind, Mark marshals stories from Jesus' time which will encourage readers to greater trust and fidelity, to follow Jesus' footsteps (which Mark describes as a "cross-carrying"). Indeed, many aspects of the gospel become more understandable if the readers are those threatened by punishments for their beliefs. Not the least of these elements of the gospel is Mark's consistent emphasis that the Jesus whom the Christians follow is not simply a Jesus who saves from predicaments—though he did that often enough in his Palestinian life. To know the deepest truth about Jesus is to know that he did not save himself at the time one would think he would—nor did God save him, either. The disciple does follow an all-powerful Lord, but the exercise of that power is not always the wisest means to true happiness.

Though the theory that Mark wrote for people in a time of persecution has much to recommend it, it still does not explain all the elements of the Marcan story, e.g., the struggles over interpretation of Jewish laws. Indeed, the more one studies Mark's gospel, the more one is convinced that Mark had multiple purposes for his writing—even though one or other purpose may be more important when weighed against others.

In my judgment, there are five goals which, taken together, adequately explain all the materials we find in the gospel of Mark. Not everything in the gospel is meant to achieve all five purposes or goals, but each element fits, in one way or another, under at least one of these goals.

First, Mark is concerned to show that Jesus, contrary to the condemnation of Jerusalem and Rome, was an innocent man. The manner of doing this is a simple re-presentation of the public life of Jesus which, if presented correctly, will show that Jesus never did or said anything wrong, and certainly nothing to deserve condemnation or crucifixion. To go through the public life of Jesus, as Mark indicates, is to understand well how false and gross the charges and misinterpretations were. By the end of the story, no matter what the "official" verdict many have said, the reader knows that Jesus was on all counts innocent and upright.

Second, and inevitably, the proper re-presentation of Jesus' public life must raise again the question: Who is he? That is to say, if the great judgment, "He is a charlatan," is wrong, what is the proper judgment to draw from all that he said and did and was? Indeed, after attention to the entire period, from John the Baptist's preaching to the words of the young man at the empty tomb, how can one conclude anything else but that Jesus was, in power and wisdom and personal integrity and holiness, the presence of God himself?

Third, if the review of Jesus' life does suggest the truth, the reality about Jesus, one must then, through certain stories, explain why this all-powerful and all-wise and all-holy person died so impotently, so shamefully, like a criminal, seated on a little perch on the vertical bar of his cross, with wrists tied and nailed to the cross, mocked as king of the Jews. If Jesus could be judged to be messiah, that one to inaugurate a new world, what sense is there to his pitiful and abrupt termination?

Fourth, if the full truth about Jesus comes clear through Mark's story, which combines the gloriousness of Jesus with his debasement and crucifixion, then an essential insight is also acquired concerning the fate of the follower of this Jesus. The disciple, too, can expect help from the power and wisdom and goodness of Jesus, but, since the messiah did not remove his disciples from the more painful aspects of this age, the disciple can expect suffering, too. Primarily it will be a suffering, subtle or flagrant, imposed by others for what he believes; but there will also be suffering involved in trying to walk the moral way Jesus did—whether in the effort to control one's own desires and to live through life's tragedies in a holy way, or in the effort to give all others the kind of love Jesus asks.

Finally, there are elements of the gospel which are best described as opportunities Mark takes to indicate why Christianity, at this time only some thirty years new, differs from the traditional, Jewish way of worshiping the one and true God. Thus, there will be moments in the life of Jesus which will serve to explain certain practices of Christianity that contrast with the practices and forms of the religion out of which Christianity grew.

These five headings, then, are an exhaustive list of goals which, one or more, will explain what Mark had in mind when he offered to Christians what we would call the "first" effort at writing such a lengthy connected narrative concerning the public life of Jesus. It is a type of narrative which, by making the reader take part in the events and in the whole arc of Jesus' life, coaxes the reader to make (again) a commitment to Jesus. It is a gospel. But why do we say it is "first"?

WAS MARK'S THE FIRST GOSPEL?

There are two ancient witnesses which do not seem to agree. One, which was referred to earlier, indicated that Mark was the secretary of Peter and thus drew the material from Peter which Mark would use for his gospel. A second ancient statement says that Matthew wrote the sayings of Jesus in the Aramaic (dialect of Hebrew) language, and the rest interpreted these as best they were able. Thus, if Mark is to be included as one of "the rest," this statement indicates that Mark got much of his gospel material from the translation Matthew made of the sayings of Jesus. And if Mark got his material from Matthew, it seems as if Matthew deserves to be called the first gospel.

Now, one can argue that gospels contain a lot more than just sayings of Jesus, that the gospels we have are not in Aramaic, but in Greek. Thus, whatever Mark may have taken from Matthew's translation, it may still be the case that Mark's gospel, as a whole, preceded Matthew's entire gospel. Still, one now hesitates as to how one should take the claim that Mark got his material from Peter, if so much of Matthew-in-Aramaic is truly at the root of Mark's work.

If we add to the above matter the fact that, since the time of St. Augustine (c. 400 A.D.), Matthew's gospel was considered the first of the four gospels (hence in our Bibles it is printed first), it was even more unlikely to say that Mark's gospel was the first. But then came the time of literary study of the gospels, of the study which considered the synoptic gospels (Matthew, Mark and Luke) purely and simply as literary works only. What did this literary study entail and what did it show about who came first?

This literary study, which has gone on for about two hundred years and actually is not over yet, starts from the literary phenomenon that in a number of places one of the synoptic gospels is practically word-for-word identical with another one or two synoptic gospels; even the order of stories is, in parts, identical. Added to these moments of "identicalness" are those times when there are great, great similarities between or among these gospels. The question must arise: How else explain these identities and similarities, if not by supposing either that one gospel copied from another, or that two (actually three) gospels copied from a source of which there is no remnant anymore?

Without going into further detail, the conclusion was slowly reached that it makes more sense to say that one of the known, existing gospels was source for the other two than to posit the existence of a fourth gospel of which we know absolutely nothing.

Moreover, and this is the key conclusion, it seemed (and still seems) better to say that Mark was read by Matthew and Luke (who did not know or read each other) than to say that Matthew or Luke was read by the other two. Thus, the study of the last two hundred years has arrived at the conclusion suggested by one of the ancient testimonies, that Mark was the earliest of the gospels; indeed, most scholars say (though there is a vocal minority in favor of Matthew as first gospel) that Mark was also a major source for Matthew and for Luke. I repeat that it is a study of the literary relationships among the gospels that yields the majority view that Mark was first and source for the others.

WHAT SOURCE(S) DID MARK HAVE?

The ancient witness seems to have answered this question: Mark used his notes from Peter's preaching to write his gospel. However, another suggestion, again based on purely literary study of the gospel, is that Mark inherited a number of stories which were fashioned, not by Peter, but by a variety of needs of the earliest church. That is to say, the earliest church, in order to exhort the believer to a better life, to defend its beliefs against attacks, to urge people to convert to Christianity, to instruct those interested in baptism—in order to do things like these, the earliest church preachers and teachers formulated stories from the events of Jesus' life. The nature of storymaking is to fit the details of an event in such a way as to achieve the purpose of the story. Four such purposes were just mentioned. One could add a fifth, the desire to communicate just precisely what happened on a certain day; the goal is nothing other than historical accuracy. Often, however, stories are formulated, not to tell all the facts or only the facts, but to expose the real meaning of an event; for this kind of story, success is measured, not by the number of facts recorded, but by the ability of the story-teller, whether by facts or other means, to expose for the reader the deepest meaning of the event.

The supposition is that the earliest church, in an effort to reach many people who were far from the time and place and mentality of Jesus, formulated many stories which sought meaning, rather than compilation of all the facts, of an event. Indeed, the purposes of the stories would eliminate those facts which would not fit the purposes. Moreover, if there was a certain accepted way of telling a story, one would adhere to that way, and thus leave out details which the literary form did not allow. (For instance, the way to tell a miracle story was to highlight the sickness, then the cure, then the reaction of people—and forget other details which had no relevance to the miracle itself.)

This supposition or hypothesis regarding how stories in our gospels originated has gained much popularity among scholars, since its emphasis in the early decades of the twentieth century. Indeed, one of the directions of scholarship has been to try to reconstruct both the original story behind the sometimes developed story we now have in the gospel and the event which lay behind the original story. If, indeed, one finds, in moving from the gospel story to the original story, that there were intervening, new formulations of the original story before the story got to its formulation as it stands in the gospel, then one happily engages in the study of the history of the story, how it first was made, how it changed and changed until it reached the way it stands in the gospel.

All of this adds up, again, to a view which differs from that ancient witness who gives the impression that Mark got the bulk of his material only from Peter and that the sequence should be kept simple: event to Peter, Peter to Mark.

MARK'S "MESSIANIC SECRET"

To talk only of what Mark received from others is to risk ignoring what Mark might have written into the gospel himself, whether it be a word or phrase (e.g., 7:19c), or introductions and conclusions to stories and summaries of events, or even the whole construction of the gospel. One major contribution of Mark in this area is his making the reader concentrate on what has been called the messianic secret. What, precisely, is the meaning of this Marcan emphasis?

"Messiah" means "anointed," and in Greek is translated by the adjective "Christos." Why is someone called "anointed"? In Jewish history, the symbol to everyone that someone is king is his anointing, just as the symbol to everyone that a person is president of the United States is his raising his right hand and pronouncing the oath of office. Anointing is a gesture indicating that the "anointed one" now has a task to perform for the good of the people. King David was perhaps the best known "anointed one" in Jewish history.

Now, in the Jewish expectation of things, God would one day establish a kingdom which would be solely and totally good, because God alone would be king; this belief was particularly strong after a small part of old Israel came back, humiliated and poor and enslaved, from its Babylonian exile (587 B.C.–538 B.C.). But to begin this kingdom of glory and goodness, God would send a human being who was "anointed" (= messiah) for the task. And here is where the problem begins, in Christian eyes.

Israel expected a messiah of power; he would erase all Israel's enemies, indeed all the enemies of human existence. If a person did not do this, he was not to be judged the messiah. Given what Jesus knew would be his fate and given what Mark, by hindsight, knew was Jesus' fate, the Christian view held that Jesus was messiah, but not the messiah as defined by Israel; indeed, Israel misconceived the true definition of messiah. Not that Jesus did not have the power to overcome all enemies, of Israel and of human existence itself. But he did not change this world or Israel's world into an age where death, humiliation, slavery, poverty, mental and physical suffering were abolished and only happiness reigned. In fact, his public life was ultimately controlled and ended by other men—surely a sign that he was not the messiah to carry out God's plan.

These clashing interpretations of messiah led Mark to highlight in his gospel Jesus' reluctance to have people call him messiah. Why call him messiah, if they do not grasp what is the true meaning of messiah, especially if they have only experienced the power of Jesus and not his final, terrible end? Indeed, will they continue to call him messiah, once they see him impotent on the cross? And so, Jesus is pictured in the gospel, particularly in the early sections, as wanting no one to call him messiah solely on the basis of his powerful deeds and his wisdom.

"Messiah," then, according to Jesus' understanding of God's plan, was not a person who would change this world by acts of power. He was a person who, though indeed all-powerful and at times showing it, did not change this world into a new one, a person who certainly taught the nearness of the kingdom of God, but whose message about the coming of this wonderful kingdom was very different from what his contemporaries expected. Can we explain this very different view of Jesus? It runs as follows.

For many people, the key to happiness is a miracle which will change circumstances: a healing, a driving out of demons, a life without pain and death. Through Jesus' life we learn that the change God seeks is the change of the human heart, of the human will. For God can control all things except a human being's free choice; to control that is to remove freedom—which is exactly the one thing that makes a human being human. Thus, God comes asking for a change of heart, a free choice to turn away from sin, a repentance, which is regret for what is against the love of God and love of neighbor, and conversion, or return to love of God and love of neighbor. This was the mission for which Jesus was anointed: to turn sinners from their sin, and thus prepare them for life with God. But there is more.

In some way there was always in Israel a conviction that sins must be expiated, made up for; without this expiation, this "making up for sins," life with God seemed impossible. Jesus became the one and only sacrifice by which the sins of the world could be and were washed away. For this supreme and unique task Jesus was anointed.

Thus, while Jesus did exercise the power and wisdom associated with the notion of the messiah, he also called for repentance and died for sins, which were necessary for life in the kingdom of God, but never thought to be the tasks of the messiah before Jesus did them. So, was Peter right in saying, halfway through the public life of Jesus, that Jesus is messiah? He was not totally wrong, but he had neither the experience nor the understanding of the truth about the messiah to be allowed to go on saying Jesus is messiah. At best he, and others, would be misleading. So Jesus asked him not to say, till after the resurrection of Jesus from the dead, that Jesus is messiah. Such is the messianic secret Mark stresses in his gospel.

There is one other observation to be made concerning the content of the messianic secret. Even after Jesus died so that sins might be forgiven and called people to repentance, and even after some did repent to follow the way of life he taught, still Jesus did not inaugurate a new age in which God alone is king. We still have suffering and failures and anguish and death as part of the very fabric of our existence. Why, if he is messiah, did he not change this world into the world-to-come?

There are no final answers, only suggestions about this part of the messiah's task. Two points are in order here. First, the Father did not even change Jesus' world into a better one, even though Jesus was his most loved of all; if he did not hasten to change the circumstances of the one most loved, he must have good reason. Second, Jesus did enter the "new age," actually, when he rose from the dead. This suggests that we, too, will enter the new age, but only by passing through, not avoiding, death and all the little deaths on our way there. Thus, God does have a kingdom of peace and joy prepared, but it is timed to come at a moment and in a way different from human expectation. Therefore, Mark can say, in the light of events and much meditation on them, that if one will allow serious changes in, but not total abandonment of, the idea, Jesus is indeed the messiah. Such, then, is the secret: the definition of messiah, the one anointed to save, fits Jesus, but it is not our definition that fits, but God's.

Let us put a cap on the introductory questions and turn now to let ourselves, as readers, become part of the story of Jesus—as Mark tells it to us.

Chapter 1

The first line of Mark's gospel is Mark's own creation and in fact is really a statement of Mark's faith. This statement can be broken down into four parts.

1. Mark is indicating that "here" is the beginning of the good news, the gospel. Surely, we know which is the first page of Mark's gospel, so he could not be pointing out to us the rather simple fact that this sentence is where the reader should begin. There are two possible explanations of what Mark intends to convey when he says, "The beginning . . ."

To help explain one possible meaning of "the beginning," we should consider a very early statement of Mark's gospel, that, whereas John baptized with water, the one coming after him will baptize with the Holy Spirit. Now, Mark never actually brings his story to the point where this prediction is specifically fulfilled. Why would Mark ever put into his story a description of Jesus which is never fulfilled? The answer is that Mark intended by his gospel to present only "the beginning" of the good news. That is, he knew there was more to the life of Jesus than what he narrated, but, for his own reasons, he chose to limit himself to Jesus' public life. By calling his story only "the beginning," Mark subtly shows his awareness of the many saving events which occurred after the close of his narrative.

SCRIPTURE TEXT

1 The beginning of the gospel of Jesus Christ, the Son
of God.
2 As it is written in Isaiah the prophet,
"Behold, I send my messenger before thy face,
who shall prepare thy way;
³the voice of one crying in the wilderness:
Prepare the way of the Lord,
make his paths straight—"
⁴John the baptizer appeared in the wilderness, preaching
a baptism of repentance for the forgiveness of sins. ⁵And
there went out to him all the country of Judea, and all
the people of Jerusalem; and they were baptized by him
in the river Jordan, confessing their sins. ⁶Now John was
clothed with camel's hair, and had a leather girdle
around his waist, and ate locusts and wild honey. ⁷And
he preached, saying, "After me comes he who is mightier
than I, the thong of whose sandals I am not worthy to
stoop down and untie. ⁸I have baptized you with water;
but he will baptize you with the Holy Spirit."

9 In those days Jesus came from Nazareth of Galilee
and was baptized by John in the Jordan. ¹⁰And when he
came up out of the water, immediately he saw the heavens opened and the Spirit descending upon him like a
dove; ¹¹and a voice came from heaven, "Thou art my
beloved Son; with thee I am well pleased."

12 The Spirit immediately drove him out into the
wilderness. ¹³And he was in the wilderness forty days,
tempted by Satan; and he was with the wild beasts; and
the angels ministered to him.

14 Now after John was arrested, Jesus came into

Galilee, preaching the gospel of God, [15]and saying, "The time is fulfilled, and the kingdom of God is at hand; repent, and believe in the gospel."

16 And passing along by the Sea of Galilee, he saw Simon and Andrew the brother of Simon casting a net in the sea; for they were fishermen. [17]And Jesus said to them, "Follow me and I will make you become fishers of men." [18]And immediately they left their nets and followed him. [19]And going on a little farther, he saw James the son of Zebedee and John his brother, who were in their boat mending the nets. [20]And immediately he called them; and they left their father Zebedee in the boat with the hired servants, and followed him.

21 And they went into Caperna-um; and immediately on the sabbath he entered the synagogue and taught. [22]And they were astonished at his teaching, for he taught them as one who had authority, and not as the scribes. [23]And immediately there was in their synagogue a man with an unclean spirit; [24]and he cried out, "What have you to do with us, Jesus of Nazareth? Have you come to destroy us? I know who you are, the Holy One of God." [25]But Jesus rebuked him, saying, "Be silent, and come out of him!" [26]And the unclean spirit, convulsing him and crying with a loud voice, came out of him. [27]And they were all amazed, so that they questioned among themselves, saying, "What is this? A new teaching! With authority he commands even the unclean spirits, and they obey him." [28]And at once his fame spread everywhere throughout all the surrounding region of Galilee.

29 And immediately he left the synagogue, and entered the house of Simon and Andrew, with James and John. [30]Now Simon's mother-in-law lay sick with a fever, and immediately they told him of her. [31]And he came and

took her by the hand and lifted her up, and the fever left her; and she served them.

32 That evening, at sundown, they brought to him all who were sick or possessed with demons. [33]And the whole city was gathered together about the door. [34]And he healed many who were sick with various diseases, and cast out many demons; and he would not permit the demons to speak, because they knew him.

35 And in the morning, a great while before day, he rose and went out to a lonely place, and there he prayed. [36]And Simon and those who were with him pursued him, [37]and they found him and said to him, "Every one is searching for you." [38]And he said to them, "Let us go on to the next towns, that I may preach there also; for that is why I came out." [39]And he went throughout all Galilee, preaching in their synagogues and casting out demons.

40 And a leper came to him beseeching him, and kneeling said to him, "If you will, you can make me clean." [41]Moved with pity, he stretched out his hand and touched him, and said to him, "I will; be clean." [42]And immediately the leprosy left him, and he was made clean. [43]And he sternly charged him, and sent him away at once, [44]and said to him, "See that you say nothing to any one; but go, show yourself to the priest, and offer for your cleansing what Moses commanded, for a proof to the people." [45]But he went out and began to talk freely about it, and to spread the news, so that Jesus could no longer openly enter a town, but was out in the country; and people came to him from every quarter.

Another, second way of explaining Mark's "the beginning" is to point to the fact that the real beginning of the good news of Jesus Christ is (as he notes immediately with verse 2) the Old Testament, which, as preparation for and explanation of Jesus, is summed up in the two citations Mark explicitly gives us here. The story of Jesus, Mark believes, begins with the expectations God sowed through his Old Testament words, and so it is with them that Mark begins.

2. Mark notes that what has its beginning in the Old Testament is the good news "of Jesus." "Good news of Jesus" can certainly mean good news "from Jesus," and can at the same time mean good news "about Jesus." But it seems best to say that "good news of Jesus" means good news "which is Jesus." By the way Mark has presented Jesus, one realizes that it is the very person of Jesus which is the source of all hope. It is his wisdom and his power which dominate all evil, which are the Christian's hope. It is his death which removes our sins, his blood which brings about the new covenant. He is the completion of Old Testament hopes and promises; beyond him, after him, there is no one else. The eventual judgment will be conducted by him; for those who follow him, his final appearance will be the moment of final salvation. Finally, Jesus, as Mark presents him, calls for faith, not just in what he says or does, but in himself. The good news, then, is not just a message or a deed, but a person, good news.

3. Mark continues his act of faith by calling Jesus "Christ." It was most unusual that Israelites of first century Palestine had a last name (Jesus would have been known as Jesus, son of Joseph); thus, "Christ" was originally really a title which Christians earlier than Mark used so often of Jesus that it became the equivalent of a last name. Whether as formal title or present last name, "Christ" is a statement of faith, that Jesus is messiah (which is Aramaic, meaning

"anointed one"). Jesus is professed, then, to be that person who will introduce God's kingdom, for such was the task people came to expect of God's messiah. The term "messiah" is most associated with royalty (though sometimes with priest and prophet), and particularly with the sons of David, whose anointing was symbol that they were kings like their father. When Jesus' contemporaries were debating whether Jesus was messiah or not, most of them were really wondering if he was the Davidic successor who would initiate God's kingdom among them. Mark says "yes," that Jesus is messiah, even a royal messiah, but only according to God's definition of messiah, not according to that of human beings. According to God, the messiah is anointed for three tasks: to call people to readiness to meet and live with God, to die for the sins of all human beings, and to be himself an example of that free gift of love to the Father which will bring one from this age, through death, to life forever. If the messiah is royal, it is in the sense that his word rules the lives of all and will eventually destroy all enemies. Mark had all this in mind, then, when he begins his gospel by confessing that Jesus is messiah.

4. The final element of Mark's opening statement of his faith is that Jesus Christ is Son of God. To many scholars, the title "Son of God," is a synonym for messiah. They point to the Old Testament language, where, indeed, the two titles are often synonymous. But since "Son of God" is not always reserved for the anointed Davidic king, but even at times tries to express divinity in some manner, it is better to look to the entire presentation of the life of Jesus for what Mark means when he calls Jesus Son of God. Without going too deeply into the matter here, one notes that only God and demons find it easy to call Jesus "Son of God"; that the words of the centurion at the cross of Jesus, perhaps not consonant with his paganism, are a response to which Mark, from his

own point of view, can give vigorous assent; that parables, while depicting great figures of Israel's past as "servants," call Jesus "God's beloved Son"; that the gospel ends with an event concerning Jesus which leaves the reader aware that he is in the presence of divinity, however it is to be explained. These elements of the gospel, and others, suggest that Mark presents not only a Jesus who functions as a faithful Son and is beloved by God as Israel's rulers in the past were loved by God; these many elements suggest that Mark knew, without giving explanation other than story, that Jesus was the presence of divinity.

THE PROPHECIES

After his statement of faith by which he introduces his work, Mark asks his reader to consider two prophecies (not one, as Mark says), which have the purpose of introducing the entire Jesus event, but particularly the figure of John the Baptist.

The sentence, "Behold, I am sending my messenger before you, who will prepare your way," is from Malachi (3:1, with help from Exodus 23:20); the rest of the citation is from Isaiah (40:30). Each deserves some comment.

When Malachi wrote, he wrote in such a way that he was quoting God; thus, the original text, as the prophet wrote it, was: "Behold I (= God) am sending my messenger before *me*, who will prepare *my* way." It is Mark who has changed the italicized pronouns, so that the text, as he gives it, indicates that the messenger God is to send is to go before "you," to prepare "your" way. In this way, Mark indicates his perception that the deeper meaning of scripture really had Jesus in mind as the one whose way a messenger was to prepare. It is conceivable that Mark thought this change slight, since he considered Jesus to be, as we have seen, the presence of God himself. In any event, it is clear that, whereas Malachi thought that Elijah, brought back to life, would be the messenger to prepare God's way, Mark has tailored the citation to fit the facts as he knew them: John the Baptist is God's messenger sent to prepare the way for Jesus.

Similarly, Mark touched up the citation from Isaiah, in order to show better how its deepest meaning applied to the Jesus event. For Isaiah, the "voice" was most likely his own, and it was "crying," but not in the desert, for Isaiah was a wealthy and influential man, who would cry, if anywhere, in the Jerusalem temple; rather, "in the desert" is meant to go with the words, "prepare the way of the Lord," thus inviting the people to go out morally, symbolically into the desert for a new cleansing, to prepare to meet the God who comes to them.

It is Mark who changes things so that the "voice crying," now John the Baptist, is a voice crying "in the desert," which is in fact the place where John cried for repentance. Moreover, though Isaiah would have understood "Lord" in his verse to mean Yahweh, it is likely that Mark, in light of what he has already professed, now understands "Lord" to be Jesus, whose paths, Isaiah continues, are to be made straight, at John's behest.

The quotations from Malachi and Isaiah are contained actually in a subordinate clause, which means that they serve to prepare for Mark's main clause. The whole ensemble of subordinate and main clauses is meant to say that, *as* God indicated in ancient times that he would send a messenger before a certain "you," *so* John came, baptizing in the desert and announcing a baptism by which the baptized professed a personal repentance which leads to forgiveness of sins (and was received enthusiastically by many people, and lived like a dedicated man) and announced that there was coming one who was greater than he, who would, like himself, baptize, but, unlike himself, baptize with the Holy Spirit. Thus, vv 2–8 are really one long rambling sentence, the essence of which should be better understood if one considers how the coming of John fits the descriptions given by Malachi and Isaiah.

Unlike other gospels, Mark's gospel offers only the essentials about John's message. John is presented as a man who is trustworthy in himself (his clothing and food indicate his sincerity and dedication) and as one who "prepares the Lord's way" by calling for repentance, reflected in baptism. What Mark presents here is a Christian theme: that repentance for sins precedes forgiveness and that outpouring of the Spirit which only Jesus could give. As repentance prepares for God's gift of forgiveness and of his own very self or Spirit, so John prepares for Jesus.

As Mark describes him, then, John is the one who prepared the way of the Lord Jesus, who will baptize with the Holy Spirit. It is at this point that Mark introduces Jesus to his readers. And it is not by chance that, just after John completes his witness to Jesus by saying that Jesus will baptize with the Holy Spirit, Jesus is described as baptized and as one into whom the Holy Spirit descends. In this way, Mark shows that Jesus, who for his own reasons underwent the lesser baptism of John, is now prepared, by virtue of the Holy Spirit's entering into him, to administer the greater baptism, that of the Holy Spirit.

But before looking to the meaning of the divine appearance and speech after Jesus' baptism, let us reflect for a moment on the baptism itself. Because Mark has described John's baptism as a baptism of that repentance which leads to forgiveness of sins, some people have thought that Jesus, by having himself baptized, is admitting that he is repentant and looking for forgiveness. Such a conclusion not only clashes with other parts of the New Testament faith, such as the expression in Hebrews 4:15, "like us in all things except sin," but contradicts the figure which comes to us through the stories Mark narrates. One is faithful to Mark if one thinks that Jesus came to John's baptism, not because Jesus was a sinner, but because Jesus wanted to embrace and encourage publicly the call to repentance which undergirded the baptism. Indeed, Jesus himself will soon appear as one calling for repentance, and this call will characterize the rest of his days in Israel and be the underpinning for all else he will say and do. The goal of John is Jesus' own goal; it is not surprising that he supports John by entering into the symbol itself. One can further think of Jesus at this baptism as one of a family or a nation or a town who, himself not guilty of sin, joins in, out of a sense of solidarity with those who are guilty, to ask for forgiveness; in this way, the baptism which begins the story foreshadows the death, for forgiveness, with which the gospel draws to a close.

Though Mark notes that Jesus is baptized, it is clear that he puts more emphasis on what occurred "as Jesus was coming out of the water," after his baptism. In brief, we have here a theophany, i.e., a divine appearance. It is limited in the sense that God himself does not appear; rather, after the heavens are rent asunder and the Holy Spirit of God, symbolized by a dove, enters into Jesus, the voice of God speaks and explains the meaning of this entrance of the Spirit into Jesus—such are the contours of this theophany.

One of the fundamental revelations of this moment is that, from now on, Jesus is possessed by and under the powerful influence of the Holy Spirit of God. It is this possession by the Holy Spirit which accounts for Jesus' immense change of life from quiet worker in out-of-the-way Nazareth to great preacher and teacher and wonder-worker and, ultimately, savior of all through his death for all. Mark does not have the habit (nor do many writers of his time) of entering into the psychology of the human Jesus. He professes that what caused Jesus to change his life and brought about what Mark will describe in the rest of his gospel is nothing less than God's own Holy Spirit in Jesus.

In no way does this entrance of the Holy Spirit into Jesus deny his divinity. Even if one explicitly says from the start that Jesus was always divine, one must still account for the sudden change in manner of life of this divine person. Clearly, the change came after Jesus was baptized by John; all gospels and the Acts of the Apostles witness to this. Matthew and Luke, as well as Mark, profess that Jesus, from this moment, is driven by the Spirit of God. Rather than considering this gift of the Spirit a contradiction to Jesus' divinity, one must (and can) integrate the divinity of Jesus with this movement of the Spirit in Jesus which the sacred writers describe.

The possession of Jesus by the Spirit, then, is not to make Jesus divine. Why, then, does the Spirit take possession of Jesus? It is the voice from heaven which clarifies this.

Of itself, calling someone "my beloved, in whom I am well-pleased," is confessing publicly one's love for this someone. Evidently, these words, spoken to Jesus (though recounted for the reader's benefit, too), are an indication to Jesus how loved he is by the Father. As they stand, one cannot miss the august implication that the one speaking considers Jesus to be his Son, so loved is he. But that is not the complete message. The complete message had the effect of changing Jesus' life completely; what more did it contain than the public affirmation of God's immense, unique love for Jesus?

Some scholars see in God's use of the term "my beloved" a subtle reference to an earlier beloved, Isaac, whom his father was willing to sacrifice out of obedience. In an imperfect comparison, it is now the Father who, for his own reasons of love, asks his "beloved" to die. In suggesting this Isaac motif, Mark would have not only given resonance to the death of Jesus, but would have shown how, as though intended by the Old Testament, Jesus' death was anticipated.

Many scholars think, however, that the term "my beloved" evokes another "beloved of God," the mysterious servant of God, described by Isaiah in four poems (42:1–7; 49:1–6; 50:4–11; 52:13–53:12), and called, precisely, "my beloved." This servant, understood in later generations as a saving figure still to come, was to preach, to heal, to suffer and, finally, to redeem; he is beloved because God can trust him with the saving task, even to death.

Given the way in which the figure of Jesus emerges from the writing of Mark, it is not surprising that Mark would have opened his gospel with God's identification of Jesus as the fulfillment of the promised servant; indeed, here, at the beginning of the gospel, we can understand this divine voice to be asking Jesus to take the mission of the servant on himself and the gift of the Spirit to be the divine movement driving the Son to change his life in order to execute the will of the Father.

Given the way in which the gospel unfolds, then, it seems best to see here in this mysterious theophany the moment in which Jesus changes his life completely, in obedience to the divine movement and direction, toward a life of ministry and sacrifice.

The post-baptism voice to Jesus, which explains to him and to us the presence of the Spirit within Jesus, indicates the direction in which the gospel will now go: Jesus, in some sense, receives the direction and inspiration of the Spirit of God which results in the rest of the gospel story. In this way the post-baptismal theophany is interpreted as the inauguration of the public life of Jesus.

Mark does not draw the lines so tightly, yet one begins to think that the theophany is not unrelated to the baptism Jesus has just undergone. The Father, in revealing to Jesus the purpose for which the Spirit is to work within him, has said to Jesus, ". . . in you I found favor." Though we translate this verb as present tense (I find favor), it actually refers to something in the past. Probably what Mark had in mind here is that God, pleased with Jesus' devotion to him in allowing himself to be baptized, now responds to this devotion by giving Jesus the mission, under the influence of the Holy Spirit, which will be developed through the length of the gospel. In this way we can see how the theophany of the Father fits well with the baptism Jesus willingly underwent.

It is probably correct to see in this baptismal and theophanic story instruction for the disciple of Jesus, who, having undergone baptism, can also expect now to have a life, in certain fundamental ways, which imitates that of his master.

Jesus, by accepting baptism, professes his devotion and love toward his Father; his Father, in turn, now asks of his Son a life of dedication as minister of salvation. It is this intimacy and unique relationship which begins to suggest that, in some mysterious way, both the Father and Jesus are divine. We cannot forget Mark's opening profession of faith, that Jesus is Messiah and Son of God.

From his experience of the theophany Jesus goes further into the desert, "thrown out there," as Mark so graphically puts it, by the Holy Spirit who now dominates Jesus' life. Clearly, the brief descriptive pictures Mark draws for the reader here suggest that this Jesus is full of mystery. Here he is, being tested or tempted by Satan himself, living among the wild animals, cared for by angels. Each of these images highlights how unique Jesus is, how he can live at the extremities of human experience.

But is Mark being more specific in his suggestiveness? Is the reader to see in the reference to "forty days" a suggestion that Jesus represents the people of Israel who wandered under temptation and testing for "forty years" through the desert? Is he more particularly to be thought of as a new Moses? That Jesus was tested or tempted by Satan—is there here a hint that we should think of him as a new Adam? That Jesus lived with the wild animals, evidently without harm—is Mark hinting that Jesus is that wonderful figure, described in Isaiah, who would bring such peace to the world that wild animals would live with him in harmony? Or is this, again, an attempt to parallel Jesus with Adam, who lived with and showed his preternatural dominion over the animal world, when he named all the animals? Perhaps, if one makes certain adjustments, one is expected to understand that Jesus is that wonderful figure of Psalm 91 who is so beloved to God that God will save him from all enemies and from all harm, even to overcoming threats from the animal kingdom and being served and protected by angels.

Whatever Mark's full purpose in this brief description of Jesus' time in the desert, he has evoked a wondrous figure, one which, in particular, is hardly preparing himself to mislead Israel. Indeed, Mark will soon convey to us that Jesus' going into desert or lonely places to pray is a fixed pattern in his public life; Judas, as he made plans for betrayal, knew that he could count on Jesus' being at prayer in the quiet garden after the last supper. Such a longing to be with the Father gives clear indication of Jesus' priorities and simplicity, of his intimacy with the Father, of his own thirst for the Father while encouraging others to repentance and reunion with God. Above all, one realizes that Jesus acts under the impulse of God's Spirit. It must be right and just action.

Though the first thirteen verses of Mark introduce Jesus,

Jesus is not yet the active force in his story. Thus, these thirteen verses are considered to be verses which introduce the story and person of Jesus. By them, the reader has been led into the mystery of Jesus' intimacy with the Father and been given clear indication of the holiness of Jesus. These verses give the reader much more information that the contemporaries of Jesus were given before they met Jesus and had to make decisions about him. Such is the value of Mark's guidance that the reader, though meeting Jesus along with others, knows in advance so much more than they; through this literary device the reader is well prepared to judge correctly just how the crowds should have reacted, just what correct decisions Jesus' words and actions called for. The reader, through this introduction, is part of the crowd, yet more knowledgeable than it. The reader, then, can offer the proper responses to the call and invitation and person of Jesus.

John the Baptist had explicitly stated that there was coming "after him" one mightier than he. Now, Jesus is reported as going into Galilee "after John's imprisonment." Jesus leaves the desert area *after* John was arrested; does he leave *because* John was arrested? John's gospel, though alone in this, notes that Jesus in his early days made and baptized more disciples than John the Baptist, and that it was when the Pharisees heard about this that Jesus moved northward again into Galilee (John 4:1–3). Though John's gospel talks about the Pharisees whereas Mark's gospel talks about John's arrest, they seem to agree in the suggestion that it was something inimical to the preaching in the desert which was the material reason for Jesus' move away, into the relatively freer area of Galilee. (Galilee was ruled by Herod Antipas and not the Roman procurator, Pilate; it also was an area less subject to the religious intensity of Jerusalem and its environs, which included the deserted areas of John and Jesus.) Luke explains that the more profound impulse to move his place of preaching came from the Holy Spirit within Jesus (4:14). In all of this, we can see how the Spirit of God worked with human causes to effect changes in Jesus' circumstances.

With the notice of John's imprisonment, Mark effectively completes John's role in the work of salvation. Only in Mark 6:14–29 will John again occupy the reader's attention, but here is only the recounting of Herod Antipas' shameful execution of John.

With verses 14–15, one senses that Jesus has now taken his place as the protagonist of Mark's work; the introduction is over. As often with such works as this gospel, these first verses present the basic program of God's representative. Here the reader's first encounter with Jesus is an encounter with him as one who announces God's good message, which can be expressed by the premises, "The time (of waiting) is completed and the kingdom of God is at hand," and by the conclusions, "Repent and believe in the good message." The four expressions, "completion of time," "kingdom of God," "repentance," and "belief in the message" are fundamental to understanding Jesus and his times, as well as the times after him. Thus, we dedicate some time to explanations of them.

"The Time Is Full." The image itself suggests that time is something which begins empty and gradually reaches its capacity by the events which pile up through the course of time. This way of imagining time underscores the limitedness of time, making clear that the events which fill time up will be only so many. Here, Jesus is indicating that, with John, the last of the representatives of the Old Testament period, gone, the Old Testament period of expectation and hope is filled up, has reached its point of completion. What was supposed to happen after the "filling up" can and will now take place.

What is to take place now? Since about 530 B.C. the conviction grew among Jews who studied their scriptures that God was planning to intervene someday in a decisive way in Israel's, and the whole world's, affairs. His love for Israel made his scriptural promises absolutely trustworthy. This sense that God would take up the cause of his chosen people overrode whatever might be the punishments Israel had to suffer because of its infidelities to Yahweh. Israel had been consistently warned that its sinful activities demanded punishment, that it could not count on its status as favorite of Yahweh to escape payment for its sins, that the prosperity experienced under God's direction and culminating in the Davidic-Solomonic monarchy of the 900's B.C. had to be lost as retribution for coldness of heart toward God and human beings. But with the release of God's loving hand for a while grew the conviction that there would come again a time when God would call "Enough!" and then once again enter into Israel's life in such a way that he would be the dominant force therein, that his blessed and just judgments would rule Israel, that Israel's beloved would remove all forces inimical to Israel, would heal Israel and bring to it a life of justice and peace, prosperity and joy—in short, the kind of life that should exist when divine love, after removing all enemies, pours itself wholly and endlessly on its beloved. Israel was confident that such divine love would one day exert itself in this thrilling fashion—and now it is Jesus' message, the good news, that the time of waiting, of promises is at last over.

"The Kingdom Has Come." The fact that Israel conceived of its future and ideal life with God as "kingdom" is for the most part historically determined. Though Israel for centuries traced its origins to Abraham, Isaac and Jacob, who were far from kings, and only hundreds of years after the exodus developed the structures which welcomed the government of a king, it is the remembrance of the kings David and Solomon that produced most of the royal images in which Israel's final future would be described. Particularly, the power and influence of old royalty were read against the pinching humiliation, slavery and poverty of the hundreds of years of suffering before the time of Jesus. God himself, Israel projected, was the one who, as in ancient days, would exert his power in such wise that Israel, freed and glorified, would itself rule in power and judgment over all the nations—a fitting role for God's chosen one. So Israel looked forward to the time when God alone would be its king, when divine power, directed by divine wisdom and love, would alone rule Israel. It is this image which Jesus called upon to express the good message he felt called upon to deliver.

There is still no total agreement among interpreters as to what Jesus meant by saying that the kingdom of God "is near." The Greek verb in Mark's gospel can mean that the kingdom is "present," but it can also mean that the kingdom is "near." Obviously, to be present is not always quite the same as to be near. Looked at from the perspective of the entire gospel, it seems best to say that in Jesus are all the seeds and powers needed to bring the kingdom to its fullest expression. That he restricted divine power and love and wisdom only to certain areas and limited them only to certain directions is a mystery. Yet Mark's conviction is that the kingdom has begun in that Jesus, the source of all power and love and wisdom, is no longer a promise, but is present forever. What he has accomplished will remain and needs only completion; this is significantly different from saying that nothing has been accomplished, that we are waiting in hope for the beginning.

"Repentance." This word includes the notion of "change of way of life," but means, first of all, a "change of one's ways of thinking, of one's evaluations." Thus, the word suggests what nature instinctively senses, that what one does very often depends on what one thinks about things, that change of habits will not go far if such change contradicts one's values, particularly one's own agreement that such a change is worthwhile. Such is the meaning of the word, but why does it form so central a place in Jesus' inaugural preaching?

For centuries, prophets of Israel had told their people that God "was coming." The corollary to this "coming" is preparation or readiness. One can further imagine that one is to go out to meet God who is coming or one is to wait for the ever closer approach of the great and mighty God. In either case, one must be ready. For all God's revelation of himself as spouse, parent, friend, covenant partner, God was still absolutely and infinitely holy and must always be given the respect and homage his awesome majesty deserves. This respect and homage translated itself not merely into liturgical worship of the Creator, but even more into a concomitant holiness on the part of the creature which would reflect that of God. In short, one must be holy to stand in the presence of God; if a creature feared the presence of its Creator, how much more would an unholy, sinful creature tremble?

This holiness was more and more called for as Israel grew to realize that its national grief and pain were punishments for its sins, its unholiness. It was a holiness which resulted from obedience to the will of the all-Holy One. The clearest expression of this will was the Mosaic law, that wonderful gift of wisdom about life, given only to Israel.

When, then, Jesus came to announce with eagerness that God is near, the logical conclusion was to call for that repentance which would make one stand worthily before God when he came. From this perspective, all of life since Jesus' fundamental message is the continual effort to be holy for the day of God's final and total presence among us. One may argue as to how much one accomplishes on one's own and how much God, in his infinite love, makes us holy; the bottom line is the conviction that, in this imagery, one must be holy to be in the presence of God—and he is near!

"Believe in the Good News!" Jesus' call for repentance is supported by his encouragement to believe what he says, namely, that God is near. Change and believe he is not far from you now!

These words become a bit more subtle in their meaning, however, from Mark's point of view. For Mark, not only is God near, but he is present in Jesus. Thus, when Mark uses Jesus' words, he wants the reader to believe not only in Jesus' good news, that God is near, but also in Mark's good news, that God is in Jesus, that Jesus is the completion of the old and the start (not just the promise) of the new. It is in the double meaning of this imperative, and of other expressions like it, that one sees how the author uses Jesus' words about good news to express his own understanding of the full good news.

Jesus' message is recorded; he begins his travels to bring it everywhere, in and out of Galilee. Inevitably, the first answer to the call to repentance is a study of the caller's credentials; who is this who asks this of me? Human beings study this person from various angles: some already skeptical, some not far from jealousy, some unwilling to change and thus looking for reasons not to, some ready to concede a bit of trust and walk further with him. It is to this mix of reactions that Mark now plunges Jesus—and his reader.

Mark has placed the main message of Jesus, framed against the hopes and desires of Israel, at the head of his gospel. Now he turns the reader's attention to the beginning of another major element of his gospel, to the gathering of some of Jesus' most intimate companions. These, the first four, will soon be expanded into what will become known as "the twelve," or "the twelve disciples," or "the twelve apostles." Mark's story here has a number of important elements to it.

First, one cannot overlook the fact that Mark places this call of four men right at the very beginning of the public life of Jesus. Evidently he has done this because he wants it clear that these men are witnesses to all that happened in the life of Jesus. If eye-witness exalts the trustworthiness of testimony, and it clearly did in ancient days, the reader knows that from the beginning the first witnesses had complete access to all of Jesus' life. A moment of reflection makes clear just how dependent Christian religion is on eye-witness. In support of Mark's testimony that Jesus early called four companions is John's similar notice in his gospel, despite the circumstances being so very different.

A second important aspect of this story is the imagery Jesus uses by which to describe what he hopes to make of these men: fishers of men. Mark's understanding of these words is clear: these fishermen work with and for Jesus to save human beings from the destructive waters. No doubt, one can go ahead to make an accurate guess that future teaching of these men will include instruction by which they will be proper fishers of men. But, one might ask, do these men ever actually "fish" in the gospel of Mark? Or is their task to be a future event, like Jesus' baptism with the Holy Spirit, not recounted in Mark's story? There are times, such as when Jesus multiplies the loaves and fish, when these men, and the others like them, help Jesus. But there is another time, one other time, when the twelve are sent off by Jesus to preach that people should repent, to drive out demons and heal the sick; the order to this type of activity is given to these chosen men once again when the gospel, at the hands of another author than Mark, records that the risen Jesus sent these men to do regularly what they did this one time in Galilee. Indeed, the choosing of the twelve, that they be with Jesus, that he might send them out to preach and have power over demons, which Mark 3:14–15 recounts, shows even more clearly what inspired Jesus' choice of these "fishers of men" in Chapter 1. These men, though only functioning once on their own as representatives of Jesus, are clearly intended to be the extension of the master who teaches and guides them for this very purpose. Thus, right at the beginning of his work Mark reveals Jesus' intention that he have certain followers, intimates of his, who would do the things he is now doing: preaching repentance, freeing from demons, healing the sick. The story of Chapter 1, in one sense complete in itself, in another sense looks for its completion in the labors of the twelve till their own deaths. The story, then, does point to a time beyond the public life of Jesus which Mark has set himself to narrate.

One cannot overlook the simple formulation of Jesus which expresses so much: *I* will make you fishers of men. In this phrasing the reader perceives how dependent are the four to be on Jesus.

One wonders if Mark intends to establish, by this special call story to Peter, James and John, some "justification" for the special moments in Jesus' life which were witnessed only by these three men; Mark offers nothing else that would explain this singularity.

Finally, one cannot fail to wonder at the naiveté which underlay the description of the dynamics between Jesus and these four men. How is it psychologically possible that these four, who show no sign of having met Jesus before, drop their nets (which stand for their lives up to now) to follow Jesus so totally? Perhaps one is supposed to know from past stories that this meeting was not the first between Jesus and these men? Yet, the story is told in such a fashion that the credibility of their reaction is strained. Is there a reason for this?

The answer seems to be that the reactions of the four men to Jesus are those that Mark knew to be the proper response to a call of the Lord. Yes, he is operating on the level of historical information, but at the same time he infuses this history with elements which are drawn from Christian faith, which are legitimated by his knowledge of the entire Jesus story and by his belief in who Jesus is. And if his goal in telling the story of Jesus is to inspire the reader to react to Jesus as the reader's faith tells him he should, Mark can, at times, overlay a "normal" psychology with a psychology which draws its logic from the believer's knowledge of who Jesus really is and what response his call really deserves. Thus, Mark is working from historical facts, but draws his characters in such a way as to inspire the reader to respond totally and immediately to Jesus' lordship.

The reader may be more interested to see if the disciples traveled a more arduous path to faith similar at all to the one the reader has traveled. Later Mark will show how difficult the disciples found the following and understanding Jesus and his teachings to be. But at this moment he wants to stress what the ideal response of the disciple to the call of the master should be; in this, the characters of the story become for the moment a means to Mark's particularized end.

With the first four disciples in place, Mark turns the reader's attention back to the work of Jesus. No longer is

Jesus pictured as one preaching repentance; rather he is here, and almost always henceforth, in the role of teacher. Is Mark's first image of Jesus to be replaced in the reader's consciousness by this second? Not really. Though the reference to Jesus as preacher of repentance will occur rarely in the future, one must understand that teaching is itself intimately linked with repentance, indeed is the extension, as it were, of preaching repentance. In short, if one actually repents, one carries out repentance by deeds which are befitting repentance, and these deeds are what Jesus taught. Teaching corresponds to the obedience which follows logically on repentance.

For his audience, already Christian and therefore already repentant and baptized, Mark concentrates on Jesus as teacher. In particular must Mark's audience hear well the teachings of Jesus which involve cross-carrying, for they have need of interweaving into their challenging situation the responses which their baptismal dedication to their Lord demands.

It is well worth considering at this initial point that it is Jesus' activity as teacher which ultimately brings about his death. Certainly, his piety and his wonder-working powers did not. Involved in this activity which so infuriated his enemies was not only irritating content which challenged their own interpretations of God's will. Underneath these teachings was the claim to authority in the matter of representing God's will. Indeed, in both what he said and what right he claimed to say it, Jesus planted the seeds of his own death. More concretely, Jesus is never represented as indicating that he thought other interpretations of the law or other, contrary advice about how to live life were as valid as his own. He was unique teacher, unique representative of God's mind. Grand, if others agreed with him, but, in differences of opinion, Jesus had the mind of God. This was a matter of immense seriousness among the religiously oriented of Jesus' time, for the history of Israel had shown that disobedience and teaching that led to disobedience to the will of God lay at the root of Israel's terrible, terrible afflictions. Any individual who appeared with teachings contrary to Israelite tradition and urged practices foreign to the normal spirituality was to justify himself—or pay a very great price.

Mark characterizes Jesus as one "who taught with authority, and not like the scribes." Indeed, it seems that the crowds were attracted to Jesus, not only for what he said, but because he evinced this authority. What is this distinction which Mark draws between Jesus and the scribes?

The scribes were those who, in a word, knew the law of Moses as well as was possible. Included in this knowledge was familiarity with the many traditional interpretations of the law of Moses which had been handed down for centuries as the law was applied to new situations which it could not have addressed before. What is most important, however, is their manner of functioning. When asked the question "How should I act in this situation?" or "What would God want me to do in these circumstances?" or "What does God's law ask of me?" the scribe would provide an answer in such a way that it was clear that he was not the authority for what he said, but that he was simply a conduit by which the laws of the past could be made to fit the present case. The scribe simply let the law speak; it was the authority behind the law that authorized this or that action.

Jesus did not operate this way. From the way he handled things, it was clear that he did not depend on anything else but his own judgment in declaring what was and what was not God's mind, God's will. Not that Jesus had no respect for the law or traditions, nor does all this mean that Jesus disagreed greatly with the Mosaic law. What it does mean is that, if Christians practice precepts of the Mosaic law, it

is because Jesus has said they are to be obeyed. For the
Christian, Jesus is the unique representative of the mind, of
the will of God—there is no surer entry thereto.

We are close to one of those insights into Jesus which
suggests that he is above all Israel's experience of God,
which suggests that perhaps he is, himself, the presence of
God, for no one has known or will ever know the mind of
God as Jesus does.

Mark, as editor, joins his emphasis on Jesus' teaching
with a story which is going to reinforce that emphasis. The
story is situated in a synagogue in Capernaum, presumably
the synagogue whose remains archeologists believe to lie
under the remains of another synagogue which are visible
to visitors today. As is usual in the telling of these vignettes,
many details which might interest readers are not recorded;
perhaps Mark himself would never have known many details,
if the story he inherited had been fashioned with only materials necessary to make "the point of the story." Since the
"point" is the manifestation of the immense power of Jesus,
the story highlights the malady of the man, but tells us nothing else about him. And there is little of description or psychology in the story. The story has been pared down to
highlight Jesus' absolute control over the demon world; the
violence in the story emphasizes the awesomeness of the
power which Jesus dominates simply by a word.

Moreover, the story calls the reader's attention to the
fact that the demon world, strangely enough like the Father
himself, knows who Jesus is and admits that it has nothing
in common with him. The hopeful suggestion of the weaker
power before the stronger power is that each go his own
way, that the one not interfere in the domain of the other.
Jesus' first response is to interfere, to free the creature from
its control. Jesus' second response is to silence any publi-
cation of his identity by the demon. Confession of Jesus'

identity, from any quarter, might seem a good thing, but until one experiences what the true meaning of such a title as "the holy one of God" is, Jesus prefers to stop any confession of his identity, particularly from the unholy one, so famous for his deceitfulness.

It is not by chance that Mark's first story about Jesus' activities has to do with domination of demons. The demonic power, unlike sicknesses, was a power from which no human being could free himself or anyone else. Only intercession with God could bring about a freedom from this evil. The first picture of Jesus, then, is a picture of divine-like power exercised by just a word. The confession of the demon only serves to enlighten feebly what the power of Jesus reveals about his identity.

Mark does not conclude his story with the expulsion of the demon, but rather with the response of the crowd, as though this response is as meaningful in its own way as is the revelation of the power of Jesus which triggered it. The response is curious. No matter how the translators polish it, the text really reflects the crowd's astonishment at both the new teaching and the new power to which it has just been exposed. One can understand why the crowd wonders at "this new authority," but why does it also fix on "this new teaching"?

Here is to be found Mark's reason for joining his description of Jesus' teaching, a teaching with authority, with a story which shows Jesus' authority over demons. The word of Jesus is authoritative, whether in teaching or in expelling demons; it brings one to happiness, whether it shows the way thereto or immediately drives out one's enemies. For an audience which, under persecution or other trial, is probably not going to enjoy the immediate intervention of God's power, Mark hopes there is consolation in knowing that the word which frees is also the word which, if obeyed, has the power to lead one to the fullest happiness. Given the power of Jesus which Mark has stressed for the reader here, it is not surprising that he ends his story by noting that the report about Jesus went everywhere throughout the environs of all Galilee. Who would not want to tell what has happened this day?

Mark next brings Jesus to the family of Peter and Andrew, in the company of James and John. The immediate object of concern here is another sick person, this time Peter's mother-in-law. No doubt, this story survived in the decades after the public life of Jesus because of Peter's fame in the church.

The house in which she lies stricken by a fever is, by the estimates of some archeologists today, about forty yards from the site of the synagogue in which Jesus had freed a man from a demon. St. Paul, years before Mark's gospel was written, asked the audience of his first letter to the Corinthians, "Do we not have the right to take about with us a wife, a believing woman, as the other apostles and brothers of the Lord and Cephas have done?" (1 Corinthians 9:5). Here is an external witness, then, to the fact that Peter (whose Aramaic name was Cephas) was married and thus had a mother-in-law.

As with other cure stories, Mark's vignette is shorn of all details other than those necessary to focus the reader's attention on the story's point. Thus, as elsewhere, we know little or nothing of the circumstances or of the personalities or of the psychology involved. What is provided is a clear presentation of disease and its cure by a power whose strength is revealed by the fact that Jesus had only to take the woman's hand and she was cured. That the woman is reported to have risen up to wait on Jesus and his companions certainly is the narrator's way of showing just how thoroughly cured the lady was. Some interpreters go a step further to say that her care for Jesus is Mark's sign of her gratitude for his cure. Finally, still others suggest that Mark is subtly encouraging his reader to learn a lesson of how one can, through the grace of the Lord, change one's life from sickness to service of others.

Certainly the cure of Peter's mother-in-law fits into a sequence which is slowly revealing itself, in Mark's first chapter, as a sequence of miracle stories. First a demoniac is cured, then a feverish woman. Finally, Mark recounts a story of generalized healing, where Jesus is, at the end of his day, crowded in Peter's house by all the townsfolk who had brought people possessed and otherwise in bad health. Again, the narrator stresses the multifold diseases and Jesus' power to deal with them all. By the end of the first full day described by Mark, it is clear that upon Capernaum has descended a power, and a willingness to use this power, which belong only to God.

As a reinforcement of the reader's memory, Mark notes in all this healing the warning of Jesus to the demons not to speak out his identity, but just to go their way. The demons did know, in a rather sterile way, the relationship of Jesus to God, but it is doubtful that they, as God's enemies, would know or understand what will be the very mysterious ending to Jesus' life. The demons are able to argue to part of Jesus' identity from his power over them, but they understand nothing of the love of Jesus for all human beings and his sacrifices for them. Thus, they are hardly the ones to interpret Jesus accurately for human beings.

The story-teller does not let miracle-working dominate the imagination or time of the reader. Revealing as miracles have been about Jesus, it is necessary to restate the purpose for which Jesus has come. He has come to preach, to preach repentance. The corollary of this purpose is that Jesus cannot stay among those who admire him and look to his power for comfort and consolation. He must visit the villages all around, in order to deliver his message concerning the nearness of the kingdom of God and the consequent need for repentance and faith.

Another sign that miracle-working is not Jesus' real purpose in life is his willingness to separate himself from human beings to spend nights in the desert with his Father. His long periods alone with his Father suggest that Jesus felt that prayer was integral to his own life as well as to his present mission.

They also help the reader to go beyond the limits Jesus' contemporaries have thus far reached about him. The very fact that they cannot understand why he is "missing," is in the desert, is unwilling to stay in one place, shows their dim perception of Jesus' own awareness of his destiny, and helps the reader to surpass them in faith.

As is characteristic of gospel writing (and other lengthy story telling), individual episodes, which serve both to convey precise notions and to entertain the imagination of the readers, are alternated with generalized descriptions, meant to fill in periods of time with what the reader understands from the individual episodes to be any day's occurrences. We have already seen this alternating style in Chapter 1: interspersed with individual vignettes are sweeping descriptions, often in one verse, of Jesus' work over an undefined period. So, his one day of loving and particularized cures is followed by a broad brush stroke: "And he went on preaching in their synagogues throughout all Galilee and driving out demons." From the particular healings the reader can imagine what all these following days must have been like.

Mark now picks out a story from an unspecified day and place in Jesus' travels. Here we have another miracle-story, true to the general purpose of the gospel's earliest section. As is to be expected of this kind of story, few details are given. The story is, therefore, all the more able to highlight the power of Jesus against the need of the poor man.

Yet from a careful reading there emerge two details or elements which are unusual for this type of story. First, there is the fact that the story-teller has not erased from his story the very profound detail that the sick man puts all the weight for his cure on Jesus' willingness to do it. This opens up a deeper revelation of Jesus when the story-teller, ever brief, notes how Jesus' very innards raced with the juices of mercy and he burst out, "Of course I want to heal you!"

A by-product of Jesus' merciful use of power is the fact that this man can now take his place as a full member of Israelite society, an effect of no small significance, though the gospel story directs attention only to the love and power which bring about this cure. Leprosy, even if the word is more restricted in its meaning today, was a social as well as a physical stigma, shunting off to the periphery of human life those unfortunately afflicted with it. The contagious nature of this disease is perhaps what prompts the way in which the leper posed his request to Jesus, "If you want..."—he realized that the cure he desired most likely involved the healer's touching him. And it is Jesus' own awareness of the leper's embarrassment at his asking Jesus to accept this danger, and Jesus' willingness to touch this leper, which made him exclaim, "Of course I want to cure you!" The story retained, right up to Mark's time, the small detail that "Jesus extended his hand and touched him."

A second aspect or element of this particular story is the time the narrator spends on its second half: Jesus' demand that the man present himself to the priests, as the Mosaic law commanded those cured of leprosy to do. Why does Mark tell us of this demand from Jesus? The best answer seems to be this: that Mark wanted early in his story to emphasize Jesus' obedience to the Mosaic law, no matter

what divinity or uniqueness among men his immense powers reveal. Jesus never flouted or showed disrespect for the
Mosaic law, and, with an eye to the future, Mark wants it
known from the start that Jesus should never be condemned
on such a charge. Given Jesus' proper attitude to the law,
one must search elsewhere for the reason why on occasion
his teaching differs from that of his contemporaries or contradicts what is written in the law of Moses.

Whether or not the cured man did go to the priests, as
Jesus directed, is not known. Mark rather tells us that the
man, contrary to the wishes of Jesus, tells everybody about
his cure. This leads, once again, to a misunderstanding of
Jesus' coming to villages and synagogues. He wants to call
to repentance; the people want miracles. Thus, Mark draws
a new generalized picture: Jesus tends more and more to
hide from crowds, whereas the crowds search him out, creating that enthusiasm and excitement which should soon
draw the ponderous attention of the Jewish and Roman leadership to him.

Since we have come to the end of Chapter 1, a word
should be said about "chaptering." When we talk of "chapters," we are talking about divisions of a book which originally had no such divisions. Indeed, the earliest manuscripts
had no chapters, no verses, no punctuation marks, no divisions between words, no variations between capital and
small letters. All such helpful markings are additions of later
ages by which people hoped to make the text clearer, both
to read and to understand. Thus, it is not Mark's, but someone else's idea that it is wise to divide the text at this point
between a first and a second chapter. All this means that
Mark, if given a chance, might prefer that a chapter begin
or end at a point other than what has been given us by later
interpreters.

Chapter 2

With the first story of Chapter 2, the reader is back in Peter's home in Capernaum. Jesus is there, and word of his presence brings ever-increasing numbers to this house. After a while, the crowds become so large that they prevent people coming through the front door. Such is the detail which orchestrates the rest of Mark's story. Four friends, wanting to put before Jesus a paralyzed man, cannot do so; cleverly, they go to the flat roof over the crowd, a roof made of a composition of tree limbs, bark, and leaves which would support dirt, and they dig a hole large enough to let the paralyzed man down right in front of Jesus.

There is no overlooking the powerful act Jesus performs in healing this paralyzed man, or the singular authority of Jesus when he says, "Stand up!" Yet, this cure takes second place to two other elements which Mark intentionally adds to the miracle-story format. First, Jesus forgives this man's sins. Jesus does not ask God to forgive the man, nor does he promise to forgive at some future time, such as after his resurrection or at the end of the world; Jesus does the forgiving.

Moreover, he forgives sins when he knows that the man sought only a physical cure. His act of forgiving in this context suggests Jesus' prophetic emphasis that sin is this man's

2 And when he returned to Caperna-um after some days, it was reported that he was at home. ²And many were gathered together, so that there was no longer room for them, not even about the door; and he was preaching the word to them. ³And they came, bringing to him a paralytic carried by four men. ⁴And when they could not get near him because of the crowd, they removed the roof above him; and when they had made an opening, they let down the pallet on which the paralytic lay. ⁵And when Jesus saw their faith, he said to the paralytic, "My son, your sins are forgiven." ⁶Now some of the scribes were sitting there, questioning in their hearts, ⁷"Why does this man speak thus? It is blasphemy! Who can forgive sins but God alone?" ⁸And immediately Jesus, perceiving in his spirit that they thus questioned within themselves, said to them, "Why do you question thus in your hearts? ⁹Which is easier, to say to the paralytic, 'Your sins are forgiven,' or to say, 'Rise, take up your pallet and walk'? ¹⁰But that you may know that the Son of man has authority on earth to forgive sins"—he said to the paralytic— ¹¹"I say to you, rise, take up your pallet and go home." ¹²And he rose, and immediately took up the pallet and went out before them all; so that they were all amazed and glorified God, saying, "We never saw anything like this!"

13 He went out again beside the sea; and all the crowd gathered about him, and he taught them. ¹⁴And as he passed on, he saw Levi the son of Alphaeus sitting at the tax office, and he said to him, "Follow me." And he rose and followed him.

15 And as he sat at table in his house, many tax collectors and sinners were sitting with Jesus and his disciples; for there were many who followed him. [16]And the scribes of the Pharisees, when they saw that he was eating with sinners and tax collectors, said to his disciples, "Why does he eat with tax collectors and sinners?" [17]And when Jesus heard it, he said to them, "Those who are well have no need of a physician, but those who are sick; I came not to call the righteous, but sinners."

18 Now John's disciples and the Pharisees were fasting; and people came and said to him, "Why do John's disciples and the disciples of the Pharisees fast, but your disciples do not fast?" [19]And Jesus said to them, "Can the wedding guests fast while the bridegroom is with them? As long as they have the bridegroom with them, they cannot fast. [20]The days will come, when the bridegroom is taken away from them, and then they will fast in that day. [21]No one sews a piece of unshrunk cloth on an old garment; if he does, the patch tears away from it, the new from the old, and a worse tear is made. [22]And no one puts new wine into old wineskins; if he does, the wine will burst the skins, and the wine is lost, and so are the skins; but new wine is for fresh skins."

23 One sabbath he was going through the grainfields; and as they made their way his disciples began to pluck heads of grain. [24]And the Pharisees said to him, "Look, why are they doing what is not lawful on the sabbath?" [25]And he said to them, "Have you never read what David did, when he was in need and was hungry, he and those who were with him: [26]how he entered the house of God, when Abiathar was high priest, and ate the bread of the Presence, which it is not lawful for any but the priests to eat, and also gave it to those who were with him?" [27]And he said to them, "The sabbath was made for

man, not man for the sabbath; [28]so the Son of man is lord even of the sabbath."

true worst enemy. Such a lesson corresponds with Jesus' mission, to call for repentance for sin, rather than to cure physical ills.

The scribes present underline the message Mark wants his readers to grasp from this story about the identity of Jesus. "Only God forgives sins!" they exclaim. Mark cherishes this logic, for the conclusion must be that Jesus is in some way divine. Jesus never again forgives sins in Mark's gospel. Evidently, this act of forgiveness is meant to underline Jesus' greater concern for spiritual healing. But one will not forget, by virtue of the scribes' reaction, the revelation about Jesus which this forgiveness of sins included.

A second element, new to this kind of story, is Mark's writing that Jesus responded to the faith of those who look to him for a cure. Here, faith is both confidence that Jesus can work a miracle and trust that he is kind enough to do it. Mark begins here to insert into many stories, directly and indirectly, the word "faith," for it will necessarily become, given the nature of his teaching and of discipleship, one of the most significant acts Jesus will call for.

Mark closes this astounding story by reporting all as awestruck, for they "had never seen anything like this." Presumably, the extraordinary thing they "saw" was the paralyzed man walking about, and in this they recognized the power of God himself in their praise of him; but the reader is equally struck and equally praising God for the revelation of Jesus, the Lord who even forgives sins. Another element of the truth about Jesus has been grasped by Mark's audience.

The second story of Chapter 2 has to do with a certain Levi and has two parts to it; in the first Levi is called to be Jesus' disciple in words which clearly recall Mark's description of the call of Peter and Andrew, James and John, and then there is the lesson to be learned from Jesus' dinner in

Levi's house. Before looking at these two Levi stories, we must recognize a problem.

The name of the tax-collector in Mark's present story is Levi. Now, both Matthew (9:9–13) and Luke (5:27–32) tell this very same story of a tax-collector called to follow Jesus, but in each of their stories the man's name is Matthew. Nowhere else in the New Testament is mention ever made of a Levi. Further, one should remember that in four places in the New Testament (Matthew 5:2–4; Mark 3:17–19; Luke 6:14–16; Acts 1:13) lists of the names of the twelve (or eleven) are given, but in every one there is mentioned Matthew, but in none of them is there a Levi. Finally, in Mark's story of the tax-collector, Levi is called "son of Alphaeus." Every other time that "son of Alphaeus" is used in the New Testament, it describes James, one of the twelve. Such, then, is the historical problem with the name of the character of our story; though most interpreters are willing to say that the man had two names, Matthew and Levi, and by chance had a father whose name (Alphaeus) was the same as that of the father of James, many acknowledge that we may not be on the right track in this matter.

Mark introduces this story with Jesus, not in synagogue or in Peter's house, but walking along the shore, presumably, the shore of the Sea of Galilee (= Lake Tiberias). As people begin to flock about him, he begins his usual, everyday task: teaching. The walk Jesus is taking brings him past a place where a certain Levi is working as tax-collector. As with the case of Peter and Andrew, James and John, Mark offers no psychological preparation for Jesus' call to Levi to follow him, nor for Levi's immediate and total response to Jesus. One can only assume that Mark, by imitating his story-telling manner of the earlier call, means to reinforce the teaching conveyed in this form: the Lord merits the complete and prompt obedience of his disciple.

It is important to understand now the kind of work Levi

did as "tax-collector." Actually, there is some division among
scholars as to its exact nature. For some, Levi is part of a
chain of people who collect taxes for Rome. The general
practice in the matter of tax-collecting was as follows. Rome
wanted such-and-such amount of money from taxes for a
given year. Mr. X would give this amount of money to the
Romans, then go to Palestine to collect for himself by taxes
the amount he had just given to the Romans—plus a per-
centage. Since he could not do all the collecting himself, he
hired men, each of which would concentrate on a particular
area. Each of these men, and any eventual helpers, would
have to be paid, obviously from taxes increased to cover
these salaries. By the time the tax-collecting was completed,
"taxes" would have been inflated to a degree that even the
simplest smelled the illegalities and cheating involved in the
collection. Suffice it to say that Jewish opinion of a tax-collector was so low that a tax-collector could never serve as
a witness in a legal trial—his word was absolutely untrust-
worthy! Such, for most scholars, is the occupation in which
Levi, called to discipleship by Jesus, is engaged.

Another possible meaning of "tax-collector" is, more
precisely, "toll-collector." At smooth points in the often rug-
ged eastern and northern boundaries of Palestine were sta-
tioned booths at which those coming into Palestine had to
pay tolls. One such level place, we know, was Capernaum,
through which passed many traders and caravans. It would
be Levi who would be the (trustworthy?) toll-collector for
foreigners entering Palestine by way of this town; here, too,
there was money to be made.

These men, toll- and tax-collectors were despised as
much as were their usual friends, "sinners" all; it is not surprising that Levi, when he gave a dinner, was joined by those
others of Palestine who were known to publicly flaunt the
law of Moses.

Mark's manner of telling this story reminds us of the

form Mark used in narrating miracles: only details are given
us which will support the main lesson of the story, little
else. In this vignette, the lesson is the response of Jesus to
the criticism of the scribes of the Pharisaic form of Judaism.
These scribes, experts in knowing the Mosaic law and the
traditions associated with it, find it reprehensible that Jesus
is so intimate with sinners that he dines with them. It is well
to recall the occasional outburst against sinners which appears in the Jewish scriptures; the psalmist in Psalm 119
speaks harshly:

> Indignation seizes me because of the wicked who for-
> sake your law (v 53).

> I hate men of divided heart, but I love your law (v
> 113).

> You, Yahweh, despise all who stray from your statutes
> (v 118).

> I watched with loathing those who denied you, Yah-
> weh (v 158).

And the psalmist of Psalm 101 is equally virulent and un-
compromising:

> I hate him who acts perversely;
> he shall not remain in my company (v 3).

> Whoever slanders his neighbor secretly,
> that one I will destroy (v 5).

> A man who practices deceit
> will never dwell in my house (v 7).

Each morning I will destroy
all the wicked of this land,
and I will uproot all evil men
from this city of Yahweh (v 8).

Pharisees, of whom these scribes are a specialist part, conclude, from God's own handling of sinners, that God does
not want holy people to mingle with sinners, lest (and Israel's history has shown it to be quite possible) the good
be won over to the bad.

Jesus' answer, meant for a small group of people at one
dinner, was kept alive for generations, for it had more than
momentary value. At the same time it explained to generations of believers and non-believers alike what for many was
confusing about him, and, to those willing to listen, it offered
further insight into his true identity.

Jesus has come for sinners, to call them to repentance.
It is certainly a prudential decision as to how to do this.
Whatever one may think of the merits of this type of asso-
ciation with sinners, Jesus' words present a strong case in
his own defense, about his own sincerity and motivation. As
to his wisdom in this, his example of physician/sick person
is extremely well chosen: How does a physician heal, if not
by contact with those who have need of him? Not only does
it serve to justify his action (and that of his disciples whom
he includes in his own), but it ultimately serves to define
Jesus anew: the physician of men and women who need
healing. Jesus represents that strong current which runs
through the Jewish scriptures: God, who loves all, is in
search of his lost ones. Jesus is now the divine voice approaching as intimately as possible to call the human heart
to conversion.

We are becoming accustomed to the gospel manner,
that one story ends quickly, even abruptly, once the main

point is expressed, and the next story begins with only a loose temporal and geographical connection to its predecessor. And so, Mark moves us from the time and place of Levi to an unknown but later time and place having to do with the disciples of John the Baptist and the Pharisees, at a moment when all these were fasting.

Piety among Jews flourished particularly in three ways: prayer, fasting and almsgiving. In the light of hope that the messiah would come soon, Jews fasted so as to be prepared for this coming and so as to hasten this coming. It is this latter motive for fasting which Jesus challenges with his own identity. He is the messiah come, or, in the words of the story, he is the bridegroom for whom the bride has been anxiously waiting. If he is now present, what is the logic of fasting? Again, this lesson, given to a few people on a certain day, has remained in Christian memory both for its defense of Jesus' actions and for its revelation of Jesus' identity. As with the case of Levi, Jesus' not fasting, which with other such actions ultimately leads to his condemnation, is interpreted absolutely falsely.

It is important to be aware how the logic of Jesus' argument works. His not-fasting is at best a suggestion, certainly not a proof, that he is the messiah; rather it is one's perception of him as messiah, owed to other facts and evaluations, which should make very understandable that fasting is not now necessary.

It is becoming increasingly clear to Jesus that, whereas some people either think him to be from God or at least are not closing their minds to this possibility, others are skeptical and unbelieving; his actions are not that of God's blessed one, and so he is to be condemned. Jesus' awareness of this growing development leads him to create two metaphors. Each of them underscores the impossibility of harmonizing two elements known as "the old" and "the new."

Old cloth, fixed with a new patch, simply will not work; both can even suffer for the effort. New wine in old wine- skins will ruin both wine and skins. Jesus is not only a com- mentator on what is developing about him. He is also showing the leap one must make to grasp him: one must be able to leave behind all that is incompatible with under- standing him, with obeying him.

Jesus' words to those fasting indicated that his own dis- ciples would someday fast indeed. By this word Mark re- minds his reader of the reality that, though the bridegroom had come, the bridegroom is now absent, to come again. In this period of absence, fasting is again in order, to prepare for his coming and to hasten it, if possible.

Mark's choice of stories, one can see, is motivated in great part by their ability to explain to many generations the innocence of Jesus as well as his identity; they are stories which can inspire future generations of Christians and an- swer questions about the way in which Jesus led his life, his reasons for this, and the direction he gave to the religious life of his followers. In recognizing this Marcan motivation, one realizes that the gospel intends to take the reader far beyond a pure history of Jesus.

The final story of Chapter 2 puts us somewhat unex- pectedly in a field of standing grain, where the disciples, to assuage their hunger, pick off heads of grain and rub the edible part out of the husks with their hands. It is the Phar- isees, who had already challenged Jesus on other important issues, who now find religious wrongdoing in this rubbing of grain. The key circumstance here is that the disciples do this *on the sabbath*.

Very early in the history of Israel the Mosaic law had reflected the holiness of the sabbath, and its many laws, meant to express this holiness and protect it, were multi- plied, as the centuries passed, till by Jesus' time many human

activities were defined as "work forbidden on the sabbath."
One of these works was "harvesting grain"; in the judgment
of the Pharisees, Jesus' disciples, by separating wheat from
husk even in very, very small quantities and for no monetary
value, were in effect "harvesting grain" and so disobeying
God's will for the sabbath.

Jesus does not agree with the interpretation of the Pharisees that the disciples are doing something here against
God's will. Jesus uses an argument which should make the
Pharisees retreat; it is the argument from scripture, the purpose of which is to return to the ground which is common
between Jesus and his opponents and seek there justification
for his position. Jesus recalls a story concerning David's eating bread which was forbidden to him. He did not eat this
bread on a sabbath, nor do all of the details of Jesus' account
square with what is in the Old Testament. The point, however, is clear: the holy bread (actually twelve loaves which,
fresh every day, were to represent Israel before God and to
be eaten, at the end of the day, only by priests) was, in a
situation of needy hunger, judged food that David could eat;
God, in other words, would not be against David's action to
curb his hunger.

This example concerning David leads to the generalized, universal statement: the sabbath was made for man,
not man for the sabbath. Though this principle is to flow
from the Old Testament story, it becomes a principle based
on human reason and potentially extends far beyond admitting some exceptions, such as David's case, to a new understanding of the law. In principle, Jesus argues, the sabbath
is "for man," i.e., to help human beings worship God better.
It calls for personal decisions and suggests that success in
keeping the Lord's day holy depends more on obedience to
one's conscience than on obedience to a list of "works forbidden on the sabbath." Going beyond simple attention to

lists of permissible and non-permissible works, one looks
more directly to God and asks oneself: How can I spend this
day so as to worship God most effectively?

Throughout the gospel, Mark presents selected teachings of Jesus. Not only are they presented because they are
in themselves persuasive; they are presented also because
they were in Jesus' public life, and continued to be in the
decades thereafter, points of contention between those who
belonged to the heritage of Israel. In view of the later discussions about the validity of the Christian way of worshiping God, the sayings and logic of Jesus are eagerly recorded.
More particularly, as Mark represents Jesus' viewpoints more
favorably than those of his opponents, the certainty grows,
as the gospel story develops linearly, that not only should
Jesus never have been opposed, but, on the contrary, there
was every reason to welcome him.

The recalling of the old story about David's eating
bread, not ordinarily allowed him, led to the principle that
"the sabbath was made for man." The fact that Jesus knows
this principle leads to the ultimate conclusion, that Jesus,
the Son of Man, is Lord over the sabbath. That is, Jesus knows
how the sabbath is to be spent because he is Lord of it.

That Jesus claims to be Lord of the sabbath is a very
significant and dangerous claim. It is significant and dangerous because there is in his self-definition not only the claim
that he knows better than all others how the sabbath is to
be conducted; there is also the hint that somehow he is
equating himself with the one who alone in history has had
the title of Lord of the sabbath. The Old Testament had asked
long ago, "Who knows the mind of God, who is his equal?"
By claiming that he knows, he equivalently says that he has
the mind of God, he is his equal. By taking to himself Yahweh's title, he is suggesting an equality with Yahweh which
is based on more than just knowledge. This was a very dan-

gerous suggestion for Jesus to make in his own lifetime—but one extremely worth cherishing and recalling to later generations of Christians who look to Jesus as their Lord.

Chapter 3

As explained earlier, sometimes the unity among stories would be more clearly visible if chapter endings could be changed. This observation is very apposite here: the first story of Chapter 3, with the concluding verse 6, surely belongs with the last story of Chapter 2. Both the story of the disciples' "working on the sabbath" by rubbing grain and the first story of Chapter 3, dealing with a cure "on the sabbath," are of a piece because they represent Jesus' "disregard" for the sabbath law. Moreover, Luke begins this first story of Chapter 3 with a reference merely to "they," showing that the antagonists of this story are those of the story that ends Chapter 2 and, thus, that this story is to continue the conflict begun in Chapter 2.

It is worth recalling, as we look at this story of the cure of the withered hand, that it was the common experience of history that to work a cure demanded real effort on the part of the healer; it was work. We are so used to the practically effortless way Jesus works the most astounding miracles that we fail to realize how "healing" was for all others real work. Occasionally Jesus does more than say a word or simply will someone to be cured, but by and large the ease with which he works miracles is understood to reveal the incomparable power of Jesus.

It is also worth remembering, in order to appreciate

3 Again he entered the synagogue, and a man was there who had a withered hand. ²And they watched him, to see whether he would heal him on the sabbath, so that they might accuse him. ³And he said to the man who had the withered hand, "Come here." ⁴And he said to them, "Is it lawful on the sabbath to do good or to do harm, to save life or to kill?" But they were silent. ⁵And he looked around at them with anger, grieved at their hardness of heart, and said to the man, "Stretch out your hand." He stretched it out, and his hand was restored. ⁶The Pharisees went out, and immediately held counsel with the Herodi-ans against him, how to destroy him.

7 Jesus withdrew with his disciples to the sea, and a great multitude from Galilee followed; also from Judea ⁸and Jerusalem and Idumea and from beyond the Jordan and from about Tyre and Sidon a great multitude, hearing all that he did, came to him. ⁹And he told his disciples to have a boat ready for him because of the crowd, lest they should crush him; ¹⁰for he had healed many, so that all who had diseases pressed upon him to touch him. ¹¹And whenever the unclean spirits beheld him, they fell down before him and cried out, "You are the Son of God." ¹²And he strictly ordered them not to make him known.

13 And he went up on the mountain, and called to him those whom he desired; and they came to him. ¹⁴And he appointed twelve, to be with him, and to be sent out to preach ¹⁵and have authority to cast out demons: ¹⁶Simon whom he surnamed Peter; ¹⁷James the son of Zebedee and John the brother of James, whom he surnamed

Bo-anerges, that is, sons of thunder; [18]Andrew, and Philip, and Bartholomew, and Matthew, and Thomas, and James the son of Alphaeus, and Thaddaeus, and Simon the Cananaean, [19]and Judas Iscariot, who betrayed him.

Then he went home; [20]and the crowd came together again, so that they could not even eat. [21]And when his family heard it, they went out to seize him, for people were saying, "He is beside himself." [22]And the scribes who came down from Jerusalem said, "He is possessed by Be-elzebul, and by the prince of demons he casts out the demons." [23]And he called them to him, and said to them in parables, "How can Satan cast out Satan? [24]If a kingdom is divided against itself, that kingdom cannot stand. [25]And if a house is divided against itself, that house will not be able to stand. [26]And if Satan has risen up against himself and is divided, he cannot stand, but is coming to an end. [27]But no one can enter a strong man's house and plunder his goods, unless he first binds the strong man; then indeed he may plunder his house.

28 "Truly, I say to you, all sins will be forgiven the sons of men, and whatever blasphemies they utter; [29]but whoever blasphemes against the Holy Spirit never has forgiveness, but is guilty of an eternal sin"— [30]for they had said, "He has an unclean spirit."

31 And his mother and his brothers came; and standing outside they sent to him and called him. [32]And a crowd was sitting about him; and they said to him, "Your mother and your brothers are outside, asking for you." [33]And he replied, "Who are my mother and my brothers?" [34]And looking around on those who sat about him, he said, "Here are my mother and my brothers! [35]Whoever does the will of God is my brother, and sister, and mother."

the thinking of Jesus' contemporaries, that synagogue official who, when confronted with a miracle just worked on the sabbath, criticized Jesus and those impressed by his healing by saying that "there are six days for working; come on those days to be cured, not on the sabbath."

Once again, we note how pared down the details of the story are, so that essential elements, need for cure and the power which so easily works the cure, are absolutely clear. In these early chapters, Mark is eager not just to publicize the cures of Jesus, but to suggest, through the ease with which Jesus heals, that the power in Jesus is inexhaustible.

Into this miracle story is interwoven, after the pattern we have seen elsewhere, elements which touch, not on the healing as such, but on the contentious reactions of those present for this event; thus, we have here interwoven with the familiar elements of the "cure story" the characteristics of what we call a "conflict story," the center of which is conflict. Mark has already indicated the dissatisfaction of certain elements of Jewish society with Jesus' attitudes to God's law; now he escalates the dissatisfaction to an outright plotting which means to "find reasons" which will stand up as accusations against Jesus in the courts of religious law. Already in the gospel the end of Jesus casts its long shadow backward.

The story interweaves the movement toward a miracle with the development of antipathies. Jesus for his part holds up the cure in order to test those who wait to trap him. His question to them reveals Jesus' own motivation for curing on the sabbath; indeed, it reveals why he is right to heal on the sabbath. Can anyone say that God, in forbidding work on the sabbath, meant that those people who could be cured should be left in their suffering? Indeed, Jesus' question is put in even sharper terms: Is it permissible on the sabbath to do good, to save a life, or is it permissible on the sabbath to do evil by not doing good, to kill by not saving a life? For not to do good is to do evil, not to save a life is to kill—and on the sabbath!

No one dares answer after hearing how Jesus formulates the question. Jesus works the cure, convinced that he knows God's mind in this matter, but he does it in anger and grief over the blindness of those who refuse to understand what he thinks so reasonable. Is it only a question of interpretation of law here, or is there, before one can interpret the law and God's mind, the need to love the man with the withered hand? Perhaps Jesus' frustration is with that lack of love which results in a wrong interpretation of God's will.

In miracle-stories so far recounted, Mark as usual ended his account by calling attention to a reaction of some sort to the miracle; such a conclusion to story-telling is technically called a "round-off" (= a rounding off of the story). The conclusion to this particular story is in place, and it is a most important one. It notes that, as a result of what Jesus had done, the Pharisees (not all Pharisees of all Palestine) joined with the Herodians to plot the destruction of Jesus. Though the Pharisees seek out the Herodians only at the conclusion of the cure of the withered hand, the reader understands that the step they are taking is a response to all that Mark has told about Jesus and his relationship with the law of Moses, from the beginning of Chapter 2.

Thus, though the stories Mark recounts are rather loosely strung together, one begins to see a certain unity among them: the ultimate end of Jesus already unites them, a distorted end which rises out of all the good Jesus has done. The cross appears early, the end which gives direction to all that has preceded it. It is this shadow of unreasonableness, hatred and pain which quickly covers everything and fills an otherwise joyful story with sorrow.

The Pharisees plot with the Herodians to overthrow and

destroy Jesus. There is an element of the improbable about this union. Pharisees, in existence in Israel from the early years of 180 B.C., enjoyed a great reputation in the time of Jesus. Pharisees had always been known for their extreme devotion to the law of Moses and the traditions flowing from it; others, like the scribes, may have understood the law better, but no one outdid the Pharisees in obedience to it. Their history, filled with martyrdom because of fidelity to the law, shone brightly when the Pharisees fought bravely with the Maccabees in the 160's B.C. to overthrow by guerrilla warfare the mighty Syrian army. At the turn of the last century B.C., when Israel began to wield that political power which the Pharisees thought to conflict with Israel's call to be only a religious state, the Pharisees again stood against all to champion the one thing that mattered: obedience to the will of God as detailed in the law of Moses. And it would be the Pharisees who would be some of the staunchest rebels against Rome in the struggle for freedom, including freedom to practice their religion as they saw fit, in the great war of 67–73 A.D. in Palestine. The Pharisees, then, brooked no one's tampering with, or disregard for, the law of Moses, i.e., the law of God.

The Herodians were people who worked for Herod Antipas, son of Herod the Great, and ruler, not of Judea and Samaria, but of Galilee (and Perea, a large tract of land on the east bank of the Jordan River). This Herod Antipas ruled Galilee from about Jesus' twelfth year to about ten years after Jesus' death. This Herod is the one who beheaded John the Baptist and met Jesus just before he was led off to crucifixion. Antipas ruled many years, a tribute to his ability to get along with many types of people. Herodians were those who worked with him and drew their livelihood from him; they did not want to lose this livelihood. Anyone who, whatever his intention, stirred up the people of Galilee to make them think of freedom, messiahship, a return to the old days of David and Solomon—such a person was suspect, for no Herodian could tolerate a "disturbance of the peace."

Pharisees had no love for the Rome-appointed ruler of Galilee or for his supporters, but they were willing, for their own goals, to form a conspiracy with the Herodians, who wanted "peace." The Herodians would act on the political level, the Pharisees on the religious level; this twin attack should deal effectively with the threat named Jesus.

Individual miracles are often followed by generalized descriptions of many and varied healings. Here we have such a description, with attention to the increased numbers and varieties of those coming to Jesus: from Judea and Jerusalem, from Idumaea (far south of Jerusalem) and from east of the Jordan River and from far north, Tyre and Sidon. So, with the plotting underway to destroy Jesus, the current of interest in him is almost a flood as he reveals power to handle with ease all sickness and possession. Jesus continues, in all of this, to forbid the demons to speak out their conviction that he is the Son of God.

The next story Mark tells follows logically from the story which describes the great press of people calling for Jesus' healing power. Jesus is in need of helpers, those who can assist him in his work, and so he picks a total number of twelve disciples, who would be most closely associated with him. We have the list of names, not perfectly consonant with the lists other gospels give us, with Jesus' first four disciples at the top.

But it becomes clear, from Mark's description here, that these twelve are meant in time to do more than just assist Jesus when large crowds press upon him. After a period which is described simply as "being with Jesus," these twelve will preach and heal and drive out demons without Jesus being present. That Jesus started to prepare a group of people who would continue his mission, without his actually being physically present, suggests Jesus' clear intention to found what has come to be called "the church." Another feature of the gospel adds support to this interpretation of Jesus' plan for his twelve: though Jesus prepared the twelve to do what he is doing, within Mark's gospel story they do this kind of work *only once*. Are we to conclude that Jesus undertook all this preparation (a preparation which lasted to the very end of Mark's gospel) just to have these twelve go out *one time* to preach and drive out demons?

That Jesus would "send out" these twelve allows us to call them "apostles," the Greek word "to send out" being *apostolein*. This term distinguishes these men from those who, though learners or disciples of the teacher, will not be "sent out." That they are called "the twelve" indicates that Christians saw in the number of these men a symbol that, as Judaism was founded on the twelve sons of Jacob and thus formed into twelve tribes, so Christianity would be formed on the twelve chosen by Jesus. Even in this way Christianity is seen to be the people of God. Each title, then—*disciple* (one who is *taught*), the *twelve* (those on whom the people of God are formed), *apostle* (one who is *sent out*)—has its own particular meaning, even though more than one term is used for the same person.

A look at the list of those who make up the twelve indicates that Mark's list is different from the lists of other New Testament writers. We do not know why this is so. Nor do we know what precisely Jesus meant by calling James and John "boanerges"; Mark translates this word to mean "sons of thunder," but this translation does not fit with our understanding of the languages involved, nor is it clear what precisely "sons of thunder" is trying to describe about these men. One might expect to find in this list St. Jude, familiar in Christianity as the patron of lost causes. Though appearing in other lists of the twelve, even as Jude Thaddaeus, he is not in Mark's list. Though in the first chapter of the gospel Peter and Andrew came before James and John, in Mark's list of the twelve the sequence is Peter, James, John, Andrew. The reason for this change in sequence seems to be that, in fact and as the gospel will show, the first three were the specially privileged among the twelve; the list reflects Jesus' unexplained preference for Peter, James and John. It is curious that two of Jesus' disciples, Philip and Andrew, have Greek names; yet it was not totally uncommon that Jews would have a second, Greek name, particularly if they come from areas (like Galilee) heavily populated by peoples other than Jews. Simon is called a Zealot, which means that Jesus called someone who was part of the movement of Jews dedicated, or zealous, to drive the Romans out of Palestine. Finally, as with so many other parts of the gospel, the list of the twelve shows the contributions of hindsight: Judas Iscariot (means "man from Cariot?") is described as "the one who handed Jesus over," clearly a betrayal which will happen only much later in the story-line; and the first in the list is called Peter, though we had only known him as Simon, and Mark never explains when or why Simon's name was changed.

The twelve, then, have been called; they are "with Jesus" and will eventually receive special teaching about the meaning of the kingdom of God and about the meaning of "following Jesus." It is they who will be responsible to carry on Jesus' work, an indispensable part of which is to witness to the significance of Jesus himself.

Having "descended the mountain," a symbol drawn from the experience of Israel as the place where God meets human beings, Jesus returns "to the house." In this case, the "house" is probably that of Simon Peter in Capernaum, though very often the "house" is meant by Mark to be a symbol of where Jesus does his special teaching of his closest disciples.

We must here take stock for a moment. Up to this point Mark has mixed into the preaching and teaching of Jesus many miracles and religious practices of Jesus which have drawn various reactions to him. Among these reactions have been one example of a kind of faith (the trust shown by those who lowered the bedridden man through the roof for healing), an ever-increasing flocking to Jesus for miracles, and a number of disagreements leading to a plot to destroy Jesus.

Mark will now settle into this pattern. He will hold up for admiration the works of Jesus, while consistently interspersing among them the varied reactions to Jesus and his works. Jesus will insist more and more on trust in himself, faith in himself, while reactions develop along the lines of greater puzzlement, refusal to repent, desire for miracles, insufficient or false interpretations and ever more bitter opposition. Mark's book does not change here, but merely escalates the interaction between Jesus and his contemporaries, so that the reader will understand with ever greater clarity why Jesus died, how unjust was that death and who the real Jesus is. The immediate goal of Mark now is Chapter 8, verses 27–31, where he has Jesus ask, on the basis of the first eight chapters, "Who do people say I am?" "Who do you say I am?"

A new story focuses on a new kind of interpretation of Jesus. It is Jesus' family, relatives from Nazareth, some twenty-five miles away from Capernaum, who, upon hearing of Jesus' feverish activities, decide that he is "beside himself." Though Mark does not say it, it must be clear that these people, most intimate with Jesus for decades, cannot harmonize what they hear of Jesus with what they knew of him for thirty years. They conclude that he is in some sense deranged. Thus, they set out to "bring him home." This interpretation of Jesus, more common in John's gospel, is rare in Mark, yet it is one which Mark sets among the variety of interpretations of Jesus which the reader will meet now in Mark's story.

A more vicious interpretation of Jesus is that offered by the scribes from Jerusalem. These experts in the interpretation of Jewish law come a long distance to evaluate this phenomenon and render their verdict: Jesus is possessed. This assessment of Jesus, much more than the one given by his family, probably was thrown up to the followers of Jesus for a long time after his death. It is particularly destructive because it is made by recognized experts in religious matters and because it is so subjective a judgment.

The logic of the scribes' interpretation, as long as it remains unexamined, seems right: like the chief of the demons (called Beelzebul, which means "lord of the flies," a replacement for the earthy Beelzebub or "lord of excrement") who controls his subjects, Jesus has power over demons; not being the chief himself, it must be that Jesus gets his power from the chief of the demons. The scribes are smart enough not to deny that Jesus drives out demons, and clever enough to say that he is an example of "like reflecting with like."

Jesus' response to this sinister claim contains two elements. First, upon closer examination of the scribes' claim, Jesus notes that it really makes no sense to say that Beelzebul is the one who gives Jesus power to drive out demons, for driving out demons is exactly what Beelzebul does *not* want to happen. To drive out demons is to make the kingdom of the demons collapse, not prosper. If some demons are trying to possess human beings and others are at the same time driving out these demons, is this not like a household which is divided against itself? The judgment of the scribes is thus seen to be illogical, false.

Jesus does not deny, however, the underlying principle of the scribes' argument, that "like belongs with like." Thus, to what should Jesus be compared, to whom does he owe his powers, if he drives out demons? Naturally, to the one who opposes demons, to God himself; it is from him who wants to destroy demons that the power to destroy them comes to Jesus. In this manner, Mark shows that the only way to interpret Jesus' driving out demons is to say that Jesus is from God; any other judgment is false.

Jesus offers a picture to his audience. The only way to rob a strong man is to overcome him first. Jesus is this in- imical thief who is trying to rob the demons; thus, he is to be understood as driving out demons so that he might take to himself those people who have been up till now the pos- sessions of the hateful spirits.

Jesus leaves self-defense in order to give a warning. Thinking that he has made clear how impossible it is that his powers come from Satan or Beelzebul, Jesus thinks he has at the same time made it clear that these powers are from God. It must be, it is another Spirit, the Holy Spirit, who in him is driving out evil spirits. Now, to deny that this is the work of the Holy Spirit is to insult the Holy Spirit, a sin which will not be forgiven.

Why will this particular sin be the only one not for- given? The answer seems to be that, once one so crassly denies signs of the presence of God's own Spirit, one has put oneself so hopelessly far from the help of this Holy Spirit that one will not accept the guidance of the Spirit to seek holiness anymore and, as the Bible sometimes expresses it, without wanting God, one will not have him.

Mark has thus scotched for his own contemporaries a wretched and deceitful interpretation of Jesus' powers by recalling what Jesus had said in his own time to his. With the debate with the scribes concluded, Mark reintroduces Jesus' family, who have now completed their anxious walk from Nazareth to Capernaum. Though the first mention of Jesus' family did not name Mary, Jesus' mother, as one of those fitfully concerned about Jesus, Mark presents her as present now and wanting to see Jesus.

At hearing that his family is present and asking for him, Jesus teaches two lessons. First, by exaggeration Jesus calls his audience his "mother and brothers." By doing this he underlines the fact that his life has been changed to such a degree that family ties no longer come before those whom he teaches about the kingdom of God. That is to say, whereas before his family, by virtue of being his family, had prior rights to his time and person, now those to whom he has been sent have these prior rights. Second, whereas before Jesus' most intimate love was reserved for his family, just because they were his family, now his fullest love goes to those who do the will of God. Sometimes it is pointed out that these criteria for love of others do not prevent Jesus from a deep love for his family, since they, particularly his mother, can well be those who want to listen to his teaching and those who do the will of God. True, but one should not forget that it will soon be Jesus' "brothers and sisters" who will show so little faith in him that he worked very few miracles. His love for family will not dictate the life of Jesus or define his values. While this story may not satisfy all one would like to ask Jesus about his love of family, it certainly makes clear who he thinks is very lovable in life—the one who listens to his word and obeys God. To this person most of all go Jesus' esteem and praise and time.

The terms "brothers and sisters of Jesus" are handled differently according to different religious beliefs. According to the dictionary, the Greek words for "brother" and "sister" can mean any person, from blood relation to fellow citizen. If the Greek words allow such a range of possibilities, which should we choose? For those who believe that Mary had only one child and no more, "brothers and sisters" must be understood as cousins or other more distant relatives. For those who believe that Mary could have had more than one child, "brothers and sisters" means that Jesus had physical brothers and sisters, sons and daughters of Mary and, no doubt, Joseph.

Mark is now about to break the rhythm he has established (miracles, teachings and reactions). He has given enough material to allow him to pause for a while over the mystery of unbelief. This mystery will be put within the context of teaching in parables about God's kingdom; indeed, though Jesus described the kingdom of God in many parables, the primary parable Mark chooses now is that which in its very makeup raises the baffling problem of unbelief.

Chapter 4

Jesus is now pictured "beside the lake (or Sea of Galilee)," and he is "teaching." Mark does without much detail here, giving just enough to let the imagination work. Mark notes that Jesus is so pressed by people that he teaches from a boat. The "boat" is a symbol for the church, a number of scholars think, the place in which, Mark underlines for his reader, the teaching of Jesus continues.

This is the first time Mark speaks of Jesus using "parables." What is a parable? Essentially, it is a comparison by which one moves from the known to the unknown. As is clear from the first parable about planting, the audience will gain understanding about the *unknown* kingdom of God, Jesus hopes, by thinking about the *very well known* activity of sowing seed. Thus, teaching through parables is a method which depends for its success on the way in which the mind learns new things from comparison with past experiences.

Before entering further into Mark's gospel text, we should take a moment to distinguish a parable from other forms like it: metaphor and simile, on the one hand, and allegory, on the other.

A parable, is distinguishable on the whole from a metaphor and simile in that, though all are based on comparisons, the parable is presented in story form, whereas the metaphor and simile are most often presented in a very brief

SCRIPTURE TEXT

4 Again he began to teach beside the sea. And a very large crowd gathered about him, so that he got into a boat and sat in it on the sea; and the whole crowd was beside the sea on the land. [2]And he taught them many things in parables, and in his teaching he said to them: [3]"Listen! A sower went out to sow. [4]And as he sowed, some seed fell along the path, and the birds came and devoured it. [5]Other seed fell on rocky ground, where it had not much soil, and immediately it sprang up, since it had no depth of soil; [6]and when the sun rose it was scorched, and since it had no root it withered away. [7]Other seed fell among thorns and the thorns grew up and choked it, and it yielded no grain. [8]And other seeds fell into good soil and brought forth grain, growing up and increasing and yielding thirtyfold and sixtyfold and a hundredfold." [9]And he said, "He who has ears to hear, let him hear."

10 And when he was alone, those who were about him with the twelve asked him concerning the parables. [11]And he said to them, "To you has been given the secret of the kingdom of God, but for those outside everything is in parables; [12]so that they may indeed see but not perceive, and may indeed hear but not understand; lest they should turn again, and be forgiven." [13]And he said to them, "Do you not understand this parable? How then will you understand all the parables? [14]The sower sows the word. [15]And these are the ones along the path, where the word is sown; when they hear, Satan immediately comes and takes away the word which is sown in them. [16]And these in like manner are the ones sown upon rocky

ground, who, when they hear the word, immediately receive it with joy; [17]and they have no root in themselves, but endure for a while; then, when tribulation or persecution arises on account of the word, immediately they fall away. [18]And others are the ones sown among thorns; they are those who hear the word, [19]but the cares of the world, and the delight in riches, and the desire for other things, enter in and choke the word, and it proves unfruitful. [20]But those that were sown upon the good soil are the ones who hear the word and accept it and bear fruit, thirtyfold and sixtyfold and a hundredfold."

21 And he said to them, "Is a lamp brought in to be put under a bushel, or under a bed, and not on a stand? [22]For there is nothing hid, except to be made manifest; nor is anything secret, except to come to light. [23]If any man has ears to hear, let him hear." [24]And he said to them, "Take heed what you hear; the measure you give will be the measure you get, and still more will be given you. [25]For to him who has will more be given; and from him who has not, even what he has will be taken away."

26 And he said, "The kingdom of God is as if a man should scatter seed upon the ground, [27]and should sleep and rise night and day, and the seed should sprout and grow, he knows not how. [28]The earth produces of itself, first the blade, then the ear, then the full grain in the ear. [29]But when the grain is ripe, at once he puts in the sickle, because the harvest has come."

30 And he said, "With what can we compare the kingdom of God, or what parable shall we use for it? [31]It is like a grain of mustard seed, which, when sown upon the ground, is the smallest of all the seeds on earth; [32]yet when it is sown it grows up and becomes the greatest of all shrubs, and puts forth large branches, so that the birds of the air can make nests in its shade."

33 With many such parables he spoke the word to them, as they were able to hear it; ³⁴he did not speak to them without a parable, but privately to his own disciples he explained everything.

35 On that day, when evening had come, he said to them, "Let us go across to the other side." ³⁶And leaving the crowd, they took him with them in the boat, just as he was. And other boats were with him. ³⁷And a great storm of wind arose, and the waves beat into the boat, so that the boat was already filling. ³⁸But he was in the stern, asleep on the cushion; and they woke him and said to him, "Teacher, do you not care if we perish?" ³⁹And he awoke and rebuked the wind, and said to the sea, "Peace! Be still!" And the wind ceased, and there was a great calm. ⁴⁰He said to them, "Why are you afraid? Have you no faith?" ⁴¹And they were filled with awe, and said to one another, "Who then is this, that even wind and sea obey him?"

form: e.g., the Chicago Bears are lions on defense (metaphor), the Chicago Bears are like lions on defense (simile). There can, of course, be cases where a parable becomes so brief that it begins to look like a metaphor, or where a simile is so extended that it tends to look like a parable.

Allegory is distinguished from parable in this way, that whereas the allegory story usually has many points which are meant to help clarify many unknowns, the parable, no matter how many details are in it, is trying to clarify just one unknown point through comparison.

Obviously, when we talk of a parable having the power to bring a person, by means of a known, to understand something that was previously unknown, we are describing how the intellect can become enlightened. We must always be aware that, no matter how clear an explanation through parable may be, if a person does not want to learn, he will not.

The best way to proceed now to interpret Mark's text is to distinguish immediately the matter regarding parables from the miracle by which Jesus calms the wind and the sea. As regards Jesus' teaching in parables, it is best to consider the entire account of Mark as an account heavily influenced by Mark himself. That is to say, Mark uses many things which are historically true, but the arrangement of everything is Mark's, not history's. A sign that Mark is orchestrating everything is the fact that, though many parables are spoken of, we actually are given only three. Even these three are loosely connected, and one of them, the sower sowing the seed on various soils, is clearly considered all-important to understanding all the others and is interpreted with an emphasis Jesus did not stress. At one point we are amidst the crowd, then alone with Jesus and those around him with the twelve, then apparently back out with the crowd. All in all, one has the impression that Mark has taken the occasion here to organize some teaching of Jesus in order to answer Mark's own questions for the good of his reader. It will be from this perspective that the following interpretation is offered.

Mark knew, of course, as did so many others, that Jesus often used parables as a way of making clear aspects of the kingdom of God which either needed emphasis or were not known at all to his listeners. Mark wants, first of all, to have Jesus give the reader three actual parables he gave to his own contemporaries; these three parables have meaning for Mark's reader. But, secondly, Mark wants to raise the questions "Why did people not respond to Jesus' teaching in parables (which are meant to clarify, not obscure)?" and "Why did Jesus keep on teaching people who he must have known would not understand him?" With these two Marcan purposes in mind—to repeat three of Jesus' parables and to answer two particularized questions—let us now follow the text as Mark has given it to us.

Mark notes that Jesus "was teaching many things in many parables." The mood now changes perceptibly. Mark moves into direct address and has Jesus call anxiously for attention, "Listen!" This call is repeated at the end of Jesus' words in even more urgent tones: "Let him who has ears, hear!" What causes this change in mood?

The words of Jesus tell a story (only later explicitly called a parable) concerning a sower who went out to sow seed. Most scholars agree that originally the story Jesus tells is meant to be optimistic in outlook: despite the failures of the seed to take hold everywhere, it will take hold somewhere and produce abundantly. But Mark is interested in the story because, as one can see from the parable itself, there is ample suggestion that often the seed can be rejected or rebuffed or choked off or thwarted, as well as be successful. It is the reality of this possible negative result of the sowing which makes Jesus' words to "hear!" so poignant. In short, through this story Mark sums up the experiences of his first three chapters wherein the preaching of Jesus has fallen on some good soil and on some bad soil as well, and indeed, from hindsight, sees reflected in Jesus' parable the reactions, positive and negative, which have occurred over the thirty years of Christian sowing of the seed.

At this point in his story, Mark interjects an event which occurred at another moment, when Jesus was finally alone with "those who were around him with the twelve." This group, Mark says, asked Jesus "as regards the parables." Are they unclear about some of them? Are they wondering why Jesus teaches through them? Whatever lies behind their question, Jesus answers them according to his own wishes.

Jesus says, in short, that he teaches "outsiders" in parables so that they may not be forgiven their sins. Here he seems to be answering the question, "Why do you keep on teaching people who you must know will not understand you?" These "outsiders" are best defined as those who refuse to be Jesus' disciples. To these people Jesus will continue to teach in parables, precisely so that they may not get to the truths contained in the parables, and, not being helped by the teaching of Jesus, these people will remain unrepentant and thus unforgiven.

There is a precedent, in the Old Testament, for Jesus' thinking here. Isaiah heard the call of God and answered, "Here I am! Send me!" God sent him, but to preach *so that* his audience would not repent; the audience was so wicked that God would make them pay double for their lack of faith, once for their rejection of him, another time for their rejection of his preaching through Isaiah. So to those who ask "Why did Jesus keep on teaching in parables to people who were his enemies?" the answer is "precisely so that they might not learn anything which would lead them to repentance and forgiveness." In other words, one must be a disciple of Jesus before parables will be means to salvation.

One can wonder if Jesus actually taught his enemies in parables for this reason Mark cites. It is not impossible—though it is also conceivable that Mark, in trying to warn his reader not to give up being a disciple of Jesus, has Jesus speak these threatening words which condemn those who do not believe, or who have believed but then give up. In any event, Jesus makes clear that only to the disciples has been given the mystery of the kingdom of God and they alone will receive clarity about it; to the others, the "outsiders," Jesus' teaching, which they did not understand or which had no salutary effect on them, was to be understood precisely as intentionally unintelligible and unhelpful—till they, too, became disciples.

One may also reflect that one is given here an explanation as to why some understood the parables and others either did not or disagreed about them: one had to be a believer in order to understand Jesus' teaching; to misrepresent his teaching was a sign that one was not Jesus' disciple.

Now, it is in the wake of this sternness toward non-disciples that Mark places the interpretation of that sower story which immediately precedes Jesus' harsh words about those who reject discipleship. Here the sower story is called a parable. Indeed it is the parable which is necessary to understand if one is to understand all the other parables. The parable's interpretation, which many scholars think is not Jesus', stresses, even more than the parable a few verses back, the negative aspects of the sowing. The circumstances which explain the failure of the seed to take hold are human circumstances, even to the mention of persecution. It seems that Mark wants to use Jesus' sower parable as a warning to his reader to remain firm to his commitment to faith in Jesus, to being a disciple. The reader can measure himself against the many threats to faith in the interpretation of the parable, and, together with the warning Jesus had given that only to disciples is given the mystery of the kingdom, can stir himself up to firmer loyalty to Jesus.

The key to understanding the parables of Jesus, then, is not always the clarity or unclarity of the parables themselves. Very often, understanding depends on prior faith in Jesus, without which the mind fails to grasp the truths taught by Jesus. Thus, the underlying question "Why did so many people fail to understand Jesus' parables?" is answered simply by the claim that unless one is first a disciple, one will not understand the master; the explanation of the mystery of the kingdom of God is not given to those who do not believe in Jesus.

The interpretation of the parable about the seed sown in various places suggests that there are a number of reasons why the word of Jesus will not be accepted or, if accepted, be ultimately rejected. There is no attention to psychology here (as elsewhere); rejection of Jesus is simply looked upon as a fact and the causes are enumerated. To sympathize with the difficulties some might find in holding onto what Jesus has taught is outside the purview of the Marcan text; the text simply wants to warn the disciple of imminent dangers so as to help the disciple remain firm. In other words, the text assumes (here, as elsewhere in the New Testament) full freedom and clarity in the disciple's choices.

It is at the interpretation of the story of the sower that the story is called a parable; indeed, it is the parable which must be understood if all others will be understood. Why is this parable so fundamental? Evidently, we are brought by another route to the same judgment made earlier, that discipleship is the presupposition for understanding properly the teaching of Jesus. If one does not understand this fact, that faith must precede comprehension of Jesus' teaching, one is in danger of not understanding anything of the realities involved here; it is letting the word in, to stay and blossom, that allows Jesus to go on and give instructions. In fact, Jesus will not enlighten further anyone who refuses to be his disciple; all he will do is confuse the person.

Jesus now adds two sets of proverbs to complete the teaching he has just given about the reception of the seed he is sowing. First, he speaks of light meant for a lampstand. As usual with proverbs, there is potential for a number of meanings. Here it seems to be the case that Jesus, suggesting the light to be himself or his word, underlines the inevitability that, once one has met him, whatever was hidden in a person will be made clear. Thus, decision is called for in meeting Jesus, whether it be of a first encounter (or series of encounters) with him, or it be of a later stage in discipleship. He it is who will make public what a person has kept hidden about his relationship with God.

The second set of proverbs has to do with the returns one receives for one's commitment to Jesus, whether in the initial acceptance of discipleship or further along in this commitment. One gets what one gives. Indeed, one can go a step further, to conclude that, if a disciple eventually turns away from Jesus, even the little the disciple had (the gift of faith itself is thought of here) will be taken away. Again, there is no look to the psychology of failure, only a relationship drawn on the objective level between commitment and its rejection.

Once Jesus has provided these two sets of proverbs to his own disciples, it seems that Mark changes the audience of Jesus back to the general crowds again. In this situation we find Jesus preaching in parables; in particular, he gives two parables which are meant to illustrate aspects of the kingdom of God. Actually, only these two comparisons, regarding the quiet growth of the seed and the potential size of what comes from the smallest seed, are the only ones in this chapter which are actually called parables and are explicitly about the kingdom of God. Again, each of them, though intelligible if given in Jesus' time, is much more descriptive of the decades which have developed from Jesus' time to Mark's writing. Thus, Mark includes them more as a commentary on what has happened after Jesus' time than during it.

One characteristic of the kingdom God rules is that, whatever one contributes to the growth of one's own faith, there is an element, as in farming, when something other than the farmer exercises an immense effort to make the seed grow. Indeed, it seems almost as if the human being has little to do with this growth. This aspect of God's role must be put beside that which Jesus has just described about the human effort to give, so that one may receive.

A second characteristic of the kingdom God rules is that, no matter how small the beginnings, God's control will grow, as it were, into a tree which can accommodate birds from all over the sky; thus, God will, though starting from a few, extend his rule throughout the Mediterranean so that the group of believers becomes large enough to welcome all who want to rest in it.

Again, there is no doubt that Jesus said these parables, but it is Mark who uses them to the advantage of his own contemporaries, in the light of some thirty years of Christian experience since the time when Jesus first began to sow the seed. In these parables and teachings, the Christians of 65 A.D. can find their identity and direction.

Mark now brings to a close a formal account of Jesus' teaching in parables (though there will be other parables given later on, to be sure). Mark's first observation, that Jesus "taught in many parables, like those" we have just read, suggests that Jesus picked and used parables "in accord with what they were able to understand." This observation indicates Jesus' concern that his teaching be understood; this is a picture quite different from Mark's earlier description that Jesus taught in parables so that his hearers might be punished.

Mark's second observation here at the close of the parables makes a distinction in regard to his first observation. There he spoke only of "them" and "they" without distinction. Here he distinguishes: to the general crowd Jesus spoke in parables only (always gearing them to what he thought they could grasp), but to his own disciples, when in private, Jesus explained everything. Thus with those already committed to him Jesus changed both his method and his content. He explained, not just spoke in parables, and he dealt with everything, not just with what he thought his audience could grasp at the moment. The distinction between audiences seems to be based, as in the earlier verses 10–12, on those who have committed themselves to Jesus as believers who want to learn as opposed to those who are curious, interested, but not yet believing and thus not yet the ones to receive "everything." Faith, then, is a presupposition for the fullest explanation and the fullest understanding. Moreover, Mark's final observation has the added merit of a suggestion to his readers that, while Jesus spoke parables generally pitched to non-believers, disciples (those who were responsible for the handing on of the complete teaching of Jesus) had everything explained to them—their teaching is valid and trustworthy.

Mark, then, has been at work in organizing this account of Jesus' parabolic teaching. Apart from the meanings of the parables themselves, which we have already described, Mark has indicated two methods Jesus had of teaching: parabolic form and explanation. The former was used for general crowds, the latter for disciples. This distinction allowed for the earlier insertion, for it is a distinction based on belief and non-belief. The earlier insertion expressed great anger at those who either refused to believe or willfully gave up belief; to them, the teaching of Jesus, meant to be helpful, is seen from hindsight to be a means to doubling the punishment for unbelief. This harsh assessment of the purpose behind Jesus' parabolic teaching was not Jesus' original purpose. It is a purpose thought visible by Mark and other Christians when they thought, "What value did the master's teaching serve for those who refused to believe? They will be punished both for refusing to believe and, in their unbelief, for rejecting the parables of Jesus." The Marcan story, then, is seen again to be a blending of Jesus' history with later Christian reflection on that history.

Mark now turns the reader's attention from Jesus' teaching to the first of the nature miracles, wherein Jesus reveals his immense power over the elements of nature. The story presents almost a perfect example of the gospel style whereby only details which serve Mark's story-telling purpose are given and all else, otherwise useful and interesting, is left out.

What seems to be Mark's unifying factor, the "clothesline" on which he hangs his stories of the moment, is the boat trip across and back again over the Sea of Galilee. Jesus, already forced to use a boat at the beginning of Chapter 4, decides to continue to use it to go to the other side of the Sea of Galilee (about seven to eight miles at its widest). Eventually he will be "forced" back to the western side of the sea, to Capernaum, and the reader by then will be at the end of Chapter 5.

The Sea of Galilee then, and now, is famous for the suddenness with which storms can blow up. Such a swift storm came upon Jesus and the disciples out on the sea. The waves reached the point of flooding over the sides of the boat so that the disciples thought they would capsize and even drown; Jesus lies in the back, head upon a cushion, fast asleep. Such then are the circumstances which lead to two lessons Mark wishes to convey from this story.

The first action highlighted by the story is the disciples' awakening Jesus with their words, "Have you no concern that we are perishing?" Jesus does not answer them immediately, but upbraids the wind and tells the sea to be quiet. Both wind and sea become calm and peaceful. The power which controls wind and sea will receive its proper acknowledgement; at this point, however, Jesus goes back to the words with which the disciples awakened him. To their question "Have you no concern that we are perishing?" Jesus responds, "Have you no faith?" The lesson Jesus teaches is that, despite all odds or human assessment, they should have trusted in him, in his power and in his love for them, to bring them safely to shore. In this way the first lesson is drawn.

With this lesson to the disciples in place, Mark completes his story by citing the reaction of the disciples. This reaction is, first of all, an immense fear or awe; the Greek word is commonly used when one is in the presence of divinity. This fear is, in turn, translated into the pregnant question, which is all the more significant for its not being answered: "Who is this that wind and sea obey him?"

The disciples have received another revelatory act of Jesus. They still cannot, however, grasp fully his identity, though their question is well phrased and promises a proper answer. While they ponder the immense power and dominance of Jesus, Jesus' question, too, hangs in the air, "Why did you not trust me?" Mark hopes his reader will have so entered into the story that he, too, will be filled with awe;

but he also hopes that the reader, in whatever difficulties he may find himself, will, unlike the disciples, trust Jesus' love to the end. This story fits with the preceding presentation of Jesus' teaching in parables, because it underlines the need for faith which, like the seed in good soil, will not end in failure, but in fruitful life. Indeed, from now until Chapter 8, Mark's stories will with great urgency focus on these two topics: faith and Jesus' identity.

Chapter 5

Immediately after the disciples ask their profound question "Who is this whom the wind and sea obey?" Mark changes scenery; Jesus and the twelve arrive at the eastern shore of the Sea of Galilee. Did nothing else happen between the calming of wind and sea and the landing? If it did, it all is lost or forgotten or ignored; Mark's next point of interest is Jesus ashore. Again, one can see why people say that Mark was not concerned to present every moment of Jesus' life or the psychology of each person involved in those moments.

Jesus and the twelve land in the territory of the Gerasenes (or, as Bibles have it, Gadera or Gergasha, the main town of which we cannot locate today). The details of Mark's story suggest that we are in a high terrain, since pigs can be described as *falling* into the sea. Certainly the area is not a Jewish locale; almost all inhabitants are surely Gentile. The town of the Gerasenes is part of a larger area known at the time as the Decapolis, which means Ten Cities. Though the actual number of the cities of the Decapolis varies from time to time, the area remains rather fixed as a territory independent from Palestine to its west and Syria to its north. Without underlining the fact, then, Mark has Jesus meet Gentiles here for the first time.

The story of the Gerasene demoniac is the longest of

5 They came to the other side of the sea, to the country of the Gerasenes. ²And when he had come out of the boat, there met him out of the tombs a man with an unclean spirit, ³who lived among the tombs; and no one could bind him any more, even with a chain; ⁴for he had often been bound with fetters and chains, but the chains he wrenched apart, and the fetters he broke in pieces; and no one had the strength to subdue him. ⁵Night and day among the tombs and on the mountains he was always crying out, and bruising himself with stones. ⁶And when he saw Jesus from afar, he ran and worshiped him; ⁷and crying out with a loud voice, he said, "What have you to do with me, Jesus, Son of the Most High God? I adjure you by God, do not torment me." ⁸For he had said to him, "Come out of the man, you unclean spirit!" ⁹And Jesus asked him, "What is your name?" He replied, "My name is Legion; for we are many." ¹⁰And he begged him eagerly not to send them out of the country. ¹¹Now a great herd of swine was feeding there on the hillside; ¹²and they begged him, "Send us to the swine, let us enter them." ¹³So he gave them leave. And the unclean spirits came out, and entered the swine; and the herd, numbering about two thousand, rushed down the steep bank into the sea, and were drowned in the sea.

14 The herdsmen fled, and told it in the city and in the country. And people came to see what it was that had happened. ¹⁵And they came to Jesus, and saw the demoniac sitting there, clothed and in his right mind, the man who had had the legion; and they were afraid. ¹⁶And those who had seen it told what had happened to the

demoniac and to the swine. ¹⁷And they began to beg
Jesus to depart from their neighborhood. ¹⁸And as he was
getting into the boat, the man who had been possessed
with demons begged him that he might be with him.
¹⁹But he refused, and said to him, "Go home to your
friends, and tell them how much the Lord has done for
you, and how he has had mercy on you." ²⁰And he went
away and began to proclaim in the Decapolis how much
Jesus had done for him; and all men marveled.

21 And when Jesus had crossed again in the boat to
the other side, a great crowd gathered about him; and he
was beside the sea. ²²Then came one of the rulers of the
synagogue, Jairus by name; and seeing him, he fell at his
feet, ²³and besought him, saying, "My little daughter is at
the point of death. Come and lay your hands on her, so
that she may be made well, and live." ²⁴And he went with
him.

And a great crowd followed him and thronged about
him. ²⁵And there was a woman who had had a flow of
blood for twelve years, ²⁶and who had suffered much
under many physicians, and had spent all that she had,
and was no better but rather grew worse. ²⁷She had heard
the reports about Jesus, and came up behind him in the
crowd and touched his garment. ²⁸For she said, "If I
touch even his garments, I shall be made well." ²⁹And
immediately the hemorrhage ceased; and she felt in her
body that she was healed of her disease. ³⁰And Jesus,
perceiving in himself that power had gone forth from
him, immediately turned about in the crowd, and said,
"Who touched my garments?" ³¹And his disciples said to
him, "You see the crowd pressing around you, and yet
you say, 'Who touched me?' " ³²And he looked around to
see who had done it. ³³But the woman, knowing what had
been done to her, came in fear and trembling and fell

down before him, and told him the whole truth. [34]And he said to her, "Daughter, your faith has made you well; go in peace, and be healed of your disease."

35 While he was still speaking, there came from the ruler's house some who said, "Your daughter is dead. Why trouble the Teacher any further?" [36]But ignoring what they said, Jesus said to the ruler of the synagogue, "Do not fear, only believe." [37]And he allowed no one to follow him except Peter and James and John the brother of James. [38]When they came to the house of the ruler of the synagogue, he saw a tumult, and people weeping and wailing loudly. [39]And when he had entered, he said to them, "Why do you make a tumult and weep? The child is not dead but sleeping." [40]And they laughed at him. But he put them all outside, and took the child's father and mother and those who were with him, and went in where the child was. [41]Taking her by the hand he said to her, "Talitha cumi"; which means, "Little girl, I say to you, arise." [42]And immediately the girl got up and walked (she was twelve years of age), and they were immediately overcome with amazement. [43]And he strictly charged them that no one should know this, and told them to give her something to eat.

the miracle stories in Mark's gospel; in some ways it is also the most colorful and most bizarre of them all. On the other hand, one cannot, despite the fuller descriptions and various moments of the story, deny that even this story has been shorn of many details and retains only what is useful to Mark's goals.

The description of the poor possessed man is chilling and frightening; it is meant to be so. When it comes to depicting a disease which is to be cured, Mark is willing to extend his description. Obviously, people learned to stay away from this violent man, which factor underlines all the more Jesus' fearlessness in meeting him.

The peculiarity of this story is that Jesus is not reported formally to heal the possessed man. Of course he does heal him, but the action of healing, contained in the words "for Jesus was saying, 'Evil spirit, come out of the man,' " is parenthetical in Mark's text. Mark's interest, while including the cure, is centered on the dialogue between Jesus and the demon. It is this relationship between these two forces that Mark wishes to highlight here.

Mark so combines the person of the demon with the person of the man possessed that the reader is not clear for a time just who it is that runs up to Jesus and does him homage, as though worshiping a superior power. Jesus' question as to who is speaking to him makes it clear that it is Legion who is doing the talking. Legion is a good name for the demon because it indicates the many demons who actually possessed this man and thus explains the savage life of the man. (Mary Magdalene was said to have been possessed of "seven demons.")

The demon has a number of things to say which are worth Mark's reporting. First, the demon wants to know why Jesus is coming into the demon's territory. Such a question.

reminds us of Satan's remark to Jesus, that "all kingdoms are mine, and I can give them to whomever I want." That is, the satanic forces were recognized as controlling various areas of the earth, despite the fact that God ultimately ruled all things. How the Jews integrated these two powers, one for the destruction of humanity and the other for its salvation, is not always easy to explain, but such was the conception of the time. Thus, the demon wants to know why Jesus comes to "alien" territory.

The demon recognizes (as had other demons before him) that Jesus is Son of the Most High God. The title is an exalted one, and surely pierces profoundly into the mystery of Jesus' identity. It is not clear just why Jesus refused to let the demons be witnesses for him. Perhaps the reason is that such a witness, which is based on knowledge without commitment to and love of Jesus, is sterile, for it acknowledges only Jesus' power and offers no comprehension of just why such a powerful person would end his life as Jesus did— and a witness without understanding of the cross is not worth much to Jesus. It cannot be denied, however, that at the same time such a confession by the demon world cannot fail to impress the reader who is, in faith, far beyond any of Jesus' contemporaries as of Chapter 5.

Evidently the command of Jesus to the demon to depart the poor man was considered by the demon as a torture, and he asked to be spared that. Here the demon, usually so mighty and unrestrainable, is brought to beg, thus revealing his real subservience before Jesus.

To this is added the more specific plea that the demon be allowed to pass into nearby swine; in this way, the reader knows that Jesus is not going to let the man remain possessed, no matter how tortured the demon feels at the exorcism. But the reader also sees that Jesus is willing not to destroy the demon. Indeed, the demon has asked not to be driven completely out of the territory and it appears that Jesus is willing to go along with this plea.

Now the pigs are under the destructive influence of the demon. They race headlong to death under its impulses. One might think that in this way the demon was actually destroyed, that Jesus only apparently acquiesced to the demon's request for some mercy. But the belief of many Jews of this time was that the devils inhabited at least two identifiable places: wild desert and the frightful bottoms of the seas. It seems, then, that Jesus did allow them to escape total destruction, as they raced off to their homes away from human beings whom they want to destroy.

The dialogue and interaction of Jesus with the demon are completed. What remains is the reactions of various people to Jesus' astounding action. These reactions are four in number. First, the swineherds run to their fields and villages to shout the news of what they had seen. These people serve to confirm to others by their eye-witness what has happened. The second group, those who have come out to see what they can, particularly the man who they knew to have been possessed, and hear on the spot the account by the eye-witnesses—this group reacts with fear, that fear which results from awareness that one stands in a place just visited by the power of the gods, and asks Jesus to take himself out of their lives. Third, the once-possessed man, showing all the signs of rationality and peace, reacts in a radical way by asking to be allowed to leave all and follow Jesus. In fact, whatever Jesus' reasons for denial of this request be, the cured man is asked to channel his bursting energies to telling in his own territories the marvelous work God has done for him—and so he does. Finally, the fourth group, like a fourth wave flowing from the divine power, is all those people of the Decapolis who "are astounded at what they hear of this event."

Mark's story, then, has many elements in it which stress the wondrous work Jesus has done, recognizably a work of divinity, and people predictably react with great fear of God, great joy at his intervention, great desire to leave all to be a part of him, for he alone is both able and willing to make the demented life a sane one. Certainly, this story is another revelation of the true identity of Jesus.

But there are two other elements important to this story. First, though the people involved are Gentiles and thus know little of the true God, their instinct tells them that Jesus is the living expression of true divine power. The ultimate sign of their belief is their request that he go away, that he not begin to take a divine hand in their human affairs. Perhaps Mark is signaling to his reader that though the Gentiles here are confused in their asking Jesus to leave, they are a promising soil on which to sow the seed of Christianity after Jesus' death.

Second, as noted earlier, the dialogue between Jesus and the demon is a major element of this story. From it one can gather, with greater clarity here than elsewhere, the balance struck by God. Though the demon is not destroyed, and thus the world is not rid of demons by Jesus, Jesus' powers in every meeting are used to free human beings, not allowing demonic possession to continue. Thus, there is a liberation for particular individuals, though no definitive freeing of the world from demons. Such seems to be the way God is willing to allow demonic presence to continue. As with all miracles of healing, one recognizes that Jesus can and will bring complete worldwide liberation someday, for he has the power and the love to do it. No longer is there need to look for the messiah to inaugurate the new age; in instances, isolated it is true, this new age has in part begun. The demon has acknowledged the presence of this power, for the demon knows it is right to call Jesus Son of the Most High God. The time of waiting is up, as Jesus had earlier said; the kingdom of God, a kingdom of physical and spiritual health, is at hand—when and where and to the extent that Jesus is present.

A final observation is in order concerning one particular element of this story. Mark notes that about two thousand swine went over off a high place to drown in the Sea of Galilee. A certain type of reflection might end in dismay that Jesus destroyed a whole herd of pigs as part of his solution in Gerasa. To draw this conclusion from the story is certainly possible, but one must assume that, whatever Jesus' reasoning here (and Mark's for telling this part of the story), the reader is to recognize the singularity of this situation so as to allow God to use his creation for his intentions; indeed, Jesus causes this type of waste only once that we know of. The Mediterranean culture, though fearful that divine plans are at times at cross-purposes to its own and thus eager to separate itself from the divine presence, acknowledged the divine right to use creation to its own ends. One might also note that, from the perspective of the Jews, pigs are an unclean animal, raised here by Gentiles; there would follow a greater tolerance at the destruction of this animal, of this property of this type of person, for God's purposes.

The only other account of Chapter 5 has to do with further miracles of great power. Here we have interwoven the plea of Jairus for his daughter's health, the cure of the woman with a hemorrhage, and the actual cure of Jairus' daughter. So neatly are these elements joined together that scholars believe Mark received this interweaving rather than creating it himself. Thus, we have here, scholars think, an example of how someone else had joined together what Mark inherited as one piece and now presents as one piece.

So pressing was the fear of the Gerasenes that Jesus, no matter what he intended by entering their territory, grants them their request, gets back into the boat with his twelve, and recrosses the Sea of Galilee. As is usual with Mark, if he has nothing to recount or does not want to recount anything, he simply moves Jesus in a sentence from one backdrop to another. We now find ourselves with him at the western side of the lake where a crowd has found him and presses upon him. Among them is Jairus, a leader of the synagogue (presumably of Capernaum, though Mark finds it unnecessary to name the town).

A synagogue was a place of prayer, meditation and reading; only the temple of Jerusalem had sacrifices and accompanying splendid liturgies. A synagogue could be established where there were just nine good Israelite men; thus, synagogues existed everywhere, and at one period in Jerusalem there were over two hundred. A synagogue usually had one synagogue leader or president, assisted by a council of leading men of the synagogue. The leading men looked to the overall well-being of the synagogue, while the synagogue leader or president took charge of the actual running of things. Often it was this synagogue leader who orchestrated the synagogue sabbath services of prayer and readings, which were followed by a homily by someone designated by him and his helpers.

Jairus was either one of these leading men of the synagogue or the leader of the synagogue himself. He sets the stage for this revelatory miracle story by asking Jesus to come to his house to cure his daughter who is critically ill; there is faith here and Jesus begins to walk with Jairus.

The distance to Jairus' house, and the pressing of the

crowd around them, allow for the insertion of another miracle story. Once again we learn only details essential for a
miracle story. Here stress upon the seriousness of the woman's condition is in the form of desperation: neither money
nor doctors can cure this woman; indeed she has only gotten worse under human professional care. But not only is
her story special for its underlining human powerlessness to
help her. The cure which is here worked is done simply by
touching Jesus, or rather touching simply his outer garment.
Indeed, Mark makes clear that Jesus did not consciously will
a cure nor did he even see the woman he had cured. Jesus
knows only that "power has gone out from himself." Jesus
makes it very clear at the end of the story that what brought
about the woman's cure (whom he gently calls "daughter")
is the interaction of three elements: his ever-present power,
his abiding willingness to use his power for the good of
others, and the woman's faith.

Once again Mark has interwoven the themes which
dominate this section of his gospel: Jesus' divine power, Jesus' good will and responsive faith in him. The reverse teaching of this story is more subtle. One has always come across
in history the use of talismans or other such objects which
supposedly have superhuman powers. Jesus here clearly
identifies the source of the cure as himself, not his clothing,
and, from a different perspective, he underlines the fact that
it was the woman's faith in him that was essential to this
cure. In this way Mark tries to separate this healing from
magic.

Mark notes that Jesus was interrupted while speaking
by people from Jairus' house. This "interruption" does not
mean that we have lost what Jesus' main point to the woman
was. Rather, "interruption" of this kind is a clever literary
way of tightly linking one scene to another, without implying
that the speaker failed to say exactly what he wanted to say.

To the sad news of the little girl's death Jesus calls for trust in himself, not fear that all is lost. In a sense, the sad words of the messengers were such that they reveal hopelessness in the presence of Jesus. It is to this despair in his presence that Jesus responds with a call for trust in himself.

The drama is heightened as Jesus is ridiculed by the officially hired and other mourners; he says the child is just sleeping, whereas all evidence to them is that she is dead. Such is the power of Jesus that, with a touch and two words, the child stood up. To show the completeness of the miracle, the child is described as standing up immediately, walking around and, soon, to be eating. The contrast between human judgment and divine power is very great here: one saying that death is beyond the power of Jesus to dominate, the other treating death as just a mere sleep from which a person, through Jesus' power, rises, walks about and then eats. Again, Mark has invited the reader to be a part of this wondrous event, to understand the perspectives of Jesus and the crowds, to grasp the reality of Jesus which is grounded not in human estimates of him but on the reality of his power.

That Jesus did not heal in the presence of all the twelve, but only before Peter, James and John (and the child's parents), is mysterious. Certainly at other key points Jesus deals directly with only these three of his twelve. It is not clear why Jesus made such a distinction among the twelve; it is not very satisfactory to say that not Jesus but the later Christians injected this distinction into the story because each of the three rose to exceptional prominence in the early years after Jesus' death. Rather, there is a remembrance here which reflects a choice of Jesus, the reasons for which are now lost. The fact remains, though, that at least through the witness of the three disciples the outlines of the story can be rooted for the early community as historical.

Mighty miracles calling for pure and total trust are cen-

tral now to Mark's story as we close Chapter 5; if the previous chapter was an opportune time in which to reflect on
the seed sown on various soils, Chapter 5 continues to press
home the need that great faith is asked of those who are
Jesus' disciples. Certainly, Jesus' miracles justify that faith;
but one is aware, from hindsight, that, despite the experience of or stories about Jesus' miracles, some people who
had enthusiastically followed Jesus later have, for one reason
or another, left his company. Mark marshals many of the
most significant miracles of Jesus for the Christian's reading,
and presents them as calls, pleas for faith. He hopes, as many
scholars suggest, that, by showing how reasonable faith and
trust in Jesus is, Mark will convince the Christian not to
waver in his commitment, even if put through the great trial,
that of martyrdom.

Chapter 6

Mark has deliberately chosen to write the account of Jesus' public life in such a way that, from the beginning stages, conflict is a visible and major thread of the story. Early on, Jesus was strongly criticized for sabbath miracles, claims to be able to forgive sins and to control the sabbath, eating with sinners and failing to fast. His closest relatives completely misunderstand him and his enemies viciously argue that he is possessed by Satan. Jesus' parabolic teaching is filled with awareness of soils which cannot receive his word successfully. Most recently, Jesus' disciples show, under pressures, a wavering trust in Jesus. Jesus for his part is now more than ever calling for trust and faith, and praising those who show trust in him. Over all this hangs the cloud Mark introduced early on: Pharisees and Herodians have conspired to destroy Jesus—no halfway measures here!

With Chapter 6 Mark moves the reader from Jairus' house in Capernaum to a new scene: we are in Nazareth and its countryside. With one brush stroke Mark notes that Jesus, accompanied by his disciples, is teaching. Immediately begins the confrontation. Those listening to Jesus are puzzled, nonplussed. The source of their confusion is "these things" which are his—wisdom, powers exercised through his hands—when they are contrasted with the Jesus they knew all their lives. The result of this contrast is "scandal";

6 He went away from there and came to his own country; and his disciples followed him. ²And on the sabbath he began to teach in the synagogue; and many who heard him were astonished, saying, "Where did this man get all this? What is the wisdom given to him? What mighty works are wrought by his hands! ³Is not this the carpenter, the son of Mary and brother of James and Joses and Judas and Simon, and are not his sisters here with us?" And they took offense at him. ⁴And Jesus said to them, "A prophet is not without honor, except in his own country, and among his own kin, and in his own house." ⁵And he could do no mighty work there, except that he laid his hands upon a few sick people and healed them. ⁶And he marveled because of their unbelief.

And he went about among the villages teaching.

7 And he called to him the twelve, and began to send them out two by two, and gave them authority over the unclean spirits. ⁸He charged them to take nothing for their journey except a staff; no bread, no bag, no money in their belts; ⁹but to wear sandals and not put on two tunics. ¹⁰And he said to them, "Where you enter a house, stay there until you leave the place. ¹¹And if any place will not receive you and they refuse to hear you, when you leave, shake off the dust that is on your feet for a testimony against them." ¹²So they went out and preached that men should repent. ¹³And they cast out many demons, and anointed with oil many that were sick and healed them.

14 King Herod heard of it; for Jesus' name had become known. Some said, "John the baptizer has been

raised from the dead; that is why these powers are at work in him." [15]But others said, "It is Elijah." And others said, "It is a prophet, like one of the prophets of old." [16]But when Herod heard of it he said, "John, whom I beheaded, has been raised." [17]For Herod had sent and seized John, and bound him in prison for the sake of Herodi-as, his brother Philip's wife; because he had married her. [18]For John said to Herod, "It is not lawful for you to have your brother's wife." [19]And Herodi-as had a grudge against him, and wanted to kill him. But she could not, [20]for Herod feared John, knowing that he was a righteous and holy man, and kept him safe. When he heard him, he was much perplexed; and yet he heard him gladly. [21]But an opportunity came when Herod on his birthday gave a banquet for his courtiers and officers and the leading men of Galilee. [22]For when Herodi-as' daughter came in and danced, she pleased Herod and his guests; and the king said to the girl, "Ask me for whatever you wish, and I will grant it." [23]And he vowed to her, "Whatever you ask me, I will give you, even half of my kingdom." [24]And she went out, and said to her mother, "What shall I ask?" And she said, "The head of John the baptizer." [25]And she came in immediately with haste to the king, and asked, saying, "I want you to give me at once the head of John the Baptist on a platter." [26]And the king was exceedingly sorry; but because of his oaths and his guests he did not want to break his word to her. [27]And immediately the king sent a soldier of the guard and gave orders to bring his head. He went and beheaded him in the prison, [28]and brought his head on a platter, and gave it to the girl; and the girl gave it to her mother. [29]When his disciples heard of it, they came and took his body, and laid it in a tomb.

30 The apostles returned to Jesus, and told him all

that they had done and taught. [31]And he said to them, "Come away by yourselves to a lonely place, and rest a while." For many were coming and going, and they had no leisure even to eat. [32]And they went away in the boat to a lonely place by themselves. [33]Now many saw them going, and knew them, and they ran there on foot from all the towns, and got there ahead of them. [34]As he went ashore he saw a great throng, and he had compassion on them, because they were like sheep without a shepherd; and he began to teach them many things. [35]And when it grew late, his disciples came to him and said, "This is a lonely place, and the hour is now late; [36]send them away, to go into the country and villages round about and buy themselves something to eat." [37]But he answered them, "You give them something to eat." And they said to him, "Shall we go and buy two hundred denarii worth of bread, and give it to them to eat?" [38]And he said to them, "How many loaves have you? Go and see." And when they had found out, they said, "Five, and two fish." [39]Then he commanded them all to sit down by companies upon the green grass. [40]So they sat down in groups, by hundreds and by fifties. [41]And taking the five loaves and the two fish he looked up to heaven, and blessed, and broke the loaves, and gave them to the disciples to set before the people; and he divided the two fish among them all. [42]And they all ate and were satisfied. [43]And they took up twelve baskets full of broken pieces and of the fish. [44]And those who ate the loaves were five thousand men.

45 Immediately he made his disciples get into the boat and go before him to the other side, to Beth-saida, while he dismissed the crowd. [46]And after he had taken leave of them, he went up on the mountain to pray. [47]And when evening came, the boat was out on the sea, and he was alone on the land. [48]And he saw that they were

making headway painfully, for the wind was against them. And about the fourth watch of the night he came to them, walking on the sea. He meant to pass by them, [49]but when they saw him walking on the sea they thought it was a ghost, and cried out; [50]for they all saw him, and were terrified. But immediately he spoke to them and said, "Take heart, it is I; have no fear." [51]And he got into the boat with them and the wind ceased. And they were utterly astounded, [52]for they did not understand about the loaves, but their hearts were hardened.

53 And when they had crossed over, they came to land at Gennesaret, and moored to the shore. [54]And when they got out of the boat, immediately the people recognized him, [55]and ran about the whole neighborhood and began to bring sick people on their pallets to any place where they heard he was. [56]And wherever he came, in villages, cities, or country, they laid the sick in the market places, and besought him that they might touch even the fringe of his garment; and as many as touched it were made well.

that is, Jesus, in their final analysis, makes these people "trip and stumble" on their way to God.

Jesus' reply to this reaction is summed up in an aphorism which appears in various forms, with various accents, elsewhere in the New Testament, as well as here. A prophet is not dishonored except in his own territory, among his own relatives, in his own household. By this saying one sees the irony that those closest, even in love, are most often those who understand least. It is a saying worth repeating, Mark thinks, to his reader.

Mark earlier had noted that Jesus' longtime neighbors wondered at his wisdom and at his miracles; evidently, their inability to believe, by means of this wisdom and these powers, that Jesus was the messiah and Son of God prevented Jesus from further miracles. Mark now stresses this inability of Jesus to work miracles for these dear ones, except for a few healings. Jesus is given the final say in this story; he is amazed at their lack of faith in those who "knew" him best. The resonances of this account are multiple. Jesus' near and dear reject him; later, his nation will reject him; finally, some of those who became his disciples will reject him. In each case one can only wonder that, indeed, it seems to be the nearest and dearest who are least able to see the truth. One sees the danger: one must *always* be able to get beyond experiences to the truth. Should one fail to believe because of one's experiences, the conclusion of the story looms unhappily: their lack of faith prevented him from using his powers on their behalf.

Mark now judges it is time to weave into his story an element he had introduced progressively earlier. At the beginning of his public life, Jesus had called four men to become "fishers of men." To these was added at least one more specific calling, that of Matthew/Levi. Next, Mark noted that Jesus later called twelve to himself, to a special relationship and to a future of preaching and healing patterned on his own mission. Strangely enough, thereafter Mark has not specifically and explicitly called attention to the twelve—though they no doubt are included in the more general title of "disciples" or "learners."

But now, in Chapter 6, Mark again introduces the twelve. If their going out to preach and heal did not actually occur at this historical moment, it is not clear just why Mark would have inserted it here. Perhaps Mark just senses that the twelve have spent enough time with Jesus to have learned to imitate him; the story is ripe for telling now.

In a story that is usually remembered for the disciples' first missionary activity apart from Jesus, there is as much time spent on prepping the disciples as in describing their actual work. The fact that the story-teller has preserved instructions about missionary life for his reader suggests that such instructions might have been of practical use still in Christian preaching of the 60's A.D.; certainly they are edifying as they reveal how single-minded and unconcerned about the things of this world Jesus wanted his twelve to be. They are practical instructions, too, for they suggest how the twelve can hope to support themselves as they dedicate themselves to the preaching.

Within Jesus' words to his twelve we can see a subtle reference to other methods of missionizing used at Jesus' time in the Mediterranean basin. It was very common for wisdom teachers and wonder-workers to gain a significant amount of wealth from their work; people gave generously to support those who brought them happiness. It is with an eye to these other wandering teachers and healers that Jesus asks his twelve to live in simplicity; in this way there is no confusion as to what the twelve think most important about life—their message.

The sign of "shaking the dust from one's feet" is a sign

that one does not want anything further to do with a person or locality, that one leaves the place or person to the results of its own decisions. Essentially, such a sign is an imitation of how the prophets of old expressed their indignation toward those who refused their words.

With advice received, the twelve go off in pairs to places unspecified. Perhaps Mark's leaving their destinations unmentioned suggests a subtle hint of the greater, limitless preaching of the generation after Jesus? The description of the twelve is intentionally reminiscent of the descriptions the reader has already seen about Jesus; in this likeness the reader sees how much the disciples simply mirror Jesus.

The description concentrates first of all on the message of repentance. One is not allowed to forget that, though Jesus is currently presented in the mode of teacher, it is repentance which is at the bottom of everything and that teaching presupposes. Teaching is simply the extension of repentance, as repentance is to be extended by deeds appropriate to repentance.

Generally, healing is the work which accompanies the call to a new way of life; particularly, Mark singles out the power of the twelve to drive out demons. In miniature, we have here in the work of the disciples the sporadic and momentary replacement of this age—sinful life, sickness, control by demons—by the longed-for life to come—a life of love, of health, of the fullest humanity. These men are indeed the extension of Jesus.

One small point asks for underlining here. The twelve are said to heal by anointing with oil. This detail may be remembered because, as a document like the letter of James (5:14) witnesses, there had grown up among Christians of various localities a practice of prayer and anointing for the cure of the sick and dying. Such a practice was more than a missionary activity; it became a community activity. In this way we learn of the beginnings of our sacrament of healing.

The twelve went off to do their assigned work. Mark does not tell us how long they spent in this work on behalf of Jesus and the kingdom; most likely their work lasted for some days. Mark's way of letting time pass till they return is to explain what happened to end the preaching career of John the Baptist; presumably Mark is interested in this fatal moment at least because it suggestively foreshadows the eventual fate of Jesus.

John the Baptist was ordered beheaded by Herod Antipas, ruler of Galilee and Perea (a large strip of land on the eastern bank of the Jordan River). Antipas, like so many of his relatives who achieved political power, carried the personal name of his father, Herod (the Great); hence, what was a personal name for one person became the royal name for his descendants.

When Herod the Great died about 4 B.C., Roman authority accepted his final will, which provided that the bulk of Palestine be unequally divided between Antipas and his brother Archelaus. Archelaus was given central and southern Palestine, i.e., Samaria and Judea; he proved so harsh and cruel that he was removed from power by 9 A.D. and replaced by a series of officials, not of the Herodian family, who were known as governors or procurators. Pontius Pilate was one of these. Archelaus is well known biblically, because it was on account of him that Joseph, according to Matthew's gospel, preferred to live in Nazareth rather than in Bethlehem or Jerusalem, when Joseph brought his wife and child out of Egypt. In this way the Holy Family is placed in Nazareth of Galilee and falls under the rule of Antipas, brother of Archelaus and the ruler of Galilee.

If at all possible, children of powerful people spent

many years in Rome seeking education and political influence. The sons of Herod were no different. It was while
Antipas was in Rome that he, though already married, fell
in love with his niece. She too happened to be married and
had a daughter, but she willingly left her husband (another
son of Herod the Great) to follow Antipas to Galilee. Her
name was Herodias (named after her grandfather, Herod the
Great) and her daughter was named Salome. Accordingly,
Antipas divested himself of his wife (for which he was eventually driven out of office) and took Herodias and Salome
as his new family.

Neither Antipas nor Herodias was Jewish in the strict
sense; thus, neither was strictly speaking bound by the Mosaic law which forbade such a marriage as Antipas now undertook. On the other hand, Antipas was ruler over the Jews
of Galilee and Perea, and thus was, in John's eyes, to live a
life in accord with Jewish law. John the Baptist made this
marital situation known far and wide, and called publicly for
repentance. This dispute was ignored by the Roman ap-
pointee in Judea and Samaria (at this time the procurator
was Pontius Pilate), and so the battle was strictly between
Antipas and John.

How John came to be murdered is easily understood
from the basic psychology of the people in Mark's story. It
is clear that, whereas one might detect a twinge of sympathy
for Herod Antipas, there is no love lost in the story for Herodias. As in most of these tragic stories, most blame is put
upon the primary mover, less blame upon the one caught
in an irony. Herod, however, remains as an excellent figure
to underline how a person, faced with obvious injustice,
cannot find the humility to reverse a terrifying decision. In
this way he carries his own peculiar part of the sin.

Though we most often associate Herod Antipas with

Galilee and thus suppose that John was imprisoned and beheaded there, many scholars believe that John's prison and
place of death was the fortress Machaerus, built by Herod
the Great on the eastern side of the Jordan River, just about
parallel with the northern end of the Dead Sea. This fortress,
like the more famous Massada and others, made up the defense line along Palestine's eastern border. Thus, John died
not too far from Jerusalem—"where the prophets are killed."

The particular circumstance by which Mark introduced
this tragic story was Herod Antipas' suggestion that Jesus was
another form of John the Baptist (whom "Herod had only
recently put to death"). Jesus, Antipas guessed, was John
come back to life. What this really means is not altogether
clear. Surely the words cannot be taken literally, that Jesus
is John risen? Yet, is it only poetry to say, not that Jesus is
like John or has John's powers and preaching, but that Jesus
is John risen?

Herod, Mark's text indicates, is not the only one trying
to guess at Jesus' true identity. Some, Mark notes, think of
him as Elijah, others think of him as one of the prophets.
By describing these guesses Mark is preparing the reader for
his Chapter 8, where the question of Jesus' identity will be
most fully answered. It is enough to know now that all kinds
of people are trying to estimate the real identity of Jesus,
even Herod the Great whose judgment is influenced by his
very recent murder of John the Baptist.

Once the story of John the Baptist is finished the twelve
reappear, bursting with joy at the success of their mission.
Note that this mission is described now as "all they did and
all they taught." Once again, "teaching" is replacing "call to
repentance." Clearly, for Mark teaching is simply the extension of this call to repentance. Jesus' reply to the return of
his twelve is to suggest a rest; he chooses a place which is

"out-of-the-way," and thus prepares for the next story whose circumstances include the necessity of feeding people who are in an "out-of-the-way place."

There is a bit of a geographical problem at this point. We seem to be at the western (probably northwestern) shore of the Sea of Galilee; the last geographical notice had Jesus in the countryside around Nazareth. It is from this northwestern point that Jesus suggests that he and his twelve depart. Which direction did they go? Mark does not say, but he does note that, when they finish their "rest," the twelve get in the boat again to "cross to Bethsaida (at the northwest corner of the lake), to the other side of the lake." When they finish this "crossing," they actually land at Gennesaret, an area or plain at the northwest shore of the Sea of Galilee. Thus, they set out from the western shore of the lake and return to the northwestern shore of the lake. One must assume, it seems, that the place of "rest," the "out-of-the-way-place," is on the eastern shore of the lake. Now, the problem lies simply in this, that the long tradition of Christian belief celebrates the multiplication of the loaves and fish on the northwestern edge of the Sea of Galilee, not on its eastern shore. There seems to be no way to harmonize calculations from Mark's text and Christian tradition.

People spotted Jesus and his twelve leaving by boat and, watching them from along the shore, so guessed as to get to Jesus' destination before him. Such was the great enthusiasm for Jesus and such was his dedication to the crowds that, "pitying them," he put aside his day of rest to teach them. Mark invokes here the long-standing biblical image, the shepherd and his sheep, to explain the total dependence of the crowd for its "food" from Jesus. Jesus responds with the food of his teaching. We do not know what precisely Jesus teaches, nor do we learn if the desire for miracles is the motive of the crowd. What is stressed is Mark's view that what so satisfyingly links Jesus and the crowd is the teaching.

What happens next is the marvelous multiplication of the loaves and fish. That this miracle is of the greatest significance can be seen from the fact that it is one of the few miracles recounted in all four gospels. Moreover, interpreters have found a number of teachings in this story, which again underlines the richness of the event the story describes.

Looking to the Old Testament for guidance, many scholars recall the powerful deeds of Elijah and his disciple, Elisha:

> "The jar of flour did not go empty nor the jug of oil run dry," as the Lord had foretold through Elijah (1 Kings 17:16).

> "Give the twenty barley loaves to the people to eat," said Elisha. But his servant replied, "How can I set this before a hundred men?" "Give it to the people ... for the Lord says, 'They shall eat and there shall be some left over'" (2 Kings 4:42–43).

In noting similarities between the stories of Elijah and Elisha (who lived in the 800's B.C.) and the story of Jesus, Mark hopes that his reader will, scholars say, see in Jesus the fullness of the power expressed in these ancient prophets of God. Indeed, were not people, Mark had only recently indicated, guessing that Jesus was a new Elijah? Here, then, is an action of Jesus which brings to Israel once again the presence of Elijah, the greatest of Israel's prophets.

Some scholars think that Mark intentionally stresses the plenteousness of bread and fish which Jesus causes. If this is the case, is Mark trying to draw attention to another won-

derful bread which fed Israel miraculously for the length of
its journey in the desert? Is Jesus, then, the new dispenser
of food which will save God's people from death? In this
interpretation, the food Jesus gives in abundance is his
teaching, his word, which will protect and give life to his
people.

One might recall that John's gospel draws the same parallel between the miraculous bread Jesus gives and the bread
of angels which fortified the Israelites in the desert. For John,
however, the bread which will give life forever is both Jesus'
teaching and Jesus' body and blood. For many scholars there
is in Mark, too, not only the resonance of life-giving teaching, but the symbolism of eucharistic bread, the body and
blood of Jesus. Certainly, the eucharist had by Mark's time
become an essential fabric of the Christian communities;
Paul himself attests to this years before Mark wrote. When
Mark describes the immediate action of Jesus before the
crowd eats, one can hardly miss the eucharistic symbolism:
"taking the bread ... looking up to heaven, he blessed and
broke the bread and gave it to his disciples. ..."

Another way of interpreting the multiplication of loaves
and fish is less symbolic than what we have so far considered. For some scholars the multiplication is simply an
astounding exercise of power. In support of this view, one
certainly is made aware very early that, according to any
human estimate, it will be impossible to feed this crowd.
Thus, Jesus emerges once again as a figure of immense, indeed unimaginable power.

Attention to one detail adjusts this interpretation a bit.
The disciples, as though they could feed the crowd, ask Jesus
if he really wants them to pay for the feeding from the purse
which supported Jesus and his twelve. Jesus, having drawn
from the disciples this question, ignores the purse and from

his own wealth lavishly bestows on the crowd more than it either needs or wants. The emphasis here is on the will to give, to spend all to please those who follow Jesus. Thus, Jesus is not only an immensely powerful being, but also one who will give generously from his stores to all.

And with the above consideration we come to the final observation about Jesus' tremendous act of power. Upon re-reading the story a few times, one realizes that there is a certain excess to Jesus' giving, something that makes it more than just an account of a miracle. The principal clue lies in the fact that, equivalently, each disciple gathers a basket filled with the leftovers of the bread and fish Jesus multi-plied. Is this gathering of baskets meant simply to argue to the power and generosity of Jesus (or, as some in the past have suggested, to his not wanting to waste food)? Indeed, the gathering of food into twelve baskets, when looked at literally, raises the perplexing question, "What did the twelve do with those baskets of food anyway?" Once one reviews the story from a certain perspective, a new empha-sis emerges.

The twelve took up twelve baskets of miraculous food. Indeed, they were the ones who brought the entire problem to Jesus' attention. They were told, "You yourselves give the people something to eat." They brought the loaves and fish to Jesus and then they, not Jesus, brought the food to the people.

From these details comes the insight that, though the twelve and their successors feel inadequate to feed from themselves the many followers of Jesus, Jesus himself will provide lavishly for his believers, in teaching and in eucha-rist; the role of the twelve will be to serve as distributors of the Lord's bounty, realizing all the while who is the real and only source of this feeding. Each of the twelve is directed to collect the food remaining, as though each one has, from Jesus, the food with which he is to go on feeding Christians.

Thus, the multiplication of the loaves suggests many things to interpreters, and it can do so precisely because of the variety of suggestive details embedded in Mark's story. It is difficult to identify what Mark is trying to emphasize above all else in this story; perhaps it is wiser in this case to appreciate all the suggestions the story makes, rather than to concentrate solely on determining what Mark wants most to underline.

After the famous story of the multiplication of the loaves and fish comes the story of Jesus' walking on the waters of the Sea of Galilee. Because John's gospel, especially in its sequence of stories, is so different from the sequences of Mark-Matthew-Luke, scholars are quick to note any agreement among all four gospels. Here is such a case. The implication of this agreement about sequence of events is that it makes most sense to say that the two stories, multiplication and walking on the waters, were put together before any of the four gospels inherited them. Thus, in the linking together of these stories we are able to peek behind the time of the evangelists to those who collected and joined the stories for later writers.

After the multiplication of the loaves and fish, Jesus sent his disciples back (westward, it seems) from the eastern shore of the Sea of Galilee toward Bethsaida. It appears to be about five in the morning. As is common enough, a storm breaks onto the sea and soon the disciples are in grave danger. The reader no doubt recalls a story Mark told not long ago, in which Jesus with great, majestic power calmed wind and sea with a word. Here too there is the suggestion that the disciples should trust in the will of Jesus, which commanded them to cross the sea, in the power of Jesus, which they have already experienced in many forms, and in the love of Jesus, which Jesus has manifested to them on many occasions.

But this story is not only another revelation of Jesus' power. Two elements are added which conspire to take the disciples and the reader ever more deeply into the truth about Jesus. The first element is the peculiar circumstance that Jesus walked on the waters, "intending to pass them by." What is one to understand to be the meaning of this peculiar action of Jesus? Strange enough is his walking on the water, but very puzzling is his intention to pass by his disciples, especially since they are in grave trouble.

Added to Jesus' behavior here is the disciples' inability to know that he who was walking on the water was not a ghost but actually Jesus. They do not even identify this image as "Jesus' " ghost (or, in Greek, *phantasma*). They simply fail to recognize him. What is at the bottom of the tension between Jesus and his disciples?

There are two signs in the Marcan story which call to mind Old Testament imagery and thus suggest that Jesus is being interpreted here in terms of the Old Testament. First, the phrasing, "to pass them by," recalls that that is the description God uses of himself in showing himself to Moses. God wanted Moses to see him, but the best that the human being could be given is a glimpse of the divine being as "he passed him by." To describe Jesus in these words, "he was passing them by," is, in the view of many interpreters, to suggest that Jesus is here revealing the divinity in him.

The second sign is the words with which Jesus responds to his disciples' cries of fear and awe. He gives them reason not to fear, because "It is I." Actually, in Greek "It is I" is *Ego eimi*. As soon as an interpreter sees the phrase *ego eimi*, and presumably Mark's audience, too, he is reminded of the name God revealed to Moses at the burning bush, when

Moses asked, "Who shall I say is sending me to free Israel from Pharaoh?" The answer was the famous name "I am who am," which from the Hebrew is Yahweh; a shortened form of "I am who am" is "I am," or, as the ancient and authoritative Greek translation has it, *ego eimi.*

With these two signs, then, many interpreters come to the conclusion that not only is Jesus revealed here as mighty Lord of nature, but he is also revealed as embodying the presence of Yahweh himself. He can use of himself the name and gesture of Yahweh, he "passes by," and say in his own case, "I am."

In supporting roles to this revelation of divinity are Jesus' domination over water and the disciples' response of fear and awe. Historically, Israel had a great fear of the seas, as is witnessed by the fact that it never had great sea-going vessels or ports; it was Yahweh who protected Israel from this violent force. From a reading of the Old Testament encounters between God and human beings, one realizes that a primary and altogether proper response to the divine presence is human fear, even a desire to flee this presence lest being too close to it might bring even death to the unworthy human being. The disciples' fear and Jesus' complete mastery over the sea, then, are further signs of the identity of Jesus.

But not only is the miracle story of calming wind and waves filled with suggestions about the divine presence in Jesus. The story does not end till Mark makes his own trenchant observation. Mark says that the disciples were astounded and dumbfounded because they did not understand about the loaves, and they did not understand about the loaves because their "hearts (which really means *minds*) were unperceptive, dull."

Precisely what Mark is getting at here is unclear. What he seems to be saying is that the disciples should never have missed recognizing Jesus and should never have been afraid, if they had perceived correctly the full meaning of the multiplication of the loaves. What is it about the miracle of the loaves that should have made the disciples recognize Jesus and unafraid in danger? Perhaps the best suggestion is that if the disciples had realized the depths of Jesus' powers and the love which governs those powers, they would have been in a better position to remain calm amidst the violent storm and to perceive in the mysterious presence on the water their own master, Jesus. The miracle of the loaves, then, was in its own way, according to this suggestion, a revelation about the divine presence and love in Jesus. If the disciples had realized this, they would have had different and proper reactions to their experience on the sea.

A final note to this story of Jesus' walking on the waters. Many scholars think that in this story (as elsewhere) Mark uses the disciples as means to an end. The end in mind is the enlightenment of Mark's community, of his readers. The disciples are described, even exaggeratedly so, in such fashion that the reader can more easily learn a lesson Mark thinks valuable. In this particular instance, what the reader has to learn is to recognize the divine presence of Jesus amidst the trials of the church. This Jesus of 65 A.D. is alive, raised from the dead. It is Jesus, though difficult to identify for those who are dull of heart. Unlike the Jesus of the story, he will not always stop his leadership "to the other side" (= heaven) in order to get into the bark (= the church) to calm the church's problems and troubles. How can the reader, Mark's contemporaries, the church, recognize the divine presence of Jesus? In the breaking of the bread, in the eucharistic meal, one finds the profound meaning (and presence) of Jesus which should calm the church and help it recognize the presence of its Lord. That the disciples saw a "phantasm," then, is a suggestion to many interpreters that

Mark is speaking to his reader about a Jesus who is difficult to perceive, but nonetheless the real, the true Jesus, the embodiment of the divine presence in the risen Lord. The Christian must be able to recognize this divine presence within the trials he endures and in the ways, some purely symbolic, in which Jesus assures his presence.

As in earlier situations of the gospel, Mark is here interpreted in a symbolic fashion; the story, apparently only recounting something that happened to the twelve, is understood to be so written as to convey a message of Mark to his readership. Thus, though there may well be history in this story, the goal of the story is not simply to present "what happened," but to teach through the way Mark writes up the event how one is to act in Mark's time.

Mark completes this section of miraculous activity with what is called a "summary," examples of which we have read earlier. Thus, again Mark uses the literary device whereby he conveys the continued powerful activity of Jesus without having to descend to particularized stories. One is thus impressed by the sheer numbers of Jesus' miracles bunched within a brief time period. Also visible is Jesus' continued willingness to help all who might come to him. In this particular summary, just a touch of the tassel of his cloak, in faith, is enough to heal, so extraordinary is the mighty power of Jesus.

Mark's "camera," then, withdraws the reader from particularized events to a general overview of Jesus' cures; more easily does one see from this perspective the masses of people Jesus reaches in his willingness to heal. It is this very massing around Jesus which really allows people to think of him as a danger to public peace and thus to plot further against him. On the other hand, the numbers of cures is in its own way an argument as to Jesus' good will and immense power. Is he the messiah?

Chapter 7

Chapter 6 contained some of the most significant parts of Jesus' preaching career: the disappointing rejection of Jesus by his family and fellow Nazareans, the first effort of the twelve to act on behalf of Jesus and the kingdom without Jesus being with them, an account of the atrocious death of John the Baptist, and many miracles, not the least of which were the feeding of five thousand people from five loaves and two fish and Jesus' own walking on the waters of the Sea of Galilee. We have noted, however, not simply the deeds themselves, but also how these events were used by Mark to speak in various ways to his reader, to his contemporaries, to his church. Mark uses past history as a means to influence contemporary behavior and thinking.

As happened earlier in the gospel, Mark alternates action with teaching. After the miracles of Chapter 3, Mark introduced the parabolic teaching of Jesus; now, after the miracles of Chapter 6, Mark gives the reader more of Jesus' teaching. The telling of the parabolic teaching of Jesus, however, was strongly influenced by Mark's own concerns with modern questions: Why did some people seem to understand Jesus' parables and others not? Why did Jesus teach only in parables, particularly to those who obviously did not understand them, whereas sometimes he did explain things to his disciples? In all of this, Mark argues that there will be

7Now when the Pharisees gathered together to him, with some of the scribes, who had come from Jerusalem, ²they saw that some of his disciples ate with hands defiled, that is, unwashed. ³(For the Pharisees, and all the Jews, do not eat unless they wash their hands, observing the tradition of the elders; ⁴and when they come from the market place, they do not eat unless they purify themselves; and there are many other traditions which they observe, the washing of cups and pots and vessels of bronze.) ⁵And the Pharisees and the scribes asked him, "Why do your disciples not live according to the tradition of the elders, but eat with hands defiled?" ⁶And he said to them, "Well did Isaiah prophesy of you hypocrites, as it is written,

'This people honors me with their lips,
   but their heart is far from me;
⁷in vain do they worship me,
   teaching as doctrines the precepts of men.'
⁸You leave the commandment of God, and hold fast the tradition of men."

9 And he said to them, "You have a fine way of rejecting the commandment of God, in order to keep your tradition! ¹⁰For Moses said, 'Honor your father and your mother'; and, 'He who speaks evil of father or mother, let him surely die'; ¹¹but you say, 'If a man tells his father or his mother, What you would have gained from me is Corban' (that is, given to God)— ¹²then you no longer permit him to do anything for his father or mother, ¹³thus making void the word of God through your

tradition which you hand on. And many such things you do."

14 And he called the people to him again, and said to them, "Hear me, all of you, and understand: [15]there is nothing outside a man which by going into him can defile him; but the things which come out of a man are what defile him." [17]And when he had entered the house, and left the people, his disciples asked him about the parable. [18]And he said to them, "Then are you also without understanding? Do you not see that whatever goes into a man from outside cannot defile him, [19]since it enters, not his heart but his stomach, and so passes on?" (Thus he declared all foods clean.) [20]And he said, "What comes out of a man is what defiles a man. [21]For from within, out of the heart of man, come evil thoughts, fornication, theft, murder, adultery, [22]coveting, wickedness, deceit, licentiousness, envy, slander, pride, foolishness. [23]All these evil things come from within, and they defile a man."

24 And from there he arose and went away to the region of Tyre and Sidon. And he entered a house, and would not have any one know it; yet he could not be hid. [25]But immediately a woman, whose little daughter was possessed by an unclean spirit, heard of him, and came and fell down at his feet. [26]Now the woman was a Greek, a Syrophoenician by birth. And she begged him to cast the demon out of her daughter. [27]And he said to her, "Let the children first be fed, for it is not right to take the children's bread and throw it to the dogs." [28]But she answered him, "Yes, Lord; yet even the dogs under the table eat the children's crumbs." [29]And he said to her, "For this saying you may go your way; the demon has left your daughter." [30]And she went home, and found the child lying in bed, and the demon gone.

31 Then he returned from the region of Tyre, and went through Sidon to the Sea of Galilee, through the region of the Decapolis. ³²And they brought to him a man who was deaf and had an impediment in his speech; and they besought him to lay his hand upon him. ³³And taking him aside from the multitude privately, he put his fingers into his ears, and he spat and touched his tongue; ³⁴and looking up to heaven, he sighed, and said to him, "Ephphatha," that is, "Be opened." ³⁵And his ears were opened, his tongue was released, and he spoke plainly. ³⁶And he charged them to tell no one; but the more he charged them, the more zealously they proclaimed it. ³⁷And they were astonished beyond measure, saying, "He has done all things well; he even makes the deaf hear and the dumb speak."

no understanding and no clarification for those who have
no faith, who have no commitment to Jesus.

Now, in Chapter 7, an analogous situation is presented.
It appears to be a simple disagreement between Jesus and
the Pharisees and scribes, which serves to show how right
Jesus was in his criticisms and thus how unjust it was to
condemn him for the positions he took in this discussion.
Yet, Mark's final purpose in describing this incident goes beyond showing Jesus right and his opponents wrong; Mark
wants to establish the justice of the Christian way of life
which no longer practices what contemporary Judaism de-
fines as God's will. It is the mind of their Lord that the Christians not follow the understanding of God's will represented
in Israel, particularly by Jesus' religious contemporaries.

Mark does not specify the time or place of the Pharisees' and scribes' confrontation with Jesus. Enough, he
thinks, to give us the occasion. Jesus' disciples were noticed
for not washing their hands before eating. "Washing,"
whether of hands or of cooking implements, of dishes and
the like, was looked upon as a form of "purifying" oneself;
one must always be pure in one's life, as all of life was lived
in the presence of the God who deserves to be lived with
only in purity. Many of the detailed prescriptions regarding
washing are conclusions drawn by later generations from the
laws of Moses, but the ultimate authority of all these derived
laws is the Mosaic law of Sinai. Thus, later generations will
say that it is the law of Moses which commands all these
particular laws.

(It is important to be aware that Mark feels he must
give his audience an explanation of the Jewish practices of
washing; this suggests that at least a good part of his readership was ignorant of these things and thus not Jewish.)

The Pharisees and scribes begin the confrontation with
the demand to know just why Jesus' disciples fail to obey

the laws handed down by their venerable ancestors. Again, Jesus is being challenged for his disregard for the law, and we are mindful of the Jewish logic which anxiously saw punishment for the nation when the law of God was eroded and flagrantly disobeyed.

Jesus' response to the scribes and Pharisees falls into three categories or stages, and ultimately goes far beyond the immediate question posed to him. The first stage has to do with the equation human beings have made between God's law and man's law; the second stage has to do with the replacement of God's law by man's law; the third stage has to do with the abolition of some of God's law. Let us look at these stages in the above order.

In preparing for Jesus' answer Mark has consistently referred to the hand-washing/purifying as a "tradition of the elders." By this phrase Mark indicates that what the Pharisees and scribes expected to be honored was a law which was not given by God to Moses, but a law which human reasoning derived from God's law to Moses. Thus, it was human reasoning which formulated this law, though claiming the while that the authority for this law ultimately resided in the divine law. Given the age of this law concerning the washing of hands, it can be said to be a decision of Israel's elders, and formally called a "tradition of the elders."

A modern example may make clear the distinction between human law which is separate from, yet dependent upon divine law. The Old Testament forbids a Jew to light a fire on the sabbath; fixed in the ancient Old Testament legislation, this law is considered to be a divine law. Many centuries later, cigarettes were invented, one way of lighting which is the lighting of a match or fire. May one, on the sabbath, light a match or fire in order to light a cigarette? What is important here at the moment is not the answer to this question (which is "no"), but the fact that it will take human judgment to answer this question, since the Old Testament contains no law specifically regarding match-lighting. Human beings will have to make a decision about cigarette matches in the light of the Old Testament laws.

Now, however the religious leaders express their objection to the disciples' disobedience concerning washing of their hands, Jesus hears them as making this human tradition, drawn, humans say, logically from the divine law, to be equal in authority with the divine law itself. To this equation he strongly objects. For him, no human law is equal in honor and authority with the divine law. As was common at this time, Jesus immediately resorts to the Old Testament for a condemnation of the scribes and Pharisees. From Isaiah he quotes words concerning Israel which is hypocritical, precisely because, while honoring God externally, it fails to honor him with its heart. What is a typical sign of this folly and imprudence? They foolishly think they are reverencing God by teaching human beings to obey the laws of human thinking.

By claiming that the scribes and Pharisees are hypocrites when they find fault with the disciples, Jesus opens the door to a deeper criticism, for their hypocrisy lies not in respect for the laws of Israel, but in their disregard for the divine laws in favor of human laws. Thus, Jesus moves from their fault in making human laws the equal of divine laws to their worse fault of replacing divine laws with human laws. The example Jesus uses to drive home the truth of his new charge is the contemporary practice of *korban*, a semitic word which means "dedicated."

One of the divine commands to Moses on Mount Sinai was the famous law, "You shall honor your mother and your father." Clearly this is a divine, not a human, law. Now, in centuries subsequent to the giving of the Sinai law, Solomon built a temple in Jerusalem, and later Jewish leaders, like

Solomon before them, insisted that all Jews should make a significant contribution to the upkeep of the Jerusalem temple (and this continued on when the new temple was built, after Solomon's was destroyed). Given the nature of things, some Jews felt an economic pinch. With all their obligations, human and divine, and their desires for the goods of this earth, they felt constricted to the point that they sought relief from these obligations. The relief came in this form: if money had been "dedicated" to payment of the temple tax, and then one's parents were found to be in difficulty, one need not transfer the temple tax money to benefit the needy parents, nor need one use other moneys for this purpose. One need simply say that the money which might have been used to aid them was already "dedicated" to the holy purpose, and so they receive no help at this time.

This *korban* practice was evidently at this time one example among many which revealed how human thinking had so worked out things that human law not only was made equal to God's law, but actually replaced it. Now, Jesus was not asked by his opponents to bring up the practice of *korban* and comment on it, but clearly the challenge as to who keeps God's law led Jesus to widen the discussion in order to reflect on the attitudes which Pharisees and scribes reveal in their own practice of obedience to the will of God.

The dialogue between Jesus and his opponents ends here; Jesus now calls the crowds to himself, but only to take up again the assumptions of the argument brought by the Pharisees and scribes against his disciples. Their argument had stressed that impurity comes from unwashed cups, from unwashed hands. Jesus is firm that it is what comes out of a person, not what affects him from the outside, that represents impurity. As earlier, Jesus gives the crowd only an axiom or a proverb, but then will explain further to his disciples, to those who believe in him, what Mark calls the "parable."

Before considering Jesus' words to his disciples about clean and unclean, we might think for a moment about the entire concept of purity/impurity. One of the basic elements in all religions is a sense that one must be worthy to be in the presence of a deity. Many religions of ancient times included in this worthiness the need for an external purity with which their deities would be pleased; such a purity was often synonymous with physical cleanness and was an essential ingredient of holiness. Israel was no exception in this regard, though it had its own definitions of objects which make one pure and impure, clean and unclean. Generally speaking, contact with things (or people) which threatened health, were disgusting, or were shameful was what made a person impure or unclean. Examples of things which caused impurity to the touch are a corpse, spit, excretions, menstrual and semen liquids, meats of animals with cloven hoof (where dirt was embedded); examples of people who caused impurity by contact are lepers and Gentiles if met in their homes. These things and these people are themselves unclean, so contact with them makes an otherwise clean person unclean and thus unworthy to stand in God's presence. In all this, what is at stake is knowledge of what makes one worthy or unworthy to stand before God. It is about this knowledge that Jesus got upset with the scribes and Pharisees.

Jesus explains his thinking about clean and unclean once he enters the privacy of the unidentified "house" (symbol of the place of revelation) to be with his disciples. He explains in more detail what he thinks makes a person truly unworthy to be with God. Here he clearly identifies the human heart as the source of the impurity which makes one unworthy of God, and he goes on to name specific actions which make unclean the person who does them.

By Jesus' teaching one becomes acutely aware of what makes one unworthy to be in God's presence. But one also can appreciate the implications of Jesus' teaching: those things which are not from the heart, but which come only from the outside, have nothing to do with clean and unclean. This is revolutionary teaching; it does away with many of the laws, not only of men, but even of those God gave to Moses. Mark himself draws one sweeping conclusion which has had inestimable consequences for Christianity; in four Greek words, Mark reads Jesus as saying that "all foods are clean." For Christians, there is no kosher law, there is no distinction between pure and impure foods; to Jesus' mind, food will not make one worthy or unworthy to stand in the presence of God. Worthiness and unworthiness are states flowing from one's moral choices, not from one's contact with foods.

It would not be fair to the Mosaic law to think that it, too, saw holiness (purity, cleanliness/impurity, uncleanness) as something determined by one's moral choices, by one's heart. Jesus is, however, unique in his religious tradition when he says that clean and unclean is a matter only of the heart. From his point of view, those who knew the law of Moses, even if they did not have the clarity of his own insights, should have sensed the difference between external and moral cleanliness and thus have been more tolerant of the disciples and more attentive in their own lives to moral cleanliness.

By Jesus' argument here, especially in that it allowed Mark to draw the conclusion which put an end to the thousand-year belief in unclean foods, one can even better understand why he was so strongly opposed and finally put to death. Certainly, involved in Jesus' stance here is a strong criticism of the religious leaders, for he even calls them hypocrites because, in his view, they live a life of external cleanness while failing in an internal life of purity. But what ultimately is at stake here is knowledge of the divine will: Who knows best what God really wants human beings to do? As Paul had expressed it earlier than Mark, "Who knows the mind of God? We do, because we have the mind of Christ!"

An historical note is in place here. Mark's words, "In saying this Jesus declared all foods clean," seem so simple, but this simplicity belies the true situation. Indeed, as the Acts of the Apostles and other documents of the New Testament show, the struggle about integration of belief in Jesus and the traditional religion of Israel was long and very difficult. Mark's simplicity represents either the conclusion of the struggle about this matter or the calm affirmation of one side without further attention to the other side. For, among Christians themselves there was a long-standing disagreement: many thought that Jews and Gentiles who wanted to be Christians should be circumcised as the premier sign of membership in God's people, and made to keep the Mosaic law. Indeed, many Jewish Christians went to their graves convinced that this was necessary for salvation. The eventual decision of the church, however, was that only one thing was necessary to be saved—belief in Jesus Christ; all else is secondary. Circumcision and those Mosaic laws not imposed anew by Jesus are left to the choice of the Christian to do or not to do; they are not to be thought of as "necessary for salvation."

The opening story of Chapter 7 is a very important episode for understanding both the particular on-going struggle Jesus had with religious authorities and the more generalized differences he created between traditional Jewish understanding of God's will and Christianity's understanding of that will. Through this story Mark has moved his narrative ever closer to the final rupture between Jesus and his opponents and at the same time given the Christian justification for the teaching about what makes one worthy or unworthy to be in the presence of God.

Mark next puts us on the path of a journey Jesus takes; the first cities mentioned on this journey are Tyre and Sidon. These two ancient and famous cities are located along the Mediterranean coast of what is now called Lebanon, Sidon being the further north of the two cities and about fifty miles north of the north border of Galilee. Though Mark does not bill this journey as a journey to pagans, scholars certainly see it as some attempt by Jesus to reach them; indeed, much scholarly opinion thinks that, even though earlier we had been led to Gentile territory (recall the possessed man in the territory of the Gerasenes), Mark is now consciously introducing the reader to a new object of Jesus' mission.

The attempt to outline clearly the limits of this journey is doomed. By the end of Chapter 7 Jesus, according to Mark, will have left the Tyrian-Sidonian territories to pass along the border (western or eastern?) of the Sea of Galilee in order to enter the area known as the Decapolis (where Jesus had met the Gerasene demoniac). Though Jesus will necessarily pass again into Palestine, it is not clear just when or where he does this. At one point (8:10) Jesus comes to Dalmanutha, but we do not know where this is—only that it is reachable by boat. At another moment Jesus reaches Bethsaida after being on the water in the northwestern quadrant of the Sea of Galilee. But soon afterward we find Jesus in Caesarea Philippi a good distance north of the Sea of Galilee, only to have Jesus thereafter reach a mountain on which he is transfigured before he enters Galilee. When Jesus has reached all these points, this journey is over and is replaced by another, the fateful journey to Jerusalem and to death. In brief, the geography of this time in Jesus' northern ministry is not altogether clear or easy to follow; we must be satisfied with references to cities or areas while not being able to see the clear pattern of travel developing between and among them.

We find ourselves about twenty-five miles north of Galilee; we are in Tyrian territory and Jesus is trying to maintain a very low profile. Yet, even in this pagan territory his fame precedes him, and thus we have once again in Mark's story the conflict and ambiguity of a Jesus who has come for the good of human beings, but for some reason or other wants silence and solitude.

Jesus is soon discovered and a woman finds her way to speak with him. This woman is identified in only two ways: she is Greek, born in Syro-Phoenicia (i.e., the Phoenicia, ancient predecessor of modern Lebanon, which was, like Palestine, to answer to the Roman ruler in Syria), and she has a little daughter who is possessed by an unclean spirit.

The cure here, as elsewhere in the gospel, is astounding. The woman hoped that Jesus would come to her house to expel the demon from her daughter; when Jesus finally decides to intervene, he shows his immense power by simply stating that the demon has gone. Jesus did not have to lift a finger or move a step, nor does he even actually order the demon to depart, so total and overwhelming is the mastery of Jesus over the demon world.

However, as elsewhere, the cure is not the whole story. Here there is a short dialogue between the woman and Jesus which is both instructive and puzzling. When the woman makes her request for a cure, Jesus refuses; he does so for a particular reason. Jesus draws a distinction between "sons" and "dogs" at a table; he wants the woman to "let the children eat what is put on the table; it is not right to take that food for the dogs" before the children have a chance at it.

The woman makes a distinction, all the while using the imagery of Jesus. She agrees that the children should have full access to the table food, but is it not possible that while the children are eating, the dogs get some crumbs or scraps from the food?

Often enough in Jewish writing, "children" or "sons" represent Israelites, "dogs" represent Gentiles. Such a terminology supports the interpretation of the imagery that Jesus, then the woman, used. Jesus indicates that his powers, like the food on the table, are meant for the people of Israel *first*; *after* they are fed, the powers of Jesus will turn to the Gentiles. The woman, not to contradict this divine sequence, suggests that, even though Jesus is now dedicating himself to Israel, he can *at the same time*, for a moment here or there, allow some of his power (like a scrap falling from the table) to extend to a Gentile.

Certainly the children's right to eat the food first is presented as a key to understanding the confines of Jesus' mission. Does Mark record this story as a subtle way of explaining to later generations of Gentile Christians why Jesus spent practically all his missionary life within the confines of Palestine, among the Jewish people, and only later did the word of God reach Gentile ears? Or is Mark even more subtly defending Christianity, so full in Mark's time of Gentile adherents, against the accusation that Jesus never really gave himself to the Jewish people, but intended to extend himself really only to Gentiles? As a first story of Jesus' journey among Gentiles, it serves to explain that, if Jesus does do anything to benefit the Gentiles, it should not be thought that he is abandoning Israel; he feeds the Gentiles, according to the image, only as dogs are fed at the table of the children.

At a first reading of this story one might be tempted to say that Jesus cured the woman's daughter only because the woman was clever, and that if the woman had not had a comeback, her daughter would have remained uncured. This would not be quite accurate as an insight into what is being said here. Certainly, Jesus reacted to the woman's words with the cure; it is not clear what he would have done if the woman had not said what she did. But the merit of the woman's words is this: she put her request in a proper perspective. That is, she was able to interpret a cure from Jesus in such a way that it would not mean that she misunderstood what Jesus in the main was about. It is not her cleverness that is rewarded by a cure; it is her ability to realize what Jesus' actual mission was that assured him that the cure of the little girl would not be misinterpreted. With this assurance that his action would not be misunderstood, Jesus gladly worked the miracle.

To put the matter another way: the miracle was worked because the woman believed in Jesus, but on condition that neither she, nor any other, think that this miracle for a Gentile in any way denied Jesus' dedication of his life to Israel.

With the lesson clearly drawn in the story of the Syro-Phoenician woman, Jesus proceeds to a cure of another Gentile, this a man both deaf and dumb. This cure takes place in the Decapolis, an area to the east of Galilee and predominantly the territory of the Gentiles.

This episode is peculiar for a number of details Mark keeps in his story. First, Jesus takes the man off by himself, actually something Jesus rarely does. Is this separation a way of symbolizing that what Jesus does for Gentiles should not be seen as part of his regular work, the work for Israel? Perhaps it is better to see it as a gesture by which Jesus, as he has so often done earlier, keeps under wraps the admiration and praise of the crowds.

Second, Jesus, in putting his fingers into the man's deaf ears and spittle on the man's unspeaking tongue, with looks to heaven and groans, shows signs of laboring for this miracle which are not seen elsewhere. Perhaps we have here a description of labor which befits other miracles Jesus worked? All the more reason would his opponents criticize Jesus for "working" cures on the sabbath.

Those who brought this deaf and dumb man to Jesus, ignoring Jesus' request for silence, announce to everyone what Jesus had done. The words they use, that he makes the deaf hear and the dumb speak (note the plurals), seem to be a Marcan hint to those who remember what the Old Testament, through Isaiah, said so joyfully about God:

> Then will the eyes of the blind be opened,
> the ears of the *deaf* be cleared;
> then will the lame leap like a stag,
> then the tongue of the *dumb* will speak (Isaiah 35:5–
> 6).

Isaiah had foreseen such mercies of God for his people one day. Jesus' actions recall such a prophecy and give reason to believe that this prophecy is being fulfilled. In this way people began to see in Jesus the fulfillment of scripture, the expression of the divine will and power to save one day. One cannot fail to note that here the power and will of God reach beyond the confines of Palestine to touch the life of a pagan. Mark understands from hindsight that what gifts have been given to his Jewish and pagan community were prefigured in this small journey of Jesus through pagan lands; someday Jesus would reach out in a consistent way to pagans as well as to Jews.

Chapter 8

We are presumably still in pagan territory. Without any attempt to give circumstances, such as time or place, Mark abruptly begins this new story with the fact that again a great crowd had come to Jesus and was without anything to eat, so Jesus calls his disciples to himself and expresses his sympathy for this crowd which has been with him three days now. Jesus is reluctant to send them away on their own, for they will find no food; those will likely perish along the way who have to go far to reach home.

In response to Jesus' anxious concern, the disciples helplessly point out the impossibility of feeding this large number of people in this deserted place. Evidently, this response is the catalyst; it is what Jesus (as well as the reader) needs to hear in order to proceed to the next step. Jesus, no longer lamenting the situation, takes immediate and full charge. He learns how much, or how little, bread is available, then orders everyone to sit, as though actually knowing that he will feed them. Finally, in words we have already read, he gives thanks for the bread, breaks it, and gives it to his disciples to distribute; then he does the same with some fish. As in the earlier story of the multiplication of loaves and fish, everyone is satisfied and still there are baskets filled with scraps left over—seven baskets actually. Without a fur-

8 In those days, when again a great crowd had gathered, and they had nothing to eat, he called his disciples to him, and said to them, [2]"I have compassion on the crowd, because they have been with me now three days, and have nothing to eat; [3]and if I send them away hungry to their homes, they will faint on the way; and some of them have come a long way." [4]And his disciples answered him, "How can one feed these men with bread here in the desert?" [5]And he asked them, "How many loaves have you?" They said, "Seven." [6]And he commanded the crowd to sit down on the ground; and he took the seven loaves, and having given thanks he broke them and gave them to his disciples to set before the people; and they set them before the crowd. [7]And they had a few small fish; and having blessed them, he commanded that these also should be set before them. [8]And they ate, and were satisfied; and they took up the broken pieces left over, seven baskets full. [9]And there were about four thousand people. [10]And he sent them away; and immediately he got into the boat with his disciples, and went to the district of Dalmanutha.

11 The Pharisees came and began to argue with him, seeking from him a sign from heaven, to test him. [12]And he sighed deeply in his spirit, and said, "Why does this generation seek a sign? Truly, I say to you, no sign shall be given to this generation." [13]And he left them, and getting into the boat again he departed to the other side.

14 Now they had forgotten to bring bread; and they had only one loaf with them in the boat. [15]And he cautioned them, saying, "Take heed, beware of the leaven of

the Pharisees and the leaven of Herod." [16]And they discussed it with one another, saying, "We have no bread." [17]And being aware of it, Jesus said to them, "Why do you discuss the fact that you have no bread? Do you not yet perceive or understand? Are your hearts hardened? [18]Having eyes do you not see, and having ears do you not hear? And do you not remember? [19]When I broke the five loaves for the five thousand, how many baskets full of broken pieces did you take up?" They said to him, "Twelve." [20]"And the seven for the four thousand, how many baskets full of broken pieces did you take up?" And they said to him, "Seven." [21]And he said to them, "Do you not yet understand?"

22 And they came to Beth-saida. And some people brought to him a blind man, and begged him to touch him. [23]And he took the blind man by the hand, and led him out of the village; and when he had spit on his eyes and laid his hands upon him, he asked him, "Do you see anything?" [24]And he looked up and said, "I see men; but they look like trees, walking." [25]Then again he laid his hands upon his eyes; and he looked intently and was restored, and saw everything clearly. [26]And he sent him away to his home, saying, "Do not even enter the village."

27 And Jesus went on with his disciples, to the villages of Caesarea Philippi; and on the way he asked his disciples, "Who do men say that I am?" [28]And they told him, "John the Baptist; and others say, Elijah; and others one of the prophets." [29]And he asked them, "But who do you say that I am?" Peter answered him, "You are the Christ." [30]And he charged them to tell no one about him.

31 And he began to teach them that the Son of man must suffer many things, and be rejected by the elders and the chief priests and the scribes, and be killed, and

after three days rise again. [32]And he said this plainly. And Peter took him, and began to rebuke him. [33]But turning and seeing his disciples, he rebuked Peter, and said, "Get behind me, Satan! For you are not on the side of God, but of men."

34 And he called to him the multitude with his disciples, and said to them, "If any man would come after me, let him deny himself and take up his cross and follow me. [35]For whoever would save his life will lose it; and whoever loses his life for my sake and the gospel's will save it. [36]For what does it profit a man, to gain the whole world and forfeit his life? [37]For what can a man give in return for his life? [38]For whoever is ashamed of me and of my words in this adulterous and sinful generation, of him will the Son of man also be ashamed, when he comes in the glory of his Father with the holy angels."

ther word Jesus and the twelve get in a boat to go to the area of Dalmanutha.

The paucity of details in this story is striking. The story-line is severe. A crowd is hungry, Jesus is sympathetic, it is impossible to feed everyone. Then the miraculous feeding takes place. Finally, without the slightest reaction to this miracle recorded, Jesus and his disciples, Mark says, go away.

As it stands, the story must be seen as a further tribute to Jesus' great, indeed immense powers over elements of this world. As mentioned earlier, the catalyst for action is the admission that no one knows "from where" all this crowd will be fed. Once the need, even desperation of the situation is clear, then Jesus proceeds to show precisely "from where" this crowd will be fed, and in abundance.

Does the story mean to do more than record, again, the majestic power of Jesus? A look at other details of the story, admittedly few and ambivalent, does suggest something else. First, Jesus is among pagans. Second, they are with him for three days; though it seems futile to say that Jesus, the Jew, was teaching non-Jews (what else would he teach but the Jewish religion?), what else can one conclude? Third, the number seven is symbolic, as Jews looked to pagans. Seven was the classical number of pagan nations which circum-scribed Israel during its ancient days. So famous did this enumeration become that, though the actual number of pa-gan nations surrounding Israel changed every now and then, the number seven remained. Finally, one cannot fail to note again the use of the eucharistic formula in the feeding of this great crowd. All of these details, taken together, add up to this interpretation: through this miracle Mark foretells that Jesus, by means of his teaching and eucharist, will feed those many pagans who will, over decades, commit them-selves to discipleship with Jesus. More broadly, this multi-plication is to be understood, exegetes say, as a companion to the multiplication of loaves which occurred earlier . The first multiplication presaged what Jesus would do for Jews who will follow him; the second multiplication indicated that Jesus would do the same for pagans who will become his disciples. Mark would strike such a balance, for the Christian community of his time contained both Jews and pagans; both would draw comfort as they see themselves reflected in the works of Jesus.

Thus, while this story certainly reveals again the might of Jesus, it also serves to alert the reader that the teaching and eucharist of Jesus is for all, Jew and Gentile.

The viewpoint which sees this miracle as a companion to the first multiplication of the loaves, together with the great similarity of details between the two multiplications, suggests to some interpreters that, historically speaking, Jesus worked only one multiplication (that for the Jews) and that Mark, for his own obvious reasons, created a story of Jesus doing this kind of work again for the pagans. The justification for Mark's doing this would be the intention of Jesus, easily readable in the makeup of Mark's church, to feed all disciples, Jew and Gentile. Certainly, the literary canons of the time would not prohibit Mark from creating a duplicate story out of the details of one actual story. In fact, his staying as close as he has to the historically based story shows how his only interest was to provide for Gentiles just what would be provided for Jews.

The response to this theory of one story being created out of another for the author's purposes is lukewarm; at best it is reckoned as possible and at worst it is rejected, precisely because the second multiplication is not simply a copy of the first, but has its own characteristics which seem better explained by assuming that there really, historically, was a second multiplication. Thus, though Mark may, in his manner of telling, underline not only the power of Jesus, but also the implied promise that Jesus will always be ready to feed pagans as well as Jews, one need not think that the second multiplication can be persuasively argued to be a created duplicate of the first multiplication.

Immediately upon the announcement of the abundant feeding of the crowd, Mark abruptly turns our attention to see Jesus and his disciples reaching Jewish Dalmanutha by boat. They presumably left from the pagan Decapolis, which is the last geographical notation Mark gave us. Dalmanutha is an area we cannot identify. A number of ancient manuscripts read Magdala, a fishing town some seven miles south of Capernaum, in place of Dalmanutha. Magdala, home of Mary of Magdala (the adjective is Magdalena), is just about at the center of the western shore of the Sea of Galilee and thus across the sea from the Decapolis. Perhaps these ancient manuscripts do reflect local knowledge which is lost to us and are right to substitute Magdala for Dalmanutha.

In this area of Dalmanutha/Magdala old opponents of Jesus reappear without any introduction. The Pharisees, unheard of for a while, suddenly are described as struggling with Jesus, testing him by asking from him a sign from heaven. This antipathy both reveals the inner agony of Jesus before these men and elicits a response which at the same time shows Jesus' personal frustration and the gulf which separates Jesus and the Pharisees.

Jesus cannot understand why this generation, i.e., the Pharisees and those like them, present and future, seek signs. One might, however, think that, on the face of it, the Pharisees' request is legitimate; they must look for heavenly guidance before they make a major commitment to Jesus. But what Jesus is upset about is the fact that, as Mark's gospel has argued, Jesus has shown all kinds of signs, whether in miracles or in teaching, by which the Pharisees could recognize him. It is not, Jesus suggests, that he has not provided

signs enough by which he can be recognized as God's representative; it is rather that the Pharisees, for whatever reasons one might suggest, are so blinded that they are
unwilling to accept the clear signs he has given.

The stand-off is just about complete. The Pharisees want
a sign in order to believe; Jesus claims no sign will lead them
to believe. Mark, of course, is writing from hindsight. He has
before him the entire course of Jesus' life, death and resurrection, and history thereafter, too. The Pharisees represent a large group of people who are a mystery precisely
because they do not believe, when so many have believed,
whether in Jesus' time or thereafter. The problem is not in
what Jesus or heaven has or has not done; the problem must
lie in the people who see, often together, the same works
and hear the same words of Jesus, even hear his resurrection
preached and feel the tug of the Holy Spirit in their lives.
Why one responds and another does not is the mystery. According to an earlier parable of Jesus, it is a question of soil,
some receptive and some not, some able to keep the seed,
some unable. Ultimately, Christians came to the conclusion
that, as John's gospel puts it, one cannot come to Jesus unless he be "taught by Jesus' Father." Here it is not Jesus who
is the source of faith, but the Father, and the doctrine of
predestination is born. But Mark is insistent that the problem
lies as well in the dispositions of the hearers and seers. That
is why Mark's ultimate judgment is that the Pharisees' case
is not one of simple ignorance, but one of willful refusal,
for whatever reason (for instance, it is because of jealousy
that Jesus is handed over to Pilate—14:10), to believe in
Jesus. It is Mark's worry that his contemporaries, his readers,
will become for whatever reason like the Pharisees of this
story.

Mark ends this brief encounter between Jesus and the

Pharisees as abruptly as he started it: Jesus gets in a boat and goes to the shore. Where he goes, whether he went with his disciples—even if his disciples were present at this dialogue with the Pharisees—we do not know.

What we do know is that suddenly we are in a new scene. We must be watching a scene in a boat on the sea, but it is not just Jesus in the boat; his disciples are there, as well. We enter the scene as the disciples are made aware that they have forgotten to bring with them any bread, except one loaf. What makes them aware of this forgetfulness is Jesus' warning to the disciples to watch out for the leaven or yeast of the Pharisees and of Herod. They, thinking he was somehow criticizing them for not having actual bread, began to argue with one another as to who failed to provide more than one loaf.

Jesus, of course, as the reader must easily already understand, is talking to his disciples on the level of symbolism, and they are showing themselves incapable of understanding him. This denseness brings Jesus to the unique point of asking his disciples seven questions in a row. They are questions coming from Jesus' frustration with the dullness of his most intimate followers, those who must be able to understand him, if anyone can. The picture of the disciples here is in part evidently a companion to that of the Pharisees just drawn by Mark; each group, in its own way, is lacking in a sensitivity, a perception of what is happening before their very eyes.

Jesus' seven questions externalize very well his frustration. Why do they argue about bread? Do they not comprehend, have they no perception? Are their minds dulled? Are they like the people, criticized by Isaiah, "who look but do not see, who listen but do not hear"? Jesus makes it clearer now as to the object of this seeing and hearing; he has multiplied bread, once to the point that twelve full baskets were left over, once to the point that seven full baskets were left over. Do they not see what that means?

What Jesus seems to find wrong with his disciples is their inability to see that, if Jesus wanted bread available (as they had concluded he did), he could easily, very easily have provided it. Clearly, then, he must have been talking about something else than just bread. Why cannot the disciples pierce through Jesus' language to his meaning? Whatever the reason, Mark thinks this tense dialogue is worth repeating to his reader, for it is possible that the reader, for his own reasons, is not able to get behind Jesus' words and deeds to their deepest meanings.

Jesus' original message to his disciples in this situation was a warning to them based on his recent encounter with the Pharisees. Whatever the cause of dullness which prevents them from seeing Jesus' symbolic meaning in his words about leaven, he clearly does not want his disciples infected with the same mentality as has struck the Pharisees. He is warning them, then, against eventually seeking for signs from heaven by which to justify or cause belief in Jesus; the signs recounted in the gospel and experienced in the church's life and teaching are clear enough, revelation enough, to justify faith.

We had noticed the swiftness with which Mark whisked Jesus and the disciples away from the scene of the multiplication of loaves for the Gentiles, the abruptness by which he switches to a demand for a sign, the suddenness by which he warns against the mentality, the "leaven" of the Pharisees. Now the seven questions of Jesus end precisely with the last question—and no answer. We are brought, in sudden change of circumstance, into Bethsaida, near the northwest shore of the Sea of Galilee. From all this jarring narrative, one gets the impression that Mark is not so much telling a smoothly developing story as he is hurrying to pile up or juxtapose stories that, together, lead to a climax about the object of so much of these stories, the profound meaning of Jesus. Rather than develop this "impression" here, however, let us consider this next story which has been so swiftly linked by Mark to the events we have just been considering; it is a story about a blind man brought to Jesus for healing.

As in the recent cure of the deaf and dumb man, Jesus "works" to heal this blind man. He takes him outside the village and, away from the crowd, uses spittle on the man's eyes as a means of healing. The peculiarity of this cure is that it needs two stages for its accomplishment. Most scholars, while not minimizing Jesus' great healing power, fix on this distinctive aspect and look here for the particular meaning of this story. What is there about a man who gains his sight from Jesus only in stages?

It is at this point that a number of elements come into play. If one has read ahead, one knows that a most disconcerting teaching awaits the disciples, that which we may summarize by the term "cross-carrying." Jesus confounds his twelve with the statement that he must die, and then goes on to indicate that in some ways they must follow him in this. All of this painful and confusing talk ends with another cure of another blind man. Many scholars see these two blind-man stories as a commentary with which Mark begins and ends this difficult teaching about the cross. The disciples are like these blind men; their perception is only gradual, their comprehension increases only by degrees. Thus, by story-telling and story-placement, rather than by explicit statement, Mark depicts the rudimentary stage of understanding the disciples had of the Christian message and their need for God's further help.

If the blind-man story of Chapter 8 underlines the need for growth in spiritual sight, one can now understand why the stories leading up to the blind-man narrative have been pushing toward a goal beyond themselves. Each of these last stories has emphasized the need for spiritual insight, something altogether missing in the Pharisees and threatening to engulf the disciples. The blind man comes to represent other people, then, who are blind in a different way. It is Jesus who, though showing signs of impatience on one level, must bring continual, fuller healing to those who follow him.

With the needs of the blind man still alive to the reader, Mark places Jesus many miles north of the place of the cure. We are now passing through various villages around the great city of Caesarea Philippi. Before Caesarea Philippi existed, there was in place a village called Panion, named after the god Pan, patron of forests, flocks and fun. This village, actually very near the ancient Israelite city of Dan, was replaced by Herod the Great with a city devoted to Caesar Augustus (ruled 27 B.C.–14 A.D)— hence the name Caesarea. Herod was succeeded by his son, Philip, who ruled the entire area in which this Caesarea was found. To better distinguish this Caesarea from others, notably that Caesarea built by Herod the Great on the shore of the Mediterranean (cf. Acts 10), Philip called his Caesarea "Caesarea Philippi" or Philip's Caesarea. Mark is very careful to say that Jesus went to the villages around Caesarea Philippi, never indicating that he entered the great city. Jesus probably avoided this city simply because it was considered out of bounds and desecrating for religious Jews. Analogously, Jesus is never reported, for all his travel around the Sea of Galilee, to have entered Tiberias; this city was built over a cemetery and thus automatically impure for all Jews.

It is while journeying around Caesarea that Jesus puts the unexpected twin question to his disciples, "Who do people say I am?" and "Who do you say I am?" The question comes out of the blue—and yet, upon reflection, one can say that it is the most natural question of all, very much to be expected, for practically all of what we have read so far has been written in an effort to lead us to grasp as much as possible of the truest, deepest identity of Jesus.

It will come clear, however, that no matter how much information we have been given in Mark's first eight chapters, we need a radically different set of data to reach the fullest truth about Jesus. The twin question will lead to this new set of data, for Jesus himself will, with Peter's reply, take the lead into this new and necessary phase of revelation about Jesus' person. In short, revelatory as is all the material of the first eight chapters, there is an aspect about Jesus which has not even been mentioned. It is a most difficult aspect to grasp, all the more so since it clashes so directly with the power and wisdom of the first eight chapters and is accepted only when the believer can integrate Jesus' earlier revelation about himself with this second and confounding revelation.

Jesus, then, asks his twelve, "Who do people say I am?" The response comes from the twelve without any differentiation among them. They report three suggestions: John the Baptist, Elijah, one of the prophets. All three of these people—John, Elijah, prophet—share a common characteristic. John, as Mark had portrayed him, asked for repentance which leads to forgiveness of sins. Elijah was the champion defender of Yahweh, pleading with the Israelites of the 800's B.C. to remain faithful to their God, to repent if they have fallen away to worship the false idols of those living with them in Israel. Indeed, it is Elijah (according first to Malachi 3:23–24) who will return someday to urge repentance upon Israel before God comes for final judgment. Each prophet, no matter what his generation or century, through cajoling and enticing asked his people for continued loyalty and sincere repentance for former sins against Yahweh and Yahweh's people. Thus, a person who has come to seek repentance, who is characterized by the power and wisdom of God himself, and who is steeped in Old Testament ways of thinking and imagining, cannot fail but to think of himself as one of those great figures of the past who, with God's strength supporting him, asked for the same repentance.

Jesus then asks, "And who do you say I am?" Here, no doubt reflecting the central position Peter played in Jesus' time and thereafter, Peter alone says, "You are the messiah." Whichever kind of messiah Peter actually had in mind (kingly, priestly, wisdom teacher), it is clear that Peter's assessment of all he has heard and seen goes far beyond the judgments of other people. For Peter, Jesus is the anointed of God in whom the change from "this age" to the "age to come" has begun. It is Jesus' power and wisdom which have led Peter to this decision, a decision based in this literary work on the stories Mark has gathered together in his first eight chapters.

Jesus' response to this profession of Peter is not given in direct address; Mark writes in summary that Jesus ordered the twelve not to speak to anyone about him. Does this mean that Jesus agreed with Peter, but asked that the twelve keep this a secret for a while? Or does this order mean that Jesus did not agree with Peter, whether Jesus thought the title wrong or Peter's understanding of messiah faulty? It is ultimately not clear as to whether or not Jesus accepted this assessment of Peter. Perhaps, in the light of Jesus' later affirmation at his trial before the high priest that he is the messiah, one can decide that here Jesus also agreed tacitly that Peter's judgment is right.

What we do know, from the way Mark tells it, is that Jesus begins publicly to describe a most shocking future for himself. This description includes the fact of "resurrection after three days," but this happy element seems lost as Peter concentrates on the tragedy of which Jesus speaks. Peter's reaction to Jesus' forecast of rejection and suffering and death is, according to Mark, to reproach Jesus. Jesus, in turn, speaks harshly to Peter, inviting him to "get out of his way," as though Peter's reaction indicates an attempt, through misunderstanding, to stop the plan of God. What is all this about? What is at the root of this bitter difference between Jesus and Peter?

One gets an inkling of the difficulty which Mark introduces here when one attends to the fact that, whereas messiah was the title Peter thought appropriate for Jesus, Jesus suddenly begins to speak of himself as the Son of Man. How do these two titles conflict? The messiah, as noted earlier, is that person who was anointed by God to begin the new age. The Son of Man, taken most likely from the description of the heavenly "one like a son of man" in Daniel (7:13–27), is a person who, after suffering much, will be glorified and given "kingship and majesty and unending dominion over all nations and peoples." The key difference between these two images is that the messiah is not foreseen to suffer, but rather to overcome all suffering and, indeed, remove it in favor of good alone.

Mark certainly knows, as does his reader, more than Peter knows as of Chapter 8, verse 32. Peter's assessment of Jesus as messiah was understandable, given that he knew only what transpired up to Chapter 8; indeed, and this is the crux of the matter on Mark's mind, the power and wisdom and authority Jesus has shown thus far seems to make it impossible that his life end in tragedy. Neither does he merit it, nor can anyone be so powerful as to inflict it upon Jesus. And yet, the tragedy, unintelligible as it seemed to Peter beforehand, occurred. There is a great mystery here, both about Jesus' life and that of a disciple, and to the announcement of this mysterious destiny Mark now devotes himself. The first indication of this is Mark's introduction of Jesus as more properly "Son of Man," because this title suggests a glory and power which will be exercised only *after* degradation and pain.

By this shift of images (from messiah to Son of Man), Mark indicates that the Old Testament did in fact foresee what eventually happened to Jesus; that is, there are elements of the Old Testament which show that what Jesus underwent at the end of his life could be interpreted as the will of God—certainly it was the will of God for the "Son of Man." That Israel of Jesus' time expected not the Son of Man but the messiah is understandable, for the messiah would answer the longings of the Israelite heart for an end to suffering and death and the beginning of a time only of joy and glory and freedom. That the early life of Jesus encouraged the assessment that he is this messiah has already been underlined. But Mark knows that the Son of Man is the more fitting image to explain the full life of Jesus, an image already defined by God himself in the Old Testament and, given the life of Jesus, a prophecy of Jesus by God himself through the prophet Daniel. It is the end of Jesus' life, and not its beginning, which is the more mysterious and thus demands the greater clarification from the Old Testament.

But it is not simply a question of "getting one's images straight," of picking the right image which will do justice particularly to the end of Jesus' life. The greater difficulty remains: How is it that the person, who to all appearances was the beginning (not just another promise) of the new age, not only did not bring about the new age (and still has not), but ended his own life so tragically? Is Peter completely wrong because he could not make any sense of all this?

Neither Jesus nor Mark spells out in simple discourse the mystery of Jesus' life. From the entire gospel story, however, one can come to some kind of answer. The answer begins by affirming that Jesus is as wise and powerful as he appears, that he is, in some sense, the beginning of the new age. He has the power and good will to change everything into good, to create that life which satisfies the human longing for perfect happiness. Indeed, someday he will do just this. Why not now?

There is, upon reflection, one thing that the power of God cannot change, cannot force, and that is human free will, or, as the Old Testament calls it, the heart. To apply force here is to destroy the very nature of "free" will. God can cajole, entice, plead, command, but choice is finally left to the creature. Now, it is this free will, this free choice which has, from the beginning of history, characterized the human contribution to the relationship between God and human beings. The entire Old Testament affirms that it is the free union of these two, God and human beings, which creates a situation in which God, for his part, uses all his powers to provide for his loved one all that his love desires to provide. The only thing the human partner to this union can provide is the free choice to be united with God.

Here we must recall the fundamental reason of Jesus' mission. He is to preach repentance. He is sent to ask for free choice on behalf of God, a free choice to return to union with God. Thus, though Jesus has the power to change everything to the good of human beings and actually longs to do it, first there must be a re-union of God and human beings. It is from this union that the happiness of the new age will come. The union itself must precede this happiness, and preceding this union must be the free choice of the human being to create this union.

Peter, then, has made the mistake of thinking that Jesus has come to create the new age. Jesus, rather, has come to ask for repentance; he has not come to change this age into the new age. This being the truth of the matter, Jesus himself is subject to the laws of this age, one of which is death, another of which is the triumph of evil people over good people. In addition to these laws there appear to be two other factors operating in the life of Jesus, as God planned this life.

First, Jesus was not only to call for repentance. He was to live it. This was not to be a momentary union with God, but a lifelong union to and through death. The uniting of himself to his Father meant for him, as for all human beings, obedience, for it is in doing the will of the other that this union consists; it is this that one freely chooses to do. For many, unknown, years Jesus evidently did the will of his Father as he lived out his life in Nazareth. At the time of his baptism, Jesus clearly changed his life completely; as Mark indicates in the appearance of the Father and Holy Spirit here, this change of life was a free response to God's will. During the early part of his new life, Jesus preached and taught and healed and cured, again responding to the will of his Father. Finally, as his life turned sour and bitter, he again responded to the will of his Father in this time of trial. In other words, it is Jesus' life, as well as his message, which he came to give. He preached repentance and lived it, not exempting himself from the laws of this age, but entering the new age only after living out thoroughly his life in this age.

There is a second consideration. Up to now, what was said of Jesus can be applied to anyone: to live in union with God must come prior to the benefits of that union, which is called the "new age," or "heaven." But Jesus is in one aspect unique. He came not only to live a life of union with God; he came, in Mark's words, to "give his life as a ransom for the multitudes." Peter never anticipated this to be part of Jesus' life. He thought Jesus had come to overthrow evil and death by power. As it eventually became clear, it was by submitting to death that Jesus overcame what the Old Testament indicated was the original source of death—sin. To put it better, by his obedience, by his freely choosing to obey, to remain united with his Father, Jesus essentially did away with the disobedience from which flow pain and death for human beings.

By his death, then, Jesus actually does put an end to this age, characterized as it is by death. That is, because Jesus has removed the cause of death, he has removed an essential element of our age and assured the eventual removal of death itself. In fact, Jesus' resurrection is the attestation of God that, for Jesus and for those like him, the new age has already begun. True, one reaches it through the death we know in this age, but one does reach it—and that is all that ultimately matters.

None of all this did Peter know, when, after thinking he had it all right, he found out that he had it mostly wrong. However, though Mark and later Christians, admittedly by virtue of hindsight and study and divine guidance, came to a correct understanding of Jesus' life in all its parts, no one has come up with the answer to the one lingering problem: If one does repent and become reunited with God, why does God not immediately bestow (as love would suggest) the perfectly happy life upon his beloved?

To this question there is no complete answer. Some remarks, however, are in order and may be helpful. First of all, it is ironic that it is God's untainted goodness that creates the problem; if God, in the Jewish and Christian tradition, was ultimately understood to be motived by evil rather than love, the answer about much human suffering would be better understood.

Second, it is difficult to say that suffering is portioned out in accord with one's sins. Jesus, sinless and most beloved of all by his Father, suffered cruelly and degradingly; if one says that this painful end of Jesus was the chosen way to expiate sins, one soon realizes that God had other ways of doing this, if he wanted.

Finally, it seems to be the divine plan that everyone live out the effects of sin in this age through death; only after the completion of this entire period does one enter the new age. This does not preclude the abrupt termination of this world and the creation of a new, perfect world, as scripture often expects. Nor does it explain why some of us suffer more, much more than others in this age. But there does seem to be a plan whereby, even if one is repentant and reunited with God, one must complete a life filled with the effects which sin, both original and personal, both private and communal, brings into this age. Until, then, the time of this age is complete and the new age begins, the harsh laws of this age continue to control the lives even of those in union with God. Jesus, then, contrary to Peter's expectations, came not to remove this age, but to ask for that reunion with God which assures entry into the perfect happiness that can follow upon death. He asked it of others, and he was asked for it himself.

Jesus eventually became known as Jesus Christ, and not long after his death, for Paul clearly uses this full name in 50 A.D. Christians had come to understand just what was implied in calling Jesus "Christ," "messiah," "anointed." At the end of Mark's eighth chapter, however, Peter and his companions need help to understand in what nuanced way messiah can be said of Jesus. Indeed, it is Mark's goal that his reader understand, through Peter's confusion, not to make the mistake Peter has made.

We can safely say that, from a total reading of the gospel, the tone of Mark's narrative changes sharply. Severely reduced in number are the miracles of Jesus; attention is paid to teaching which is difficult to bear; conflict becomes ever more the staple of Jesus' days, as his life draws perceptibly to an end. This new tone reflects the new concern of Mark that the disciple realize the full meaning of what commitment to Jesus can bring.

Jesus notes that he will be rejected by "the elders, the chief priests and the scribes." These three groups of people, together with the high priest, make up the Sanhedrin (which means simply "sit together"), the supreme judicial, legislative and executive body in Israel. Actually, there were smaller legal bodies belonging to smaller geographical units of Palestine; the Sanhedrin of which the gospels speak, however, is the supreme body of Israel housed next to the temple in Jerusalem.

"Elders" are those who belong to long-established Israelite families. These men, wealthy and thus powerful, obviously want a direct say and participation in the body which makes ultimate decisions about life in Palestine. "Chief priests," in number about eight, are appointees of the high priest to help him run the immense work of the temple of Israel in Jerusalem. These priests were full-time priests; the ordinary priests were part-time, serving as priests in various ways only eight weeks or so out of every year. "Scribes" are those men proven for their knowledge of the entire corpus of Jewish law. Pharisees and Sadducees are not appointed to the Sanhedrin. However, many people who are members of the Sanhedrin espouse the religious convictions of Pharisees and Sadducees; in this indirect way, the Pharisees and Sadducees also make their voices heard in this august legal body. Whoever is chosen as high priest for a given year is automatically president of the Sanhedrin, and he brings the complete number of members of the Sanhedrin to seventy-one. It is this group that Jesus will meet eventually in Jerusalem; it is they whom he sees now in his future.

As if to underline the close relationship between master and disciple, Mark swiftly turns from Jesus' self-description to the implications of it for the disciple. Like the master, the disciple can expect to suffer. In the light of the actual type of suffering Jesus endured, the disciple's suffering is summed up as "cross-carrying."

The disciple is advised, "Let him deny himself." Presumably, this command or exhortation first looks to a control over oneself which will allow one to accept persecution or death for one's convictions, if it comes to the disciple, as it did to Jesus. A second meaning of this "denial," however, is this, that the disciple must be ready to accept that cross or difficulty which is involved when one must choose the right way to live rather than the wrong way one may prefer. To obey the teaching of Jesus may well be a difficult cross. A third sense of the word "cross" refers to those parts of life which are painful because they are imposed not by enemies but simply by life itself, e.g., sickness and untimely death of dear ones. There is a way to suffer with trust in God and a way to suffer not with trust in God; it is the willingness to suffer with trust in God's care that one can find difficult, a cross. Finally, there has developed in the history of Christian discipleship an understanding of Jesus' words which allows one to actively seek crosses, suffering; penances and heroic service of others are examples of this. Thus, over the centuries Christians have come to understand "cross-carrying" to apply to a number of situations. For Mark's immediate purpose, however, Jesus warns that fidelity to him can bring to the disciple what his own obedience to his convictions brought to him: death.

The lengthy verses which conclude Jesus' words in Chapter 8 are characterized by the Greek word *gar*, which often is left untranslated. This little word means "for" or "because," and the sentence it is in serves as the reason for what has just been said. Thus, the first *gar*-sentence, verse 35, explains why Jesus' statement in verse 34 is true. Jesus had said that to be a disciple meant that one must carry his cross and follow Jesus. Verse 35 says that this is true from the point of view that the death implied in this cross-carrying on behalf of Jesus and his gospel is the way to life, that to try to have life by not carrying the cross is the sure way to lose life. Verse 36 suggests that the attempt to have life by having everything except Jesus, even if the latter includes cross-carrying, is futile, for only in following Jesus does one get life. Jesus leads one to life, whatever the means may be; to think of having life any other way is futile. Verse 37 carries on the argument of verse 36: since life is reached only by following Jesus, how could one think that, in exchanging discipleship for the illusion of life through possessions, one has made a just exchange? Verse 38 picks up another strain of the argument in favor of discipleship, even if it includes cross-carrying: to deny Jesus (especially in front of a sinful generation) will be met someday by Jesus' denial of the disciple (in front of the true and virtuous society). In these verses 35–38, then, Jesus gives solid arguments why discipleship, painful as it may be, is the only way to life, for nothing else but the following of Jesus will lead to true life.

With these words Chapter 8 ends. What had begun as a chapter which continued the miracles of Jesus amidst growing opposition by enemies and incomprehension by friends culminates in questions about Jesus' identity. Almost doomed to fail to know the true meaning of Jesus, because he had not lived his full life as yet, Peter, representing the twelve, reveals his incomprehension in such a way as to threaten his friendship with Jesus. Jesus points to his real future and then suggests that such a future awaits anyone who wishes to follow him. It is a future deprived of miracles, but, he insists, the only way to life. Perhaps, over the centuries, the type of cross-carrying has changed for some disciples; nonetheless, it is universally agreed that no one who follows Jesus avoids a cross. Thus, Jesus' words offer the truest advice: to search for a path to life other than the following of Jesus may appear to be the way to life, but it is not—only the following of Jesus truly leads one to life. These are hard words to believe before one starts the search for happiness. The life of Jesus, which ended in life forever, is the major gospel argument that his words truly are the words which lead to life.

Chapter 9

Traditionally, Mark's Chapter 8 ends with Jesus speaking about the judgment of disciples at a time when the Son of Man comes in the glory of his Father and with his angels. This time of the Son of Man usually was linked to the end of this age, whenever that might occur. It is possible that the coming of the Son of Man would be thought to be so far away that it would really serve as no motivation to move a disciple to faithful discipleship, particularly to cross-carrying. In an attempt to cut short this type of thinking, Mark brings into play a saying of Jesus, that before at least some of those listening to him died, the kingdom, which Jesus had been preaching was near, would have come in power.

Some interpreters think that Jesus wants to identify "the coming of the Son of Man with the angels" (usually understood as the end of this world) with "the kingdom come in power." With this kind of identification, however, Jesus will be proved wrong, for obviously every one of Jesus' audience died without seeing the "coming of the Son of Man with the angels." Perhaps, though, at Mark's writing some of Jesus' listeners had not yet died, and so Mark thought Jesus' saying was still capable of fulfillment, that the kingdom in power, i.e., the Son of Man with his angels, was to come soon.

Jesus did not make this kind of mistake. Certainly, he intended to make clear to his audience that soon, within the

9 And he said to them, "Truly, I say to you, there are some standing here who will not taste death before they see that the kingdom of God has come with power."

2 And after six days Jesus took with him Peter and James and John, and led them up a high mountain apart by themselves; and he was transfigured before them, ³and his garments became glistening, intensely white, as no fuller on earth could bleach them. ⁴And there appeared to them Elijah with Moses; and they were talking to Jesus. ⁵And Peter said to Jesus, "Master, it is well that we are here; let us make three booths, one for you and one for Moses and one for Elijah." ⁶For he did not know what to say, for they were exceedingly afraid. ⁷And a cloud overshadowed them, and a voice came out of the cloud, "This is my beloved Son; listen to him." ⁸And suddenly looking around they no longer saw any one with them but Jesus only.

9 And as they were coming down the mountain, he charged them to tell no one what they had seen, until the Son of man should have risen from the dead. ¹⁰So they kept the matter to themselves, questioning what the rising from the dead meant. ¹¹And they asked him, "Why do the scribes say that first Elijah must come?" ¹²And he said to them, "Elijah does come first to restore all things; and how is it written of the Son of man, that he should suffer many things and be treated with contempt? ¹³But I tell you that Elijah has come, and they did to him whatever they pleased, as it is written of him."

14 And when they came to the disciples, they saw a great crowd about them, and scribes arguing with

them. [15]And immediately all the crowd, when they saw him, were greatly amazed, and ran up to him and greeted him. [16]And he asked them, "What are you discussing with them?" [17]And one of the crowd answered him, "Teacher, I brought my son to you, for he has a dumb spirit; [18]and wherever it seizes him, it dashes him down; and he foams and grinds his teeth and becomes rigid; and I asked your disciples to cast it out, and they were not able." [19]And he answered them, "O faithless generation, how long am I to be with you? How long am I to bear with you? Bring him to me." [20]And they brought the boy to him; and when the spirit saw him, immediately it convulsed the boy, and he fell on the ground and rolled about, foaming at the mouth. [21]And Jesus asked his father, "How long has he had this?" And he said, "From childhood. [22]And it has often cast him into the fire and into the water, to destroy him; but if you can do anything, have pity on us and help us." [23]And Jesus said to him, "If you can! All things are possible to him who believes." [24]Immediately the father of the child cried out and said, "I believe; help my unbelief!" [25]And when Jesus saw that a crowd came running together, he rebuked the unclean spirit, saying to it, "You dumb and deaf spirit, I command you, come out of him, and never enter him again." [26]And after crying out and convulsing him terribly, it came out, and the boy was like a corpse; so that most of them said, "He is dead." [27]But Jesus took him by the hand and lifted him up, and he arose. [28]And when he had entered the house, his disciples asked him privately, "Why could we not cast it out?" [29]And he said to them, "This kind cannot be driven out by anything but prayer."

30 They went on from there and passed through Galilee. And he would not have any one know it; [31]for he was teaching his disciples, saying to them, "The Son of

man will be delivered into the hands of men, and they will kill him; and when he is killed, after three days he will rise." ³²But they did not understand the saying, and they were afraid to ask him.

33 And they came to Caperna-um; and when he was in the house he asked them, "What were you discussing on the way?" ³⁴But they were silent; for on the way they had discussed with one another who was the greatest. ³⁵And he sat down and called the twelve; and he said to them, "If any one would be first, he must be last of all and servant of all." ³⁶And he took a child, and put him in the midst of them; and taking him in his arms, he said to them, ³⁷"Whoever receives one such child in my name receives me; and whoever receives me, receives not me but him who sent me."

38 John said to him, "Teacher, we saw a man casting out demons in your name, and we forbade him, because he was not following us." ³⁹But Jesus said, "Do not forbid him; for no one who does a mighty work in my name will be able soon after to speak evil of me. ⁴⁰For he that is not against us is for us. ⁴¹For truly, I say to you, whoever gives you a cup of water to drink because you bear the name of Christ, will by no means lose his reward.

42 "Whoever causes one of these little ones who believe in me to sin, it would be better for him if a great millstone were hung round his neck and he were thrown into the sea. ⁴³And if your hand causes you to sin, cut it off; it is better for you to enter life maimed than with two hands to go to hell, to the unquenchable fire. ⁴⁵And if your foot causes you to sin, cut it off; it is better for you to enter life lame than with two feet to be thrown into hell. ⁴⁷And if your eye causes you to sin, pluck it out; it is better for you to enter the kingdom of God with one eye than with two eyes to be thrown into hell, ⁴⁸where

their worm does not die, and the fire is not quenched. [49]For every one will be salted with fire. [50]Salt is good; but if the salt has lost its saltness, how will you season it? Have salt in yourselves, and be at peace with one another."

lifetime of at least some of them, the kingdom would actually be recognizable because of the powerful act which
established it. This need not be the coming of the Son of
Man with his angels, but another divine action which would
serve as warning not to be lulled into thinking that God's
ultimate coming is so far away as to be unimportant. Some
scholars think this divine, powerful action, to occur within
the lifetime of some of Jesus' listeners, is Jesus' own resurrection. This resurrection is certainly a forceful step toward
ending this age and beginning the next, a warning that this
age will not go on interminably. Other scholars think that
this divine, powerful act is the Pentecostal outpouring of
the Holy Spirit, interpreted by some (e.g., the Acts of the
Apostles) as something which occurred "in the last days" of
this age. Still other interpreters think that Jesus has in mind
the establishment of his church, in a certain sense the kingdom of God come in power. All of these interpretations are
possible; the point is that Jesus, aware that the coming of
the Son of Man may lose its motivational force because it
will not happen soon, keeps his disciples aware that God is
still entering forcefully into their history, particularly by
bringing about his kingdom soon in power. This should
arouse the disciples to fidelity to the way of Jesus, even if
the Son of Man should not come soon.

A number of scholars think that the next story, that of
the transfiguration, is put here because in its own way it
foretells a time of Jesus' life (the glorification of Jesus) which
can be considered that "kingdom of God come in power"
of which Jesus had just spoken. Certainly, the raising and
glorification of Jesus is an act of God which destroys the
kingdom of Satan and goes far toward the establishment of
God's own sway over all creation.

Transfiguration is a Latin word which means that a person's exterior looks or body (*figura*) is changed radically in

some way (*trans*). In this case, Jesus' "form was changed," as the Greek word (*metemorphothe*, which gives us our word metamorphosis) literally describes it. The few details which begin the story are suggestive. We are six days from the strained experience of Caesarea Philippi and its talk of death. Only the innermost three disciples will witness this transformation of Jesus and its sequel. It all occurs on a high mountain, unnamed (though later identified as Mount Tabor, south of the Sea of Galilee) and thus all the more probably thought of by Mark as a symbol for a place of special divine presence and revelation. Moses and Elijah are seen talking with Jesus. As in an earlier time, a voice identifies Jesus as "my Son." Finally, there is Peter's "foolish suggestion," and the mysterious envelopment by a cloud. What does all this add up to?

No doubt, Jesus' temporary appearance, as described by Mark, is meant to underline the reality of glory that always belongs to Jesus, because of his relationship with his Father, and will be visibly manifest from his resurrection onward, once he has passed through the suffering and humiliation of the crucifixion. Glorious physical changes often signaled to those brought up in Old Testament imagery both the reality underlying what they normally see and the presence of divinity.

That conversation with Moses and Elijah is added to this glorious change suggests that, as Moses (standing for the law of Israel) and Elijah (standing for the prophets of Israel) represented works which foretold the death and resurrection of Jesus, so now they visually stand with Jesus and speak of—what else?—his imminent death and resurrection. The old is now being fulfilled in the new.

Such a visual representation of prophecy and fulfillment, culminating in the glorification of Jesus, serves as a counter to the concentration of earlier conversation between Jesus and his disciples on the suffering which is about to take place. Many interpreters see in this contrast Mark's final encouragement: as you pass through the darkness of the cross, remember the person you saw as glorified; his glory is what will ultimately result from all this suffering and will be the only eternal reality. And if this is true of the master, will glory not also be the final and only lasting state of the disciple? In this understanding, the transfiguration not only enlightens one about the true identity of Jesus, but also serves as an encouragement and motivation for fidelity in the disciple.

Peter's desire that Jesus, Moses and Elijah remain with him and his companions is understandable, from a certain point of view. On the other hand, it clearly shows that Peter has no understanding of what role Moses and Elijah are playing in this vision, nor does he understand that the glorification of Jesus is to come, not now, but only after suffering and death.

At this point a cloud envelops the disciples. Traditionally in the Old Testament imagery a cloud was often a vehicle signifying revelation or divine communication; it linked heaven and earth. Here, enveloped in the divine revelation, Peter and his companions hear the revelatory voice. This divine voice speaks of two things. First, it reinforces the identity of Jesus as God's Son, almost repeating totally what had been said at the beginning of Jesus' mission. The identification of Jesus as God's Son is further testimony to the glory that ultimately will be visible in Jesus forever. Second, the voice, unlike the voice at Jesus' baptismal experience, adds the order, "Pay attention to him." Here, the intimacy of Jesus with his Father gives reason why what Jesus is teaching deserves the fullest credence; he is God's Son, so what he says is just and true.

The Father's identity of his Son serves a purpose different from that identity given by the Father at Jesus' baptism. At the baptism God spoke primarily to Jesus, to alert him that now is the time to begin his mission as servant of Yahweh. Now, God speaks in order to spur on the disciples to trust in the painful teachings of Jesus. What are these teachings which the disciples are ordered to "hear"? They are the teachings regarding the fate of Jesus and the corollaries regarding the similar fates of the disciples—hard teaching, after one had concluded that his master was indomitable, truly Lord, immensely powerful and most wise, Son of God, come to bring about the new age. Far from a permanent place with the glorious figures of Jesus, Moses and Elijah, the disciples are to return to "life," that succession of events which lead to suffering and death. The memory of this vision, however, will continue to live in the storytelling of the Christian communities, for by it future disciples are to draw courage and understanding to live out successfully the trials that their commitment to Jesus brings upon them.

By the words, "they saw no one but Jesus with them," Mark not only closes the transfiguration experience, but also underlines the reality of the world in which the disciples are to live. As at earlier moments, Jesus warns these three disciples to say nothing about what they had seen. Why he asks this of them is not so clear—perhaps, as the three had misunderstood much of its significance during the experience, others would continue to make the same mistake when hearing about it. On the other hand, the silence Jesus imposed was to last "till he was raised from the dead." Presumably, once this event occurred, the transfiguration experience could be properly interpreted. Unfortunately, mention of his resurrection from the dead was itself unintelligible to the disciples, thus throwing everything into confusion and ignorance. In portraying the disciples as totally confounded, Mark makes his case that one can really understand the meaning of the life of Jesus only after one has seen it all and come to proper terms with it all; no one, not even those closest to Jesus, understood much of the reality of things before Jesus had lived out his full life on earth.

To come down the mountain, then, was to come back to the reality of things in this world of Jesus and his twelve. One element of the transfiguration experience, however, remained in the minds of the three disciples. Having seen Elijah, they ask about the old prophecy of Malachi (4:5–6): scribes still taught, they say, that Elijah was to come again (he never did actually die, but was carried up to heaven on a chariot) to do for the final generations what he had done for his own: to prepare them to meet their God. Jesus affirms that such a figure will come, and indeed has come—and been treated evilly. Here Jesus seems to be identifying John the Baptist as this Elijah-returned. He had tried to prepare the people for the coming of God's kingdom, and for the appearance of God's messiah who would begin that kingdom. Though overpowered by the forces of evil, John served as the Elijah and thus Jesus can, once again, impress on his disciples that the kingdom of God is at hand. (Many exegetes find in this identification of John with Elijah the Christian explanation of how John, a mighty religious figure in his own right and a contemporary of Jesus, is to be rightly related to Jesus.)

In answering his disciples' question about scripture's prophecy about Elijah, Jesus takes the opportunity to direct the discussion toward a more significant and pressing point: What about the scripture which speaks of the Son of Man's suffering and being emptied? Are they interested in it? Do they understand its vital importance, especially now, for themselves as well as for Jesus? Do they have any sense as to what is about to happen to Jesus, any way of understanding it?

Interwoven artistically with the story of the transfiguration is the story about a cure of a possessed boy. Mark so narrates the cure that the beginnings of this event occur as the transfiguration event is coming to an end. The cure story stresses two points, and for this reason the story, at least as regards the description of the condition of the possessed boy, is lengthened. On the one hand, Jesus is presented with the fact that his disciples were asked for a cure, but could not do it. On the other hand, the terrible condition of the boy tests his father's trust in Jesus' ability and willingness to overcome the demon.

Though Jesus' disciples had driven out demons in an earlier chapter, Mark sees no contradiction in their unsuccess here. Why they were unsuccessful comes clear only at the very end of the story, when the disciples, in that "house" which seems characterized by revelations not given elsewhere, learn that in some cases they must have recourse to prayer for success. This lesson may seem a small one, but for the later Christian communities it was a corrective to people's thinking that they had power themselves to exorcise, to people's forgetting to whom one must appeal for healing. If this story is truly meant to correct wrong attitudes of a later generation, Mark is justified in citing Jesus' exasperation with people who do not understand where the true power over the evils of this world comes from.

Equally central to the story is the dialogue between the boy's father and Jesus. In the most extreme circumstances Jesus calls for trust; the man's cry, "Help my unbelief," is stark witness to the inability to believe caused by the immensity of the evil present. The mind finds it practically impossible to trust; it needs not only help to overcome the demon, but also help to believe that Jesus can do it. Mark is underlining more and more, as he draws closer to the death of Jesus and calls up the painful and confounding teachings about discipleship, the need for faith in the most trying circumstances. It is only this faith which will bring the disciple to the glory that lies beyond the cross.

After the stories associated with the "mountain" (which, though a real place, has become for Mark a symbol of the place of revelation), Jesus returns to Galilee. He is back, but in secret because, as Mark notes, he was, again, teaching his disciples about his imminent death and resurrection. Evidently, Jesus now restricts this special teaching to only those nearest him; the activity of Jesus to which we had become accustomed in the first eight chapters is sharply changed. For their part, the disciples given this teaching understand nothing; not only that, they are afraid to ask for clarity. So much more confounding is this time than when the disciples had no fear of asking for clarification of parables they did not understand.

From now to the end of this Chapter 9, Mark presents Jesus as teaching. Once again, Jesus, now in Capernaum, teaches in the "house," probably the house of Peter, but not a symbolic place of private teaching. Here Mark has gathered once again teaching which is difficult to practice, as though to say, for a second time, that certain teaching should be dealt with only in the light of Jesus' own cross-carrying.

The first teaching Mark gives here arises from a concrete situation among the disciples. We know the problem only to the extent that it serves to teach a correct attitude. The problem seems to be that the disciples were arguing among themselves as to who was greater, or the greatest among them. Perhaps this was occasioned by the fact that three were allowed to be present for the transfiguration while nine were incapable of performing an exorcism. Evidently, they know such a discussion was improper, for they would not admit to having had it. In response to their discussion, Jesus sits (this is the position of the teacher). He calls to himself the twelve. Evidently it is these men, most qualified to call themselves the greatest among the disciples of Jesus, who need Jesus' teaching most.

Jesus changes the words of the situation slightly. Instead of talking about "the greatest," he will talk about "the first" and "the last" and "the servant." By doing this the subject is more clearly focused upon as a matter not of intrinsic value, but of place of honor. Thus, there may be disciples who are "greater" than others from a certain perspective, but how is that translated in reference to honor, to serving and being served?

Jesus makes his point by gesture and word. First, he speaks, like a wisdom teacher, words which seem contradictory: if one wants to be first, he will be last of all and servant of all. How can one be first by being last? Then Jesus takes a child and wraps his arms around him. A child is, at this time, legally the least important person in mature, human society. To this gesture of identification with the child, Jesus adds the words which indicate the true worth of this littlest person: to receive the child as one somehow sent by Jesus is to receive Jesus himself, just as to receive Jesus is to receive the one who sent Jesus.

The lesson to be learned here, under the shadow of cross-carrying, calls on those disciples who are "greatest," by virtue of gifts given them, to achieve honor by serving those least protected and gifted. These least can be received "in my name," i.e., as ones sent by Jesus, as ones loved by Jesus. As in the case of other human situations, one sent by another represents the sender and so is honored, if for no other reason, because of the sender. Jesus does not preclude here other motives for helping the least of society; he is concerned to make clear that should love for the littlest not be present, respect for Jesus, who sends the least, should make sure that the least be well served. Nor does Jesus say that one should not seek to be "first." He only wants to make sure that what is necessary to being "first" is clearly understood. Many interpreters, while admitting that the disciples had already in Jesus' time begun to claim honors for themselves, suspect that Mark sees need in his own generation for the lesson of this story.

Mark next brings to the reader's attention Jesus' remarks about people who, though not his followers, use his name to cast out demons. According to the logic of the disciples these people should be stopped, precisely because they do not "follow Jesus." Now, it is common enough at this time in history that exorcisms, as well as other types of healing, were often done by calling on names of various powerful people or deities. Since Jesus has had great success without appeal to anyone else's name, other healers tended to use his name in their own curing, without ever knowing much about Jesus, not to mention being a committed follower of his. Perhaps this situation continued on into Mark's time of writing, and so made this story especially worthwhile to recount.

Jesus again gives teaching that goes against the logic of his followers. He gives two reasons why the disciples should not stop these people using Jesus' name. First, a person who is successful in healing by use of Jesus' name is not easily going to turn around and speak wickedly of Jesus. Thus, though the person is not a follower of Jesus, he will do no harm to Jesus. This reflection leads to the second and more general observation: the person who is not against you is thereby on your side. Jesus probably means more than that this type of person is "on your side" because he doesn't hurt you. Such a person as this, who knows why he is successful in healing, will positively (whatever concretely this may mean) be on the side of the person in whose name he heals, even if he be not one of his followers.

Jesus' next remark brings up another situation, which, however, falls under the same heading as what he has discussed so far. If a child is "in my name," and a person, who is not Jesus' follower, heals "in my name," it is "my name" which must be seen as a major circumstance governing one's actions toward the child and the person. In a third situation, if one gives water to the disciples as representatives of Christ (i.e., as those who come "in my name"), that person will receive his reward—not necessarily from the disciples, but necessarily from the one whose "name" was honored. Diverse, then, are those who carry the name of Jesus; some have it because they use it with respect, some have it because they are loved by Jesus, and some have it because they are Jesus' representatives. Because of this name, however it was gotten, great respect is to be shown to those who stand in Christ's place, as his representatives, as his loved ones. Again, this teaching of Jesus is not easy to grasp; it produces relationships of respect and love where human thinking does not create love and respect. Human beings, as the disciples are showing, do not instinctively think Jesus' way. Thus, Jesus urges them to change to his reality, not to remain in illusion; this change is a death to the past and a cross-carrying, which, ironically, issues in creative love, or resurrection and new life.

A final teaching of Jesus in this chapter is actually a continuation of his earlier thoughts about the "little people." Here he is not speaking solely of a child, but rather of all those who can be called the "little ones who believe in me." Again, the attention of the twelve is called to their relationships with the least of the Christian community. Jesus' concern here is with scandalizing one of these least, even just one. To "scandalize" means to put something in the way of a person's believing, so that the person believes less from one's action. Having simply stated his concern and without describing what kind of scandal he is thinking of (evidently the reader is to know what is and is not scandalous), Jesus spends much time in emphasizing how bad scandal is. The examples he uses are very expressive and, one might say, harsh. They are exaggerations, in the sense that Jesus did not expect people actually to cut off limbs or, having given scandal, to commit suicide. Nor do these examples show the mercy for which Jesus is justly famous, for they were not constructed with mercy in mind. Jesus, as is usual with him and other wisdom teachers, is trying to teach one thing and the examples used aim only at this one thing. Here he tries to underline as graphically as possible the tragedy that scandal causes; the way to comprehend this is to hear what the one who causes scandal deserves, to hear what efforts one should make to avoid the tragedy scandal causes. One is not to cut off a limb as though it were the limb that causes the scandal; one is rather, from this example, to understand the effort one must make in one's will which governs the foot and the eye and the hand. One should understand that even a bitter and painful death is not ultimately as harmful as the loss of faith that scandal causes in the follower of Jesus. Jesus' hearers were used to what we call "semitic exaggeration." They knew that Jesus was not calling for death or amputation. They learned rather just what efforts the human will should make to avoid harming fellow Christians. This, like the other lessons Jesus has just given, presents people with a way of caring about others which is contrary to the usual, human way of thinking. Jesus asks for change, which in its own way is another form of cross-carrying.

In speaking about the ugly place we today call hell and Jesus called Gehenna, Jesus is referring his audience to a specific locale in a valley just south of the city walls of Jerusalem. This area drew its name from a man named *Hinnom* (in Aramaic, *Henna*) who, a long time before Christ, owned this property in this valley (which word is *ge* in Hebrew). At one time in Israel's history this area was used for offering children live to pagan gods; thus the area was always symbolic of evil. In Jesus' time, this Gehenna was actually the city garbage dump. As such, it was on fire almost continually, as otherwise the refuse piled up there would be intolerable. Among all this garbage, too, were those vermin whose numbers never ceased. It is this ugly image which Jesus invokes as he tries to draw a picture of what befits the scandal which destroys faith.

Jesus' description of hell includes mention of a "fire which never goes out" (v 48). Verse 49 explains that everyone cast into this fire will be "salted" with fire, a frightful image which recalls that as salt is rubbed closely into meat, so closely will fire be rubbed into those cast into Gehenna.

The mention of "salting" brings up a useful metaphor about salt, but the context is not of punishment. Salt is good, Jesus says, but, should its saltiness be lost, how can it be regained? Jesus' point is that if one has what it takes to love others, to respect others, to treat others as they should be treated, to enjoy peace, one should not lose it, at the peril of not ever being able to regain it. It is not easy to pinpoint just what it is that creates a person who loves and what creates a person who does not love, but it is abundantly clear when one has passed from one kind of person to the other. Jesus exhorts his disciples to keep the "salt" in themselves and not to lose it.

Chapter 10

Mark now changes scenes; we last were listening to Jesus' teaching in the "house" in Capernaum, and now we are going southward through the hills of Judea and eastward across the Jordan River. Only by reading ahead does one realize that, with this movement, Jesus definitively leaves Galilee and ultimately will arrive in Jerusalem where he dies. Jesus, then, is moving in a southeasterly direction, probably following the Jordan valley to a point near Jericho where he will turn westward again to reach Jerusalem. While on his journey, crowds come to him and he responds as usual with teaching.

We should recall that, though we are in a new chapter and though the scene has changed appreciably, we are still under the shadow of the cross and cross-carrying, as far as Jesus' teaching is concerned. That is, we can expect more "difficult" lessons, lessons which separate the Christian from ordinary human thinking about people. We can also recall from time to time that most all of the teaching Mark cites is cited because Mark thinks his reader can profit from it as much as could the original hearers of Jesus.

Mark says that Jesus teaches; as on other occasions, Mark does not detail in just what this teaching consisted. It is the approach and questioning of the Pharisees which brings us a concrete and out-of-the-ordinary teaching from

10 And he left there and went to the region of Judea and beyond the Jordan, and crowds gathered to him again; and again, as his custom was, he taught them.

2 And Pharisees came up and in order to test him asked, "Is it lawful for a man to divorce his wife?" [3]He answered them, "What did Moses command you?" [4]They said, "Moses allowed a man to write a certificate of divorce, and to put her away." [5]But Jesus said to them, "For your hardness of heart he wrote you this commandment. [6]But from the beginning of creation, 'God made them male and female.' [7]For this reason a man shall leave his father and mother and be joined to his wife, [8]and the two shall become one flesh.' So they are no longer two but one flesh. [9]What therefore God has joined together, let not man put asunder."

10 And in the house the disciples asked him again about this matter. [11]And he said to them, "Whoever divorces his wife and marries another, commits adultery against her; [12]and if she divorces her husband and marries another, she commits adultery."

13 And they were bringing children to him, that he might touch them; and the disciples rebuked them. [14]But when Jesus saw it he was indignant, and said to them, "Let the children come to me, do not hinder them; for to such belongs the kingdom of God. [15]Truly, I say to you, whoever does not receive the kingdom of God like a child shall not enter it." [16]And he took them in his arms and blessed them, laying his hands upon them.

17 And as he was setting out on his journey, a man ran up and knelt before him, and asked him, "Good

Teacher, what must I do to inherit eternal life?" [18]And Jesus said to him, "Why do you call me good? No one is good but God alone. [19]You know the commandments: 'Do not kill, Do not commit adultery, Do not steal, Do not bear false witness, Do not defraud, Honor your father and mother.' " [20]And he said to him, "Teacher, all these I have observed from my youth." [21]And Jesus looking upon him loved him, and said to him, "You lack one thing; go, sell what you have, and give to the poor, and you will have treasure in heaven; and come, follow me." [22]At that saying his countenance fell, and he went away sorrowful; for he had great possessions.

23 And Jesus looked around and said to his disciples, "How hard it will be for those who have riches to enter the kingdom of God!" [24]And the disciples were amazed at his words. But Jesus said to them again, "Children, how hard it is to enter the kingdom of God! [25]It is easier for a camel to go through the eye of a needle than for a rich man to enter the kingdom of God." [26]And they were exceedingly astonished, and said to him, "Then who can be saved?" [27]Jesus looked at them and said, "With men it is impossible, but not with God; for all things are possible with God." [28]Peter began to say to him, "Lo, we have left everything and followed you." [29]Jesus said, "Truly, I say to you, there is no one who has left house or brothers or sisters or mother or father or children or lands, for my sake and for the gospel, [30]who will not receive a hundredfold now in this time, houses and brothers and sisters and mothers and children and lands, with persecutions, and in the age to come eternal life. [31]But many that are first will be last, and the last first."

32 And they were on the road, going up to Jerusalem, and Jesus was walking ahead of them; and they were amazed, and those who followed were afraid. And taking

the twelve again, he began to tell them what was to happen to him, [33]saying, "Behold, we are going up to Jerusalem; and the Son of man will be delivered to the chief priests and the scribes, and they will condemn him to death, and deliver him to the Gentiles; [34]and they will mock him, and spit upon him, and scourge him, and kill him; and after three days he will rise."

35 And James and John, the sons of Zebedee, came forward to him, and said to him, "Teacher, we want you to do for us whatever we ask of you." [36]And he said to them, "What do you want me to do for you?" [37]And they said to him, "Grant us to sit, one at your right hand and one at your left, in your glory." [38]But Jesus said to them, "You do not know what you are asking. Are you able to drink the cup that I drink, or to be baptized with the baptism with which I am baptized?" [39]And they said to him, "We are able." And Jesus said to them, "The cup that I drink you will drink; and with the baptism with which I am baptized, you will be baptized; [40]but to sit at my right hand or at my left is not mine to grant, but it is for those for whom it has been prepared." [41]And when the ten heard it, they began to be indignant at James and John. [42]And Jesus called them to him and said to them, "You know that those who are supposed to rule over the Gentiles lord it over them, and their great men exercise authority over them. [43]But it shall not be so among you; but whoever would be great among you must be your servant, [44]and whoever would be first among you must be slave of all. [45]For the Son of man also came not to be served but to serve, and to give his life as a ransom for many."

46 And they came to Jericho; and as he was leaving Jericho with his disciples and a great multitude, Barti-maeus, a blind beggar, the son of Timaeus, was sitting by

the roadside. [47]And when he heard that it was Jesus of Nazareth, he began to cry out and say, "Jesus, Son of David, have mercy on me!" [48]And many rebuked him, telling him to be silent; but he cried out all the more, "Son of David, have mercy on me!" [49]And Jesus stopped and said, "Call him." And they called the blind man, saying to him, "Take heart; rise, he is calling you." [50]And throwing off his mantle he sprang up and came to Jesus. [51]And Jesus said to him, "What do you want me to do for you?" And the blind man said to him, "Master, let me receive my sight." [52]And Jesus said to him, "Go your way; your faith has made you well." And immediately he received his sight and followed him on the way.

Jesus. The Pharisees, always now the testers of Jesus, want
to put him in a difficult position. They ask him whether or
not a man may divorce his wife. If he says yes, Jesus shows
that he is a follower of Moses and is not deserving of adu-
lation that makes him equal to or greater than Moses; eventually, the Pharisees think perhaps, Jesus will be shown to
belong to the Mosaic law tradition. If he says no, Jesus is
again in opposition to the Mosaic law and, in the eyes of
many, ever more the troublemaker, belligerent and destructive.

As with most arguments of the type proposed by the
Pharisees, the battleground is the Old Testament wherein
one finds the mind of God. The Pharisees evidently take the
side that says that Moses permitted divorce; actually, they
cannot and do not say this about Moses, but they think they
can conclude to it from Moses' order that a document of
divorce be drawn up when a divorce occurred. What else
could Moses be interpreted as doing if not permitting divorce, when he says that a man must first give his wife a
document attesting to the divorce and then let her go?

Jesus does not deny what Moses wrote, that a decree
terminating the marriage was obligatory before a divorce
took place. But two questions arise from this writing. First,
why did Moses write what he wrote? Second, does his writing really mean to say that Moses permitted divorce? Moses
demanded a document which formally freed the woman
from her husband. He did this because the Jews were so
hard-hearted that, first, they would have divorced women
without any clear sign that the women were divorced; and
without this clear, documented sign women caught with another man would automatically be stoned to death as adul-
terers; second, they would not have had the love of neighbor
necessary to maintain the woman in a dignified manner if
the marriage were to continue.

Jesus does not challenge Moses, but rather shows why Moses did what he did. Moses' decision was based on the sinfulness of his contemporaries, the basis for exception perhaps, but not the basis for law itself. The law, Jesus insists, is very clear. It is contained, not in the Mosaic instructions, but in the very act of creation of male and female.

Male and female God made them; the intention here is to stress unity by complementarity. Because of this peculiar fact, the two when joined become one flesh, with the result, Jesus concludes, that there are no longer two fleshes but there is only one flesh. What can separate this one flesh into two separate, separated bodies again? The husband? Even though a man chose to unite himself to his wife, he cannot effect a breaking up of that union, once it is made. For he has consented to joining in a type of union the nature of which (not one's consent) makes the union unbreakable except by God. Not all contracts humans freely enter into are of this type, but marriage is.

Jesus, then, will not allow divorce because of his understanding of God's plan. Moses cannot be said to contradict God's plan, for Moses' decision about divorce was governed, not by God's plan, but by man's hard-heartedness. Moses, Jesus presumes, would agree with him, if Moses spoke only on the level of what God's plan intended.

Once again we find ourselves in "the house," except that now we definitely are not in the usual house of Capernaum, but far south and east of it. In this symbolic place of revelation, Jesus answers further questions about divorce put to him by his disciples. Specifically, Jesus moves beyond the question of the Pharisees— "Is it permissible to divorce one's wife?"—to the question, "Is it permissible that a man divorce and remarry?"

In answering this second question Jesus points up a new evil which a man incurs by divorcing and remarrying: the woman he marries after his divorce is adulterated; the man, in other words, is guilty of adultery. Thus, not only does the man destroy the union which only God should break; he also soils the woman of his second marriage.

In answering this second question, Jesus talks about women who divorce and remarry, as well as about men. How is it that the Pharisees' question spoke only of men who divorce, whereas now Jesus speaks of both men and women who divorce their partners? The answer seems to depend on what law code one is using. According to Jewish law, only the man could initiate a divorce, never the woman; according to Roman law, either a man or a woman could initiate a divorce. Such legal differences have led interpreters to think that Jesus' answer to the Pharisees was an actual answer he gave to a problem of his society, whereas Jesus' answer to his disciples "in the house" was not something explicitly said by Jesus, but something which Roman Christians deduced from what he did say in Palestine; they deduced it to meet a need arising from their own law code (which allowed a woman to initiate a divorce), a need Jesus never had to face and thus never explicitly addressed (because Jewish law never allowed a woman to initiate a divorce).

Jesus' teaching about divorce was unique in Palestine, for all teachers admitted some divorce, differing only on the causes which made a divorce legitimate. Thus, Jesus once again, claiming to know the mind of God (and Israel's own scriptures) better than anyone else, presents teaching which is difficult to comprehend, another "cross-carrying."

Mark swiftly replaces one scene with another. Are we still in the house? Does this situation arise immediately after Jesus' teaching about divorce? We do not know for sure about these details. All we know is that children are brought to Jesus for him to touch, and his disciples, *thinking* to

know what is the correct thing, forbid the children to dis-
turb Jesus. Is their judgment correct in this matter, or must
they come to a new understanding?

Jesus catches sight of what his disciples are doing, becomes indignant and utters the following teaching: let them
come, "because the kingdom of heaven belongs to such as
these." Precisely why the kingdom belongs to such as these
has been greatly disputed over the centuries, as people try
to see what it is in children that makes the kingdom belong
to people like children. Certainly, simplicity and unpreten-
tiousness and a willingness to trust are qualities usually associated most with children. In this way of thinking, it is a
child's virtue that makes it an "owner" of the kingdom.

Another way of looking at this is that the kingdom is to
be given to all, but especially to those most in need. Jesus
is not so much pointing out a child's worthiness to enter
the kingdom, as he is the child's need and dependence—
and God's corresponding desire to step forward to give the
kingdom to such a needy one. Finally, one might simply say
that just the coming to Jesus is reason enough to say that
the kingdom is theirs. We have seen in this narrative about
Jesus' public life how few really come to him. Just to put
faith in him, to "come to him to be touched," lets one into
Jesus' presence, into the kingdom of God which he is beginning to let happen.

Jesus, however, goes a step further in his teaching when
he insists that one will enter the kingdom only if one receives the kingdom as a child receives it. Here we are again
faced with the same question as before: What is peculiar
and laudatory about a child's way of receiving the kingdom?
Perhaps again what Jesus intends to praise here is the simple
fact that the children, admittedly with the help of others,
tried to reach him, wanted to reach him, knew that his touch

was good for them. Such an attitude may be the attitude which alone allows one to enter the kingdom of God.

In any event, in this case Mark brings his story beyond the teaching of Jesus to Jesus' action: he embraces the children and blesses them with his hands upon them. This is not just a warm ending to the story. However one explains the teaching of Jesus, it is the children, in fact, who do reach Jesus, who do receive his embrace and blessing. Whatever brought this meeting together, the children did enter into the intimate presence of him who is, as beginner, the kingdom of God. The gesture teaches in action what the words of Jesus want to convey: the kingdom is for those who, like children, make their way to Jesus.

Jesus is next seen "on the road," without further attempt at a more precise geography. A man runs up to Jesus, kneels before him (clearly a sign of respect), and puts the question to Jesus, "Good master, what must I do to gain eternal life?" One cannot fail to see how fitting it is that Mark puts this story right after Jesus' remarks about whose is the kingdom, about who will enter it.

The unnamed man addresses Jesus as "good" master or teacher. Jesus objects to being called "good," on the grounds that God alone is good. This objection may seem excessive on Jesus' part, but it serves to turn praise away from the human teacher, who ultimately only mediates God's wisdom, to the truly wise God, who, in the last analysis, is the only source of wisdom and thus the only one fully deserving praise for it. Again, one must recognize in this way of Jesus' response to others a normal type of exaggeration used by semitic teachers to underline a truth they were convinced of. By this exaggeration, then, Jesus shows his own self-conception: he is dependent on his Father for his knowledge.

In direct response to the man's question, Jesus gives

what one might call the expected answer: to reach eternal life one must do God's will. The man's response shows how good a life he had led and explains why he was searching as he was. According to Jesus' answer, the man is on his way to enter eternal life, and Jesus never denies this. What follows, however, complicates matters.

Jesus is now said to love this man; why, we do not know, nor is Mark interested in explaining why. This love is noted only as a cause for what Jesus does next. Jesus offers the man the opportunity to follow Jesus, to be a disciple journeying with Jesus, to enjoy a life with Jesus. One thing this desirable life entails, however, is getting rid of what one owns, for such a life as Jesus leads in Palestine makes one poor. Jesus, in suggesting that the man follow him, likewise suggests that the man sell all he has and, like a good Jew, give it to the poor, for the Jews knew that such a charitable action won them treasure or reward in heaven. Jesus is pushing the man to respond to him with love, corresponding to the love with which Jesus had first responded to the man.

The man could not take advantage of this unique offer. It was not that he could not or would not love Jesus; he just could not accept the means to this life with Jesus, that is, the selling off of all his wealth for the good of others and for treasure in heaven. (One might suggest that the man could have "banked" his wealth instead of selling it, and then followed Jesus, and then at some future date he could regain his wealth—but this is not the offer of Jesus to this man.)

The man now disappears; we are left to listen to Jesus twice draw a conclusion: to the degree that following Jesus leads one into the kingdom, how hard it will be for those who have wealth to enter it—indeed, as Jesus broadens his remark, how hard it will be (without reference to wealth) to enter the kingdom of heaven! The camel, largest of animals in Jerusalem, will find it easier to pass through a needle's eye, the smallest of openings, than will a rich man to enter the kingdom. Thus, we may conclude that, though the rich man did observe the commandments of God, it is possible that decisions will be made which, though not about commandments of the law, will either lead or not lead a person into the kingdom. Commandments of the law, then, do lead to eternal life, but, since they do not cover all situations, it is possible that one may still not reach eternal life. Concretely, the commandments do not forbid wealth; yet, as the story shows, the man turned away from Jesus to save his wealth—can he reject this grace and other graces, and still enter the kingdom?

More specifically, is it possible that wealth be such an attraction that, when the moment comes to use it for the benefit of others, love of wealth will keep one from so using it? Can one, then, say he will enter life or, as the man seemed to say to Jesus, "I have kept all the commandments of God"?

The Jewish law did not forbid owning things, even great wealth; it seems to have been Jesus' understanding of human nature that provoked this conflict between law and wealth, as though to say that the law of Moses may actually *not* be able to lead one through all of this life's situations into eternal life. In short, wealth (and perhaps other things, too, which are not forbidden by the Jewish law) takes its toll in one's efforts to love God and love one's neighbor. Perhaps Jesus exaggerates about the difficulty of a rich man entering heaven. Even so, his point, devoid of exaggeration, is well made, as anyone can attest who knows how people are influenced in their actions by the love of wealth.

The disciples, as is typical of them in this section which follows the prediction of Jesus' crucifixion, find this teaching hard. It is another form of cross-carrying. They ask Jesus rather frustratedly, "Then who can be saved?" This question arises from their very innermost selves, for they know just

how impossible it is for people to give up wealth in order
to follow Jesus. Indeed, the twelve have, Mark reported,
given up everything to follow Jesus; the question, then, is
put more properly about others, particularly about future
disciples, and most particularly about Mark's contemporaries: What will keep them from following Jesus? How will
they be saved?

Jesus' answer moves us to another plane or level of the
Christian reality. It is somehow the power of God which will
lead people to make the sacrifices which people of themselves have not the strength to make. Nothing more is said
of this principle, but, in accord with other statements given
elsewhere in the New Testament, Christians have come to
understand better the tension their theology must accept:
the human being, free to choose, must choose God to have
life; yet, without the decisive help of God, no one will
choose so as to have life eternal.

Mark, through Peter, now approaches the subject of
wealth, and sacrifice of it, from a different perspective. Having learned how difficult it is to enter heaven as a wealthy
person, Peter reflects the situation of the twelve who have,
as the early stage of the gospel told us, left everything and
followed Jesus. What is the future for these men? Jesus' response suggests a great abundance of gifts in return; indeed,
it seems as though one has not made a sacrifice, but increased his relations and possessions by a hundredfold in
this age and gained eternal life (which is what the rich man
was after at the beginning of this story) in the next age.

Why does one, who appears to lose, gain so much? The
reason seems to be embedded in the phrase "to leave all
things *for my sake and for the sake of the gospel*." It is this
motive which brings forth from God such a richness of gifts;
ultimately, what is mysteriously at stake here is an exchange

of love, something which Jesus is said to have offered the rich man and something the rich man could not offer Jesus.

Together with the return a sacrificing disciple receives is a share in persecutions. There is a certain realism here, directed, we think, to the Christians whom Mark is encouraging to fidelity in time of Roman persecution. No doubt, the lives of the Christians, often separated from pagan family members by their new religion, have found "mothers and sisters and brothers and children," but they have also found persecution. This persecution, however, is placed in Jesus' speech amidst the benefits from God, in order to help one understand that suffering is to be seen and borne against the great background of blessings. One's commitments to Jesus will be richly returned but reality must admit that there will be suffering in this new life and amidst these blessings.

Jesus closes his answer to Peter by a proverb which appears often in the New Testament: many first shall be last and many last shall be first. This saw has many applications. In the context of Jesus' remarks to Peter, it means that those who appear to be "last" because they accepted nothing in place of everything are, by virtue of God's love, the equivalent of the "first," the most honored, whether in this age or in the age to come. Conversely, those who have the most in this age, the "first," by irony merit to be called the "last," for they mirror the rich man who turned away from Jesus while others accepted him, and, although he kept the commandments of God, clearly becomes the "last" in the story.

The lessons following the first prediction of Jesus' suffering form a unit, as do the lessons following the second prediction of Jesus' suffering. Now Mark gives us the third and final prediction, more intense and more detailed, as the time of fulfillment draws ever nearer. Sensing the tragedy and reflecting it for the reader are those traveling with Jesus.

Those accompanying Jesus are anxiously mystified, whereas his disciples are simply, starkly afraid.

For the first time Mark clearly tells us that we are going up to Jerusalem. (Since Jerusalem was about 2,800 feet above sea level and since the city was the most honored of all cities, one always goes "up" to Jerusalem.) Amidst the anxiety and fear, Jesus calls his twelve aside to spell out in more detail the fate awaiting the Son of Man. More clearly than before, we learn that this fate includes betrayal to chief priests and scribes, a Jewish condemnation, and the handing over of Jesus to Gentiles who will mock and spit upon and whip and kill him; but after three days he will rise up. Thus, more suffering than just death awaits Jesus, and it will be a suffering caused by both Jew and Gentile. One effect of this description is that the reader will realize that little that happened to Jesus at the end of his life was a surprise to him. His going to Jerusalem, then, was not a walk into the unknown; all the greater is his devotion to his Father that, knowing what lay ahead of him, he went right to it.

It is only right to recall that each of the three predictions of suffering go hand in hand with predictions of resurrection. The resurrection is never forgotten as the predictable end to all the suffering. The emphasis of the gospel, before one reaches these final events of Jesus' life, is, however, on the inexplicable suffering that Jesus (and later his followers) must undergo for his claims. The balance between suffering and resurrection is, then, in favor of the former in this gospel, though one never is allowed to forget the impact of the latter.

As one might expect, Mark follows the prediction of suffering with another "hard" lesson. This teaching comes from a blatant request of James and John that, in the time of glory, one be assigned to Jesus' left and the other to Jesus' right. This request reflects the imagery Jesus' contemporaries used to express the kingdom in which the messiah rules as king. Over the centuries, Israel, so beaten and humiliated, depicted its salvation as a restoration to its rightful place as the beloved of God. In kingdom imagery, this place of preference is at the right and left sides of God; there Israel would be recognized for the beloved it was and would, with God, judge those who had judged it. Now, James and John ask for these places of honor and power.

As often happens in gospel writing, a story which ends a unit reflects a story which began the unit. Here, the request of James and John, which closes the "hard" teaching of Jesus in the light of the cross, reflects the opening of the "hard" teaching of Jesus (who will be "first"?) which followed his second prediction of suffering. This story of the request of James and John has two parts; first it deals with James and John, then it deals with the twelve after the request of James and John came to their attention.

Ultimately, the request of James and John is not for Jesus to fulfill, or apparently even to intercede for. Here we have one of those places in the New Testament where a distinction between the role of Jesus and the role of the Father in salvation is kept very clear. Jesus assumes the functions of God when he is professed as savior and judge, but there are certain areas which are not credited to him by all the New Testament documents.

The point of the story, however, is not a simple "I can't do what you ask." The point lies in the response to the request for glory and honor and closeness to Jesus in glory. This response, using language signifying suffering, asks if the disciples can suffer with Jesus; the logic seems to be that, if one really wants to sit in positions of honor and power, he will have to do it by means of suffering—as Jesus had just noted about himself he will suffer first, then after three days rise. (For clarity's sake, the word baptism, in its Greek root, means a "dipping" or an "immersion." Thus, Jesus looks upon his imminent future as a "dipping" or "immersion" into suffering and death.)

The disciples say that they can drink as Jesus will, can be baptized as Jesus will. Jesus himself affirms that they will. (Perhaps this affirmation of Jesus is particularly recalled, since at least James had been martyred by the time Mark wrote his gospel.) Thus, suffering is indicated for these two disciples as well as for the master. To the readers of Mark's time, this story suggests the pervasive presence of a martyr's death whenever one looks to entering eternal life.

One may not be too surprised to hear that the other ten were upset with James and John for what they had asked of Jesus. Underlying their argument against these two brothers seems to be a conviction that others than James and John are the greatest, the first, and that these deserve the places of honor James and John had unduly requested for themselves. Again, Jesus tries to teach reality, hard and difficult though it be to understand and accept. His teaching represents a death to "human" thinking, and as such it is a form of cross-carrying.

Admitting that some disciples are to rule over others, that some are "greater" than others in a certain sense, Jesus stresses that the use of power and authority is to be conceived of as a service and that the bearing of a user of power and authority is to be that of one who looks to the good of another, and not to his own good. Human rulers do not use power and authority as a service to others, but to their own service. This will not do in the Christian community, whether that of Jesus' or that of a later generation. Human rulers so use their authority and power that their own self-esteem is heightened and that those who obey are humbled. Not so in the Christian community. One must use authority authoritatively (as did Jesus), but the pervading attitude is not that one is humbling another, but working out love for the other. The more exact and detailed psychology of authority-obedience is not worked out here, but left to human prudence; the principle of rule is clear, however, that one rule in such a way that one is not seen as self-seeking or self-aggrandizing, but loving the one who is to obey.

Mark concludes this teaching under the shadow of the cross by having the disciple look to Jesus to see what attitude dictated his life. He came to serve, not to be served; because he came in this way, he will be first and greatest in honor. Jesus will not directly quarrel with his disciples' desire to be first and greatest in honor, but their firstness and greatness will only be the result of their serving others. To be served in this life is no sign that one has achieved "firstness" or that one is "the greatest." So it was with Jesus: he first became human to the point of service by crucifixion, and then he was raised up in glory. This is the rhythm of Christian leadership in any generation after Jesus.

A most crucial belief of Christianity is embedded in Jesus' final remark here. In describing his life of service, he is most specific about the fact that he is giving his life as a ransom for the multitudes. Mark's gospel, like others, does not intend to tackle head-on this belief that Jesus' death was a ransom for others; by and large, the gospel view is usually that Jesus' death is a death foreseen by God (and thus not an obstacle to belief in Jesus) and it is the death of a just man (and thus no reason to think that Jesus is not the embodiment of divine power, wisdom and goodness). However, in Mark's work, here and in the words of consecration at the last supper, Jesus clearly identifies his death as a ransom.

When speaking of his death as a "ransom," Jesus is clearly using a human metaphor to express a mysterious reality. According to the metaphor, human beings belonged originally to God, but, in some way, became the prisoners or possessions of an enemy (to God and to human beings); under this possession human beings ultimately would be destroyed. This element of the metaphor explains in imagery the perceived reality that human beings are estranged from God and under the domination of power which continually leads them from reconciliation with God.

Human beings are essentially helpless, and doomed thereby. The solution lies in the unilateral restoration of the human being to a friendship he could not regain of himself. According to the metaphor we have been using, this restoration was done by a payment on behalf of those who could not help themselves. The payment was, as another New Testament work puts it, not in gold or silver, but in blood, the blood of Jesus. By this freely given blood human beings are returned to their original owner, God. This is Jesus' primary service and the example he offers of how one achieves "firstness."

The chapter ends with the story of the cure of a blind man, Bartimaeus (*bar* is Aramaic for "son of"; *timaeus* is the Greek for the Hebrew Timai, a man's name). But this story also is seen as the end to this long section Mark has presented to the reader, intending to interweave predictions of Jesus' imminent suffering with teachings which are often very hard to understand and to put into practice—which in their own ways, then, are types of crosses.

The cure of Bartimaeus, on the one hand, continues to recall the power and love of Jesus; for Mark's own reasons, these miracles are less now since the crucial question "Who am I?" and the introduction of predictions about Jesus' fate in Jerusalem. Still, we are periodically reminded of this aspect of Jesus' mysterious identity.

Also underlined in this story is the fact that Jesus attributes the man's cure to his faith: "Your faith has saved you." Faith, too, has been a theme which Mark has stressed, particularly as the time approaches when very difficult and challenging events will take place. In these situations which seem impossible of joyous resolution, Jesus insists on trust, on faith in himself as the key response which will lead to peace and joy.

The cure of Bartimaeus, on the other hand, has certain features which suggest that this story is placed here for a specific reason. The disciples had tried to prevent the children from disturbing Jesus; against that story, the crowd's trying to prevent Bartimaeus' reaching Jesus seems intended by Mark to reinforce the difference between Jesus' thinking and that of his fellow Jews. The story, however, does not look only backward, but in a small way anticipates what is to come next. In the next story Jesus will enter Jerusalem in the symbolic form of royal messiah, the longed-for "Son of David," who will begin again to rule as did his glorious ancestor, David. In the Bartimaeus story, Jesus is called by the very rare title, Jesus Son of David, apparently a preview to the royal entry into Jerusalem.

But perhaps most important of all in the Bartimaeus story is Mark's highlighting the granting of sight which eventuates in Bartimaeus' following Jesus on the road. So central is the need for and request for sight and the granting of it that many interpreters see the Bartimaeus event as a twin to that earlier cure of the blind man which preceded the lengthy section Mark has devoted to predictions of the cross and descriptions of disciples' cross-carrying. That is, many interpreters think that Mark intentionally put on either side of the difficult teaching about the cross a story about blindness and the cure only Jesus can effect. This structure is meant to underline, not just that Jesus could cure blind people, but that the disciples need Jesus' help to remove their peculiar blindness by which they are unable to comprehend, to "see" things the way Jesus sees them. To the degree, then, that Jesus' way contradicts human thinking and human ways of acting, to that degree disciples need Jesus to remove their confusion, their incomprehension, their blindness. His teaching will do this in part, and to this will be added the other part: his grace which enlightens.

Another symbolic aspect in the Bartimaeus story is the very last line of it: he saw and followed him on the way. Not only is God-given sight necessary to understand the difficult events of Jesus' life and his teachings regarding discipleship, but, once this sight is given, the result is that one follows Jesus on the way. Thus, through a particular manner of story-telling, Mark urges his reader to seek the insights of Jesus and, with faith in him and God-given understanding, to follow Jesus on his way—to suffer, but then to rise. Mark's hope is that the disciple will respond with trust in Jesus and his teachings, with enlightenment drawn from those teachings and God's grace, to the challenges presented in his life by crosses which, left to themselves, may destroy faith, destroy the seed once so gladly received, and eventually cause one to lose that life which is obtainable only through suffering.

Mark has intentionally joined the difficult teachings of Jesus with the difficult fate of Jesus himself. Thereby, he hopes that the disciple will be comforted by the knowledge that he is imitating the Lord, and thus not alone, in his cross-carrying. If God himself took this road, there is comfort indeed that it leads only to life, for who else, if not God, knows the way to eternal life?

Chapter 11

With ten chapters completed, Mark is just about ready to bring Jesus into Jerusalem. That life of Jesus which was composed of preaching, teaching and miracle-working ended some time ago, when Jesus asked the question, "Who do you say I am?" From that moment on, Mark restricted Jesus' life-story to teachings about his fate and the meaning and consequences of discipleship. Now, as Jesus climbs from Jericho (some 600 feet below sea-level) up to Jerusalem (some 2,800 feet above sea-level), Mark picks him up just as he is about to reach the top of the mountain (Mount of Olives) which stands directly east of the mountain-top, Jerusalem. Once Jesus crosses the top of the Mount of Olives, he need only go down into a deep valley (Kedron) and then start walking up till he walks right into Jerusalem.

As Jesus approaches the ancient city of David, his famous royal ancestor, Jesus decides to assert in symbolic fashion a sense of his mission which he has not thus far shown. Whereas Galilee was Jesus' home area and Nazareth his home town, he evidently thought of Jerusalem as "his" to the extent that he, the Son of David, was the inheritor of the throne of his ancestral father. Precisely what more Jesus intended to after this claim, in symbolism, to the throne of David, we do not know nor will it be made clear. Perhaps it was enough that Jesus by sign identified himself as the

11 And when they drew near to Jerusalem, to Bethphage and Bethany, at the Mount of Olives, he sent two of his disciples, ²and said to them, "Go into the village opposite you, and immediately as you enter it you will find a colt tied, on which no one has ever sat; untie it and bring it. ³If any one says to you, 'Why are you doing this?' say, 'The Lord has need of it and will send it back here immediately.' " ⁴And they went away, and found a colt tied at the door out in the open street; and they untied it. ⁵And those who stood there said to them, "What are you doing, untying the colt?" ⁶And they told them what Jesus had said; and they let them go. ⁷And they brought the colt to Jesus, and threw their garments on it; and he sat upon it. ⁸And many spread their garments on the road, and others spread leafy branches which they had cut from the fields. ⁹And those who went before and those who followed cried out, "Hosanna! Blessed is he who comes in the name of the Lord! ¹⁰Blessed is the kingdom of our father David that is coming! Hosanna in the highest!"

11 And he entered Jerusalem, and went into the temple; and when he had looked round at everything, as it was already late, he went out to Bethany with the twelve.

12 On the following day, when they came from Bethany, he was hungry. ¹³And seeing in the distance a fig tree in leaf, he went to see if he could find anything on it. When he came to it, he found nothing but leaves, for it was not the season for figs. ¹⁴And he said to it, "May

no one ever eat fruit from you again." And his disciples heard it.

15 And they came to Jerusalem. And he entered the temple and began to drive out those who sold and those who bought in the temple, and he overturned the tables of the money-changers and the seats of those who sold pigeons; [16]and he would not allow any one to carry anything through the temple. [17]And he taught, and said to them, "Is it not written, 'My house shall be called a house of prayer for all the nations'? But you have made it a den of robbers." [18]And the chief priests and the scribes heard it and sought a way to destroy him; for they feared him, because all the multitude was astonished at his teaching. [19]And when evening came they went out of the city.

20 As they passed by in the morning, they saw the fig tree withered away to its roots. [21]And Peter remembered and said to him, "Master, look! The fig tree which you cursed has withered." [22]And Jesus answered them, "Have faith in God. [23]Truly, I say to you, whoever says to this mountain, 'Be taken up and cast into the sea,' and does not doubt in his heart, but believes that what he says will come to pass, it will be done for him. [24]Therefore I tell you, whatever you ask in prayer, believe that you have received it, and it will be yours. [25]And whenever you stand praying, forgive, if you have anything against any one; so that your Father also who is in heaven may forgive you your trespasses."

27 And they came again to Jerusalem. And as he was walking in the temple, the chief priests and the scribes and the elders came to him, [28]and they said to him, "By what authority are you doing these things, or who gave you this authority to do them?" [29]Jesus said to them, "I will ask you a question; answer me, and I will tell you by

what authority I do these things. [30]Was the baptism of John from heaven or from men? Answer me." [31]And they argued with one another, "If we say, 'From heaven,' he will say, 'Why then did you not believe him?' [32]But shall we say, 'From men'?"—they were afraid of the people, for all held that John was a real prophet. [33]So they answered Jesus, "We do not know." And Jesus said to them, "Neither will I tell you by what authority I do these things."

divinely intended successor of David, the one God designated to bring a divine peace and wisdom to Jerusalem.

Mark tells us that Jesus and his followers draw near to two towns which lie just about at the top of the Mount of Olives, the mountain across from Jerusalem. Bethphage means, in Aramaic, house of unripe figs (*beth* = "house of," *phage* = "unripe figs"; Bethany likely means, in Aramaic, house of Ananias (*beth* = "house of," *any*, probably short for a proper name Ananiah"). Bethany lies two miles east of Jerusalem, Bethphage slightly less.

As Jesus approaches these two towns, he sends two of his twelve ahead to requisition a young mule. Mark spends some time over this requisitioning. Why? As with most prophets, the setting up of a symbolic act is mysterious and puzzling; so is this action of Jesus. But even more startling is Jesus' foreknowledge of just where to pick up this animal and how the scene will play itself out. Perhaps most important of all is the fact that, when people learn that it is the master who wants this animal, no further objection is made. Now, one could work up a theory that these people all knew Jesus (we learn from other gospels that Jesus was good friends with Lazarus, Martha and Mary who live in Bethany and host Jesus every night when he is in the Jerusalem area); thus, when they learn that he wants the mule, they gladly entrust it to him. But this kind of information is not given, precisely so as to highlight the mastery and lordship of the word and will of Jesus. It is his control of the situation, his knowledge of all its details, which Mark stresses here at the beginning of the period in which Jesus would appear to be caught unprepared and powerless; no, everything is being done as the plan indicated and the reader is to be impressed by this opening detail.

One may wonder why Jesus chose "riding on a colt" as his means of entering Jerusalem. Actually, it is the core of the symbolism we perceive in this story. Matthew's gospel is clearer about this, but Mark seems clear enough. Centuries ago, the prophet Zechariah, upon looking into the future of Israel, caught sight of someone, unnamed, about whom he could say:

> Rejoice heartily, O daughter Zion,
> shout for joy, O daughter Jerusalem!
> See, your king shall come to you;
> a just savior is he,
> meek, and riding on an ass,
> on a colt, the foal of an ass.
> He shall banish the chariot...
> and the horse of war....
> The warrior's bow shall be banished,
> and he shall proclaim peace to the nations.
> His dominion will be from sea to sea,
> from the Euphrates to the ends of the earth (Zechariah 9:9–10).

A great and significant gesture, then, is Jesus' call for a colt on which to ride into Jerusalem, and Mark's description of the particulars of Jesus' call for this colt contains much for the reader to ponder.

The disciples bring the young colt to Jesus, and then throw their cloaks over it for Jesus to sit on; as the colt begins its movement over the top of the Mount of Olives, Passover crowds, evidently impressed, join the disciples, front and rear of the animal, to accompany Jesus to Jerusalem. As a gesture of reverence people throw their cloaks for the colt, bearer of Jesus, to walk on; others put down reeds, cut from the fields, before the colt. To their gestures the people add words of praise and call for salvation. "Hosanna" rises like a liturgical refrain at either end of their cry.

Hosanna means "please save us" and fits the ancient prophecy of Zechariah which looked for a savior to enter Jerusalem. Great blessing is called upon the one who enters now
in the name of the Lord. This is a refrain taken from a psalm
(thought then to be written by David), which psalm ironically speaks of one who is coming to God's temple to praise
God after God wonderfully saved him from most probable
death. The people think of Jesus as the one who comes from
God, probably as prophet of God (earlier, the twelve had
said to Jesus that many people thought of him as prophet).

But their cries not only ask for salvation and wish well
to the one who comes on behalf of God; the people also
ask for a blessing on the kingdom of David, which, they
think, is to be reborn with Jesus' entry into Jerusalem. In
the light of their total song, the people seem to be professing
Jesus to be not only prophet, but royal successor to David.
Mark sees this as an inkling of the greater and more pene-
trating perception that Jesus is the messiah. But why, after
all Jesus' efforts to avoid being called messiah, does he do
something which might lead to a public awareness of this
personage? It seems that what Jesus intends here is to make
a claim to Jerusalem in such wise as to elicit from the inhabitants of Jerusalem (whom he has not really met yet) at
least an initial acceptance of himself. He expects people
there to hear the crowds and to understand the symbolism
of the colt, and thereby to give him a generous hearing and
ultimately total response. Clearly, it did not work out that
way.

Having used the great confession about Jesus as his
opening gambit, Mark quickly brings the scene to a close
by noting nothing else but that Jesus entered the city and
its temple, looked it all over, and then retired to Bethany
with the twelve. Where Jesus would have entered the city
precisely is disputed. Some scholars think it would have

been through what is today known as the Golden Gate, set pretty much in the center of the wall that runs north to south and faces the Mount of Olives. Others think that he eventually went through the south wall by stairs that led onto the temple platform. It is interesting to note that Jesus spent no nights in Jerusalem. Certainly, the city was immensely crowded at this Passover time, when all adult males were expected to be in Jerusalem. Moreover, Jesus had very good friends in Bethany, just two miles' walk (climb) away. Perhaps most suggestive in this brief description is Mark's notice that Jesus looked everything over, then left. Is it a proprietary look, the look of one who thinks that what he is looking at is his? From the way Mark has introduced Jesus' entry into Jerusalem, such an interpretation seems likely.

It is the next day and Jesus is setting out with the disciples for the day in Jerusalem. Mark now tells a peculiar story about a fig tree. The story is peculiar for its placement (which we will discuss later), as well as for an apparent lack of logic.

Jesus is hungry. This simple fact is the cause of his going to a fig tree for something to eat. Why did he go to the fig tree rather than wait a bit longer for something to eat? Because he saw from a distance that the tree had leaves on it. It is this leafing of the tree which gives Jesus hope of finding fruit; appearance seemed to imply a reality. Once Jesus stood at the tree, however, he realized that there was nothing on it except the leaves. So he cursed the tree.

Is this a story meant to exemplify Jesus' power? We will see, but only at a later moment in this chapter, that it was interpreted in this direction. For now, we only know that the tree was cursed. What other reason would Mark have for telling this story? Many interpreters think that the key to understanding this story is its placement before the story of the cleansing of the temple. We will look more carefully at the account of Jesus' cleansing the temple in a moment, but now we draw attention to the likeness between the two stories (fig tree and cleansing), so that the condemned fig tree can be seen to be a prophecy concerning the temple.

The key to the fig tree story is the interplay between the appearance of bearing fruit and actual barrenness. Here is a symbol for the fruitlessness of temple worship, even though appearance seemed to say that worship was valid and acceptable before God. What explains the fruitlessness of temple sacrifice despite the appearance of fruitfulness? One can point, first, to the criticism of the gospel leveled against the hypocrisy (apparent fruitfulness, but real fruitlessness) of leading religious groups; they concerned themselves with only a part of the law of God, and that part is only the external part. But, in the long run, the Christians will suggest that the temple sacrifice is fruitless if Jesus is rejected. The rejection of the messiah, a king and a priest, makes sacrifice without him a fruitless sacrifice. Thus, the cursing of the apparently fruitful tree is a prophetic symbol, for many exegetes, which introduces the story about the cleansing of the temple, and, indeed, hints darkly at the eventual destruction of the holy city, Jerusalem, by the Roman forces in 70 A.D.

The fig tree story is peculiar for its logic. Unlike Matthew, who also recounts this story, Mark adds his own notation that Jesus found nothing but leaves on the fig tree, "because it was not the season for figs." This "because" causes problems. Why would Jesus curse a tree for not producing fruit if it was not yet the season for producing fruit? Jesus seems to be unreasonable. Moreover, even though the tree had leaves on it, why would Jesus go looking for figs if it was not the season for figs? Jesus seems to be ignorant of the seasons for fig production, even though he has lived in the country for over thirty years.

Interpreters have for long tried to explain why Jesus was justly angry with and cursed the fruitless tree, but no one is satisfied with any explanation given thus far. Perhaps the best one can say is this. The leafing of the tree, taken as the natural leafing which suggests at least some fruit developing (though figs would not be there in full bloom), is a leafing which only appeared to be the leafing of the natural process. Not only was it not the season for figs, but also not the season for those leaves which prepare for the figs. The leaves, then, appear to be what they are not; they deceived Jesus, for they "pretended" to be legitimate signs of the beginning of figs, but were, in fact, false signs. It is for this causing false hope through false appearances that Jesus is justly angry with and curses the tree.

However one explains this action of Jesus toward the fig tree, many see it as a prophetic action, strategically put by Mark as an introduction to Jesus' criticism of the temple. Mark ends his story, however, with a detail which will be picked up when Mark, after the cleansing of the temple, returns to consider again the cursed fig tree. What is this detail? "Jesus' disciples heard Jesus' curse."

Leaving the scene of the fig tree, with Jesus next to it and his disciples overhearing from a distance his curse, Mark introduces us to a new scene. He tells us that they enter Jerusalem, and that, without further ado, Jesus is said to enter the temple area (situated at what was then the northeastern corner of Jerusalem) to begin pushing out those selling and buying in the temple; he overturns the tables of the money-changers and the stalls of the men who sell doves, and he does not allow anyone to pass through the temple. Again, we have a prophetic action by Jesus which calls for explanation. We will give it, but first it is best to explain something of the background to this scene.

The mountain on which the temple was built (whether

that of Solomon in the tenth century B.C. or its poorer replacement at the end of the fifth century B.C.) was not flat
and smooth to hold a temple building and its serving buildings. Somehow a flat platform had to be constructed for
these buildings. The method finally used was that of raising
up columns from the sides of the mountain in such a way
that they could hold a flat quadrangle of great size. This great
quadrangle, larger than a football or soccer field, was
reached by walking up stairs till one could step onto the
quadrangle. This quadrangle was, from earliest times, called
the "temple" or the "temple area (platform, precincts)." On
it were a number of buildings, but the main building, which
faced east and was backed up against the western wall of
the quadrangle or temple area, was the famous and glorious
house of God (or house of God's name, or house of God's
glory). Just outside this house, on its eastern porch, the animal sacrifices were offered. Just inside its first room, beyond
where animals were offered, was the room where incense
was offered and showbreads were placed. (This first interior
room was called "the holy place" or "the holies.") Finally,
in the second room was to be found the throne of God (no
longer present in Jesus' time) which only the high priest
once a year (at Yom Kippur, or Day of Atonement for sins)
could come to. This room is the holiest room, the holiest
place on earth, and is thus called "the holy of holies" or
"holiest place." Here God, or God's name, or God's glory,
was believed to rest. What was this unique building called
which housed the throne of God, the offerings of incense
and showbreads, before which the animal sacrifices were
offered? It is called the temple. But is not this the title for
the large quadrangle on which the temple building is built?
It is. That is to say, both the quadrangle on which the house
is built and the house itself are called the temple.

When Mark says that Jesus cleansed the temple by his

vigorous actions, is he saying that Jesus cleansed the building
or the quadrangle, each of which is called the temple? Mark
means that Jesus cleansed the quadrangle, the temple area,
the temple precincts.

Why were dove-sellers in this large quadrangle area?
One of the most frequently offered animals offered in sacrifice before the temple building was the offering of doves.
In order to serve the needs of many, the priests (chief
priests, that is) who ran the temple worship allowed the
selling of doves right near the place of sacrifice; it is basically
a convenience for the worshipers. Why were money-changers in this large temple area? Because to buy things used in
temple sacrifice, it was decided that one had to use sacred
money; money used in ordinary daily transactions was not
holy money, and holy money should be used for buying
things intended for holy use. Finally, if one realizes the size
of the quadrangle on which the temple building and its service buildings stood and the fact that the quadrangle was a
favorite gathering place of Jews and Gentiles and, further,
that using this quadrangle was really the simplest and
smoothest path by which to pass from certain parts of Jerusalem to certain other parts—if one realizes all this, one
can understand why Jesus would have found the temple area
used by people not for worship, but as an easy road by
which to cross the mountain of Jerusalem.

Mark has chosen to open up the Jerusalem stay of Jesus
with Jesus' action in the temple area of the capital city: the
cleansing of the temple precincts. How long his purifying
action lasted is hard to say. Certainly, though Jesus was very
serious in his criticism, his was only a prophetic gesture,
rather than the establishment of a long-term policy. Did his
action dominate the activity of the morning? It is quite possible that, given the sizable crowd that would be milling
about at this time of Passover in the temple area, not ev-

eryone there would have noticed what Jesus was doing; indeed, usually the money-changing and dove-selling was restricted to the northern section of the temple quadrangle, so that those in the southern part, blocked by the temple building itself, might have seen nothing and heard only rumbles reverberating from the northern side. Jesus' action was grave and revealing, though prophetic and limited in scope and immediate audience.

Jesus' prophetic gesture is given meaning by this teaching from the words of the prophets Isaiah (56:7) and Jeremiah (7:11). Each prophet in his own time identified the temple as a place of worship. Isaiah concluded to the nature of the temple (a house of prayer) from the type of holy action which would flow from conversion to the true God: from conversion comes prayer to Yahweh, and thus the temple is a house of prayer to God. Jeremiah had railed against the hypocrisy of loud crying, "Look at me, I am in the house of God," which is followed by action most suitable to a den of thieves. Whatever the reasons which in theory legitimated selling doves and changing money and using the temple quadrangle as a thoroughfare, Jesus saw that the actual intentions of these contradicted the age-old purposes of the temple area. Indeed, one might read the text to say that the temple area become a "den of thieves" suggests that practices of unfair pricing, whether in the sales of animals to the poor or in the selling of money, were particularly what Jesus railed against in the temple quadrangle. Thus, he reacted with the violence and anger which all Jews would understand: it was the reaction of one who championed the cause of the pure worship of Yahweh and opposed the corruption brought about by human venality and selfishness openly visible in the temple area.

Jesus' action befits his earlier attitude of the day before, the attitude of one who came to Jerusalem and the temple

as their owner, or as representative of the owner of this most
holy site. Jesus claims authority to right what he decides is
wrong here, even if only in prophetic gesture.

Because of his action, limited as it was, discussions begin on how to "get rid of" Jesus. Earlier such discussions
were conducted by the Pharisees and Herodians, but then
we were in Galilee. Now these discussions are being held
by the powerful chief priests (members of the ruling Sanhedrin) and the scribes of Jerusalem. These men, some responsible for the area and activity Jesus is criticizing and
others responsible for the knowledge of the law of Israel in
this matter, want to get rid of Jesus as soon as possible, for
the crowds, who sense the rightness of Jesus' action and
teaching, will only grow larger and more supportive as the
Passover day draws nearer. Mark, then, makes us look to the
imminent future and suggests just why, in three chapters,
Jesus will be on trial. Jesus, for his part, returns at eventide
to Bethany, his resting place in his visit to Jerusalem.

Day one in Jerusalem is completed, though Mark has
described for us only one thing Jesus did all this day, one
reaction of the Jewish leaders, one reaction of the crowd.
We should be used to this trait of Mark whereby he feels
free to give us as much or as little as he wishes. Often, it is
true, Mark is restricted by the limited information handed
down to him, but just as often he freely shapes his stories
to convey what he wishes—and other things are left aside.

With the next scene Mark brings us, we are again early
on the road from Bethany to Jesus' day in Jerusalem. Again
we pass by the fig tree cursed by Jesus yesterday morning.
Peter, remembering (as Mark had hinted he would) what
Jesus had done, calls Jesus' attention to the shriveled tree.
This gives Jesus the opportunity to teach a second lesson
from this cursed tree.

Cursing involved calling on God to act in a severe and

punishing manner; as such it was a prayer to God. Fastening on this aspect of the curse, and in full view of the results of this prayer, Jesus encourages his disciples to have that attitude in prayer that he has. Because he trusted his Father to execute this particular curse or prayer concerning the fig tree, he urges his disciples to pray with the same kind of trust. Without trust prayer will not be heard. This is not the first time that Jesus, in the gospel of Mark, asks for trust behind requests made for help.

Jesus insists that prayer made with faith, faith in God's power and his love to give, is the prayer which will gain favor. To ask, without real trust, is hardly complimentary to anyone, particularly to God. Prayer made with absolute trust in God can accomplish the impossible, if God wants it so; such trust, to use Jesus' own example, can move the Mount of Olives.

Jesus is talking here about what, from the human side, will make prayer effective. One thing necessary is absolute trust. Another thing that is necessary, if one is seeking forgiveness from God, is one's own first forgiving one's enemies. Forgiveness is a familiar refrain of Jesus' teaching, something always on his mind. This reference to a particular kind of prayer at this juncture is apt, for Jesus has been dealing with prayer from a very human perspective. One cannot ask God to fulfill one's petitions if one at the same time has doubts about God; and one cannot hope for forgiveness if one cannot forgive others.

The scene changes radically; we come to Jerusalem and right into the temple area. The temple quadrangle is enclosed by a high wall on all sides. Jutting out into the quadrangle from the top of this enclosing wall for about fifty feet or so was a roof, supported by columns, so that in great heat or rain one could remain cool or dry in the temple area. Often somewhere under this roof Jesus would teach. Today,

day two of his time in Jerusalem, Jesus was walking around
in the large open area of the quadrangle, and so was seen
by chief priests, scribes and elders (all members of the Sanhedrin, the highest Jewish authority in Palestine). These men
take the occasion to challenge Jesus, particularly for what
he had done two days ago in his entry into Jerusalem, and
for what he had done yesterday by his prophetic cleansing
of the temple area—but, as part of a larger story, this challenge can be understood to be a challenge to all that Jesus
has done and taught in his career.

The leaders of Jerusalem and Israel ask about the source
of Jesus' authority and power to do what he has done. His
response is clever; from a certain point of view, Jesus' claim
to have authority from God would fuel the antipathy already
lit against him and hasten his punishment, even his death.
Perhaps that is Jesus' thinking, but in any event he decides
to answer them only if they first answer him—and no doubt
he suspected that they would think the way in which Mark
describes their thoughts and so would not answer, and so
he would not have to answer them.

But there is possibly a bit more to this gambit of Jesus.
If Jesus could get these men to admit that John the Baptist
preached with God's authority behind him, then he might
be able to by comparison and analogy get them to admit
that God is the authority by which he preaches and acts.
But these men will not admit God's presence behind the
preaching of John, though great numbers of Jews did.

The enthusiasm of many Jews for John the Baptist helps
us to understand why John is so strategic an element in the
general Christian defense of Jesus, whether in Mark's gospel
or elsewhere in the New Testament. We know that in 50
A.D. there were still disciples of John who followed his
teaching and honored him, rather than Jesus. If such a "neu-
tral" and trustworthy figure, in a sense outside the Jewish

and Christian camps, could be used by one side in support of its belief, the reasons for belief would be even stronger.

In this story we have another small nod to the fact that the leaders of Jerusalem wanted to do nothing which would so upset the crowds who admired Jesus that the crowds would oppose their leaders when the decisive moment came. The crowds are not part of the plotting underway against Jesus, but their confused help at the right moment is necessary.

Chapter 12

This chapter (together with the last story of the previous chapter) is sometimes referred to as Jesus' "ministry in Jerusalem." One must be cautious about this title, for it can obscure a significant aspect of Jesus' self-understanding. It is true that Mark does describe Jesus as teaching the people in the temple precincts; to the extent that he does teach here, we can say that he is exercising a ministry, not unlike that exercised in Galilee. What causes hesitation in the use of this term "ministry" is the fact that Jesus is not in Jerusalem except by obedience to the Mosaic law that he come for Passover. It is because he is here a few days in advance of the actual celebration day of Passover that he has the time and occasion to do what he wishes; there is no indication Jesus looks on Jerusalem as one of the places to which he comes solely for the reason of preaching the good news of the kingdom. In short, if Jesus ministers in Jerusalem by teaching, he will do so only until the feast is over; then he will return to Galilee where his real mission seems to be. Actually, at the time of the last supper and at the time of the revelation of Jesus' resurrection, the disciples are reminded that, once the brief stay in Jerusalem is over, they will meet Jesus in Galilee, not in Jerusalem.

The first story of Chapter 12 starts with the notice that Jesus was speaking to "them" in "parables." Though Mark

12 And he began to speak to them in parables. "A man planted a vineyard, and set a hedge around it, and dug a pit for the wine press, and built a tower, and let it out to tenants, and went into another country. [2]When the time came, he sent a servant to the tenants, to get from them some of the fruit of the vineyard. [3]And they took him and beat him, and sent him away empty-handed. [4]Again he sent to them another servant, and they wounded him in the head, and treated him shamefully. [5]And he sent another, and him they killed; and so with many others, some they beat and some they killed. [6]He had still one other, a beloved son; finally he sent him to them, saying, 'They will respect my son.' [7]But those tenants said to one another, 'This is the heir; come, let us kill him, and the inheritance will be ours.' [8]And they took him and killed him, and cast him out of the vineyard. [9]What will the owner of the vineyard do? He will come and destroy the tenants, and give the vineyard to others. [10]Have you not read this scripture:

'The very stone which the builders rejected
has become the head of the corner;
[11]this was the Lord's doing,
and it is marvelous in our eyes'?"

12 And they tried to arrest him, but feared the multitude, for they perceived that he had told the parable against them; so they left him and went away.

13 And they sent to him some of the Pharisees and some of the Herodi-ans, to entrap him in his talk. [14]And they came and said to him, "Teacher, we know that you are true, and care for no man; for you do not regard the

position of men, but truly teach the way of God. Is it lawful to pay taxes to Caesar, or not? [15]Should we pay them, or should we not?" But knowing their hypocrisy, he said to them, "Why put me to the test? Bring me a coin, and let me look at it." [16]And they brought one. And he said to them, "Whose likeness and inscription is this?" They said to him, "Caesar's." [17]Jesus said to them, "Render to Caesar the things that are Caesar's, and to God the things that are God's." And they were amazed at him.

18 And Sadducees came to him, who say that there is no resurrection; and they asked him a question, saying, [19]"Teacher, Moses wrote for us that if a man's brother dies and leaves a wife, but leaves no child, the man must take the wife, and raise up children for his brother. [20]There were seven brothers; the first took a wife, and when he died left no children; [21]and the second took her, and died, leaving no children; and the third likewise; [22]and the seven left no children. Last of all the woman also died. [23]In the resurrection whose wife will she be? For the seven had her as wife."

24 Jesus said to them, "Is not this why you are wrong, that you know neither the scriptures nor the power of God? [25]For when they rise from the dead, they neither marry nor are given in marriage, but are like angels in heaven. [26]And as for the dead being raised, have you not read in the book of Moses, in the passage about the bush, how God said to him, 'I am the God of Abraham, and the God of Isaac, and the God of Jacob'? [27]He is not God of the dead, but of the living; you are quite wrong."

28 And one of the scribes came up and heard them disputing with one another, and seeing that he answered them well, asked him, "Which commandment is the first of all?" [29]Jesus answered, "The first is, 'Hear, O Israel: The Lord our God, the Lord is one; [30]and you shall love the

Lord your God with all your heart, and with all your soul, and with all your mind, and with all your strength.' [31]The second is this, 'You shall love your neighbor as yourself.' There is no other commandment greater than these." [32]And the scribe said to him, "You are right, Teacher; you have truly said that he is one, and there is no other but he; [33]and to love him with all the heart, and with all the understanding, and with all the strength, and to love one's neighbor as oneself, is much more than all whole burnt offerings and sacrifices." [34]And when Jesus saw that he answered wisely, he said to him, "You are not far from the kingdom of God." And after that no one dared to ask him any question.

35 And as Jesus taught in the temple, he said, "How can the scribes say that the Christ is the son of David? [36]David himself, inspired by the Holy Spirit, declared,

'The Lord said to my Lord,

Sit at my right hand,

till I put thy enemies under thy feet.'

[37]David himself calls him Lord; so how is he his son?" And the great throng heard him gladly.

38 And in his teaching he said, "Beware of the scribes, who like to go about in long robes, and to have salutations in the market places [39]and the best seats in the synagogues and the places of honor at feasts, [40]who devour widows' houses and for a pretense make long prayers. They will receive the greater condemnation."

41 And he sat down opposite the treasury, and watched the multitude putting money into the treasury. Many rich people put in large sums. [42]And a poor widow came, and put in two copper coins, which make a penny. [43]And he called his disciples to him, and said to them, "Truly, I say to you, this poor widow has put in more than all those who are contributing to the treasury. [44]For they

all contributed out of their abundance; but she out of her poverty has put in everything she had, her whole living."

chooses to say that Jesus spoke in "parables," he gives to the reader only one parable. Evidently, we must conclude, it is only this one that he thinks necessary or sufficient for his reader at this time. As regards the identity of the people behind the word "them," one is inclined to say that the pronoun refers to a group already mentioned, and the only group already mentioned is that of the chief priests, scribes and elders. This parable, then, is a parable specifically for these Sanhedrin members. Knowing the tensions already existing between Jesus and these men, the parable should be a dandy.

To understand Jesus' story of a vineyard, one must hear certain preliminary facts. First, absentee-landlordism was a reality of life in Palestine; the supposition of the story, therefore, has a definitely true-to-life aspect to it. Second, it was a rule that, should the heir(s) of the absent landlord die, the workers of the land would have first right to possess the land. Thus, the workers of the story are not wrong in saying that, if they kill the son, the vineyard would be theirs. Third, though (and perhaps because) vineyards were so ordinary, many prophets and teachers used the vineyard as a symbol for Israel, "planted and tended by God to bring forth good fruit." Brought up in such symbolism, it was easy for Jesus' audience to understand almost immediately what the vineyard of his story represented.

The story Jesus tells is rather straightforward. The unwillingness of the workers to give their lord his due seems extreme, and one is left to one's own devices to figure out just why the workers are so vicious. Once one transfers the story from a simple vineyard problem to the history of Israel, one understands much better the source of the workers' violence: the leaders of Israel had often rebelled against God and would not give him his due, and were so determined in this disobedience that anyone sent to them to call them to repentance was harshly dealt with. The story, then, is pointing to a tragic history in which the present leaders are now playing the same part their ancestors had played.

The ultimate solution of the lord of the vineyard is to send his son, "the beloved son" (and we recall that these same words were used from the heavens at Jesus' baptism and from the cloud at Jesus' transfiguration). The judgment of the lord may be questioned, but one would think that the truest representative of the lord would be recognized for what he was, and thus respected. Not so, and he is put to death, symbolically thrown outside the vineyard so as not to defile what "soon will belong to others."

Jesus asks the Jewish leaders to reflect: What will the lord of the vineyard do about all this? Jesus tells them. The lord will finally come himself and destroy the workers, then give the management of the vineyard to others.

(For clarity's sake, we should be explicit and say that some elements of Jesus' story are not applicable to the contemporary leaders of Jerusalem. For instance, in Jesus' story the workers of the vineyard hurt or kill many messengers as well as the son; in the application of the story, only the son (not other past historical figures) is mistreated by the "workers," i.e., the leaders of Jerusalem. Moreover, there is no thought to the leaders of Jerusalem inheriting anything, though the workers of the story hope to do so. Also, who these "others" are to whom the vineyard will be given is not clear: does it mean "other Jews" or "Christians" or "Christian Jews"? Finally, it is not clear just how one is to apply to Jesus' contemporaries the fact that the workers of the story did not give the lord his due of the fruit. Is this to be interpreted that, while the people of Israel are producing good fruit, their leaders somehow arrange that this good fruit go not to God, but rather to themselves? In short, then, we have here a parable which is in part applicable to a situation outside itself, in part only meant to stay within its own literary self to develop its own story-line.)

To the parable Jesus adds a further word, a citation from Psalm 118:22-23. This psalm is used more than once in the New Testament, for it explains in a nutshell a fundamental understanding of the particulars of the death and resurrection of Jesus. Ironically, the stone of the psalm originally referred to a great hero of Israel whom God saved from the deadly threats of men. Now it is used to describe Jesus whom God will restore to life after he has been "rejected" by the builders, or leaders of Israel.

The psalm gives new direction to Jesus' lesson here. The vineyard story concludes with the warning that the workers will be killed and the vineyard will be given to others. The psalm, on the other hand, promises that what has been thrown away will be brought back by God to be the cornerstone. Attention has switched from the action of God against the workers to the action of God on behalf of the "stone rejected." The effect, however, is similar in that in both pictures it is God who is going to straighten out what the Jerusalem leaders have mishandled.

There is still some discussion among scholars as to the exact function of the resurrected stone. Is it to be a cornerstone or is it to be that stone which is the last to go into an arch and thus the one that holds the arch together? Whatever be the correct identity of the stone, it is clear that what men thought absolutely of no value is now the essential element of God's construction.

Finally, one notes the stress put on the fact that it is God who is responsible for the wondrous change. Jesus is rejected by men, but approved by God. It is important to put the expression this way, for, at a time when it was still debated just how Jesus was to be taken, God's support in favor of Jesus was of immeasurable significance.

The leaders of the people had no trouble interpreting this particular parable; it described them, they knew, and specifically their rejection of Jesus. Fear of upsetting the crowd again looms large in their reaction; they decide to leave things be for now.

From a distance, however, these leaders of the people challenge Jesus again. This time they send representatives, some Pharisees and some Herodians, enemies become friends a long time ago in Galilee in an effort to get rid of Jesus. (Herod Antipas usually came to Jerusalem for the Passover, staying in the palace his father had built there; with him would come his supporters, the "Herodians.") These Pharisees and Herodians, though now careful friends, are still, in matters other than Jesus, enemies. For a Pharisee, payment of taxes to Caesar was an abomination, a fundamental act reflecting slavery to him. Anyone who encouraged payment of taxes was reductively an enemy of the people of Israel. On the other hand, the Herodians knew that their livelihoods were tied to keeping peace with Rome, for Herod was really only a representative of Caesar. Anyone who encouraged people not to pay taxes owed to Rome disturbed the peace and was to be silenced. It is these two groups, one for paying the taxes and the other against paying the taxes, who now ask Jesus, "Should we pay taxes to Rome?"

The Pharisees and Herodians begin by flattering Jesus, no doubt a ploy to suck him into an argument—a dilemma—from which, they think, he will be unable to extricate himself. Jesus recognizes this flattery, and thus shows himself to be no fool, where other men might well be. He is not deceived by anyone and chills the air with his question, "Why do you test me?"

As to the substance of their question, Jesus uses a common ploy: he does not answer, but rather asks another question. The question Jesus asks is based on a principle they all accept, which says that a thing belongs to the person whose mark is on it. A slave, for instance, always wore a brand mark which indicated the person to whom the slave belonged. So, Jesus asks for a coin, a denarius, which he knows has Caesar's image and inscription on it. With this in hand and having made his examiners say that Caesar's image and inscription are on the coin, he need only draw for them the logical conclusion: the money piece belongs to Caesar. And, of course, if the money is Caesar's, it should be given to him.

Jesus' argument is smooth, even slick; it has a certain validity, at least enough validity to let him escape while his opponents are trying to figure out just how he frustrated them. Actually, he never says simply that taxes are to be paid to Caesar, or that they are not to be paid to Caesar. He creates two statements, "the coin is Caesar's" and "give to Caesar what is his," but he does not say that taxes belong to Caesar. His opponents realize that they have been led to agree that at least coins belong to Caesar and that it is then logical to give him what is his. But where does that lead one in the discussion about paying or not paying taxes? Perplexed for the moment they can do nothing—and Jesus faces new opponents.

One cannot overlook the extra advice Jesus gives: give to God what is God's. Jesus is not interested ultimately in taxes; his mission, as always, is to call people to repentance, to the fruits of repentance. He takes advantage of the opportunity to remind his opponents of this fundamental obligation. He is not separating Caesar from God, civil duties from religious duties. He is simply reminding his opponents, who are so concerned about "debts," that there is an entire world of debts that they should pay, whether Caesar exists or not. It is God to whom they owe so very much.

Jesus has been recognized for the divine wisdom of his teaching, but part of his overall intelligence is his human cleverness in debate and his ability to answer all problems successfully. Such cleverness may not be essential to teaching wisdom, but it does reveal the human agility and attractiveness of Jesus among his contemporaries, many of whom made his life hang on the response he could give them without preparation. Indeed, on this day of the visit to Jerusalem and its temple, it seems that Jesus is in for a series of tests, failure in which would at the very least lose him the admiration of the crowds. But it is not just chance that Jesus is put to a series of testings now; the hand of Mark is visible here, as he lines up, for a final time before the next stage of his gospel begins, the enemies of Jesus. Each group is given its head to ask the question which it finds most difficult to answer; if Jesus slips in this final assault, he will find himself humiliated, if not also in great trouble. Jesus first criticized the leaders of the temple worship by his cleansing the temple and his subsequent parable. The first retort came from the Pharisees and Herodians, sent by the chief priests and scribes. Now it is the turn of the Sadducees.

The Sadducees (meaning either "descendants of Sadok," David's high priest, or "just ones") were a relatively small group in Jesus' time, but influential all the same. Their origins go back almost two hundred years before Jesus' time of preaching. Presumably they grew up as a religious group intent on living the Jewish religion as they understood it.

The Sadducees believed that, though all the Jewish writings were of great benefit to a religious life, only the first five books of the Bible, i.e., the books of Moses, or the Pentateuch— Genesis, Exodus, Leviticus, Numbers and Deuteronomy—were the revealed basis for Jewish belief. Thus, if something was not clearly stated in one of these five books, it need not be and should not be believed as revealed by God.

From a conservative reading of the Pentateuch one would find it very difficult to say that any of the five books professes a belief in the resurrection from the dead (or in angels or spirits). And so, the Sadducees, quite the opposite of the Pharisees, believed that no one rises from the dead—clearly a point of opposition to Jesus, and the central point of their question to him now.

It may appear, at a first reading, that the law which allowed a woman to marry seven times is the issue here. Actually, her bizarre situation is only a pretext by which the Sadducees hope to show how silly belief in the afterlife really is. If one keeps in mind that the real challenge to Jesus here is concerned with the existence of the life after death, the passage is much easier to read.

The basis of the Sadducees' argument, put in story form, is an ancient law of Israel, called the Levirate law (*levir,* in Latin, means "brother-in-law"). According to this law, if a man died without an heir, a close kin of the deceased was to have intercourse with his widow (considered a marriage) in order to raise up an heir to the dead man. Israel, one must understand, was always anxious to keep land in the hands of the tribe to which the land originally belonged; the same, with a bit less anxiety, was true of other possessions. The way to assure this kind of possession was to have another member of the same tribe, even of the same family, raise up an heir who would, of course, be of the same tribe and thus preserve the possessions within his father's tribe and family, to boot.

Whether or not the Levirate law was actually in practice at Jesus' time, his powers of interpretation were put to the test. The story concocted by the Sadducees has this woman married seven times—a bizarre situation, but not against any law or belief of Israel. But the Sadducees now look to an awkward result of obedience to the law of Moses: In the next life, whose wife will she be, since she was wife here of all seven? The Sadducees do not expect a clear answer, but rather they expect Jesus to be baffled and humiliated for his belief in the afterlife, for surely the situation the Sadducees describe forces one to admit that to believe in an afterlife now looks very silly and foolish. The very idea that a woman, who here had one husband *after* another, will there have all seven husbands *at the same time*. Surely the afterlife is a ridiculous belief!

Jesus' answer is very valuable for a number of reasons. First, he shows how far off base is the conception of the Sadducees about life after death. Their question supposes that the woman will be wife to some one of the seven men in the next life in the sense that she is wife in this life— here the latter six men had to marry the woman because of a need for an heir. In the next life there will be no need for an heir to the first dead man, for the first dead man will be alive. Obviously, then, if the Sadducees understand the next life properly, that it is life forever, they will not be confused by seven (or seventy) marriages during life on earth. Ultimately, it is the Sadducees who do not understand, not Jesus.

Second, and here Jesus goes directly at the real question of the Sadducees, the dead must rise because God has revealed that "I am the God of Abraham and God of Isaac and God of Jacob." When God said this, Abraham, Isaac and Jacob were long dead; yet he said, "I *am*" their God, not "I *was*" or "I used to be." Now, Israel's God was not, as Jesus says and presumes the Sadducees to agree, a God of dead people. Thus, when he says "I *am*" their God, they must be alive, at least to him if not to us.

Finally, one can note the exasperation in the words with which Jesus begins and ends his answer to the Sadducees, "You are wrong... You are dead wrong." Jesus reveals through his response how unfounded was the argument of the Sadducees and how shallow their understanding of their own God was. The latter is the more frustrating: they do not even understand the implications of their own belief, that to belong to God—and God says that Abraham, Isaac and Jacob *belong* (not "used to belong") to him—*means that one must live.* And what text of scripture, of God's own word, did Jesus use to make his argument? He took a text right from the midst of the scripture the Sadducees accepted! They do not understand their own books!

Jesus' revelation about God is extremely precious. It is one of the clearest expressions as to why one can be sure that one who is faithful to God, who remains "his" so that he can say "I am God of..."—that this person will rise from the dead. To belong to God means that one can only live; to him, and he decides everything, reality cannot be any other way.

The Sadducees, as earlier the Pharisees and Herodians, have had their chance, their last chance to outwit Jesus— and on their own terms. Now Mark quickly brings forward a representative of the scribes, that group which asks only one thing of anyone who wants to join it: thorough knowledge of the entire corpus of Jewish law, i.e., the law of Moses and all laws which have been derived from it. Scribes had challenged Jesus before and found him up to the challenge. But then it had been a question regarding a particular law the scribes thought Jesus broke. Now, this scribe puts to Jesus what was equivalently the test of tests among the experts themselves.

This scribe has watched the previous encounters and, Mark notes, has recognized that Jesus has answered well. Just what effect this recognition had on the scribe is unclear. Perhaps he has gained a certain admiration of Jesus and so is willing to test him as the great scribes were tested; but perhaps he is, conversely, out to show that, though others could not trip Jesus up, he can. Whatever his motivation, he puts to Jesus the great question, "Which is the first commandment of all?"

What this question really means is this, that of all the laws of Israel, which is the one which gives coherence to all the rest, which is the one from which all others flow and all others draw their validity? As an example of what the scribe is after we can think of the modern law against reckless driving; it is a valid law because it enforces in a particular way the more general law which commands care and respect for another's person. Thus, one law is valid because a higher law is valid; one law is valid because it is simply a specification of a higher law. Looking at the entire corpus of Jewish law, then, which is that law which justifies all others, of which all others are specific applications?

The answer of Jesus is very well known—it begins: the greatest law is the one which says that Yahweh, Israel's God, is the only Lord; therefore to him alone is given the love of one's entire heart and soul and mind and strength. Thus far, one can explain the entire law code of Israel as a code which in various ways promotes and encourages love of Yahweh and of no other god. It is a code which recognizes that the love which everyone recognizes God alone deserves is to be given to Yahweh and to no other god. Every law, then, according to Jesus serves to further and protect the love of Yahweh. The worth and goodness of every law is found in its ability to encourage love of Yahweh.

Before anyone can say anything to what Jesus has just uttered, and consciously going beyond the limits of the question put to him, Jesus adds, "and what is the second

really belongs with the first: love your neighbor as you want
to be loved; it is these two laws together (which can be
read in Deuteronomy 6:4-5 and Leviticus 19:18) which are
the greatest laws." Why did Jesus add this "second law" to
the "first law"? Because the question of the scribe really
wanted to know "which law is the center of all other laws"
and the complete answer, as far as Jesus is concerned, involves two laws. Why?

We must adjust what we have earlier said so as to be
complete and perfect. All the laws of Israel aim at either
assuring love of God or love of neighbor. There is no law
which is justified by any other consideration, and no law has
any other purpose or justification except to lead one to express greater love of God or of neighbor. Thus, for example,
each of the famous ten commandments makes sense only
because it promotes love of God or love of neighbor; the
same must be said even of the laws of kosher and other laws
which are often difficult to understand or explain.

Law was one of the friction points between Judaism and
the new group which followed Jesus. What caused the
church to disagree with classical Israel was in part the fact
that, under the teaching of Jesus and the guidance of the
Holy Spirit in human experiences, the church realized that
certain laws which Israel professed to be necessary for love
of God or love of neighbor were not, in Christian eyes, any
longer necessary. An excellent example is the law of circumcision; though in some situations a good health law,
Christians did not see it as required for love of God or love
of neighbor; for this reason, then (as well as for others), the
Christian leaders did not oblige Christians to practice it.

Though further explanation of the differences between
Christianity and Judaism regarding traditional Jewish laws
would take us too far afield, it is worthwhile to note that
often Jesus, with an eye to promoting and assuring love of

God and love of neighbor, made certain Jewish laws more stringent (e.g., divorce) and refocused others (e.g., adultery); his changes did not consist in merely dropping laws.

One may well ask why, if asked about one "greatest" law, Jesus cites "two as the greatest." Is not love of neighbor a law which should be subsumed under the law of love of God? Put that way, yes it is, because the perfect love of God consists in love of neighbor (and proper love of self, for that matter). But the structure of the actual law code of Israel makes it more practical to cite two sources of Jewish law: God and neighbor, so that one can see more perfectly just what is the purpose of every kind of Jewish law. It should be said, however, that though one might well argue that love of God demands love of neighbor, nowhere is this intimate connection really thoroughly explained in the Bible. God says it is so, but he does not thoroughly explain why it is so; most of the time he presumes it to be reasonable.

The scribe (unlike Jesus' other examiners) responds favorably and seconds, by repetition, Jesus' wise answer. The scribe, however, goes a step further; he affirms that the laws Jesus had identified as greater than all other laws are also worth more than all temple sacrifices and offerings. This is quite a statement, considering that it is said in the shadow, so to speak, of the very place of sacrifices and offerings.

Jesus recognizes the profound value the scribe is emphasizing here and praises him for it. To understand what the scribe and Jesus are affirming here, we must go back into the history of Israel. Often, from the time of Moses' Israel in the desert, through the times of the judges and the kings, to more recent and even contemporary times, Israelites had found themselves able to offer sacrifices in their temple and still not truly love God; at the same time, their love for their neighbors was hardly existent. Indeed, Israel's teachers and prophets often, far too often, railed against hypocrisy, whether toward God or toward other human beings. It is against this background that Jesus praises this scribe who has come to see the crucial significance of repentance and the deeds proper to repentance; external offerings should exist, but one must get at the heart of worship—this is love of God, and God asks love of neighbor so that worship may be acceptable to him.

The scribe's words to Jesus indicate that, in Jesus' judgment, the scribe is near to the kingdom of God. Here the image suggests, not that the kingdom is coming or being brought to a person, but that the person can draw near to the kingdom by a proper understanding, which involves a proper appreciation of the repentance needed to enter the kingdom. Given his insight about life, the scribe is not far from entering this kingdom.

Some interpreters suggest a more subtle meaning here. They think that Jesus' words indicate that the scribe, not far from the kingdom of God, is really not far from Jesus himself, for Jesus is in a radical sense the kingdom of God. The scribe is moving away from the Judaism which opposes Jesus and coming closer to embracing Jesus himself. In this way, the scribe is drawing closer to "the kingdom of God."

With a single sentence Mark draws the testing of Jesus to a close: "And no one dared any longer to ask him anything." But, as a part of the gospel as a whole, this sentence also brings to an end the entire gospel effort of the Jewish leaders to trap Jesus, the wisdom teacher. Miracle working had long ago stopped. The call to repentance is hardly heard in a Jerusalem apparently unprepared for it. All that is left is to proceed to the final act of the drama.

Before doing this, however, Mark has three final elements to offer, all having to do with words of Jesus, each in its own way revealing the depths of Jesus' intelligence and comprehension.

The scene changes, to the extent that no enemies of Jesus are after him, but rather Jesus is teaching in the temple area, probably under the roof which runs along the eastern wall of the temple quadrangle. Jesus puts before the crowd a problem of scriptural interpretation; such problems of interpretation were a favorite way of teaching the will of God. Jesus first notes that the scribes say that the messiah is the Son of David. Against this authoritative interpretation Jesus puts the words of David himself (who was thought by all to have written all the psalms): The Lord said to my lord, "Sit at my right hand, so that I may put your enemies (like a footstool) under your feet." The first "Lord" of the psalm verse is clearly Yahweh, God of Israel. The word "my" is a pronoun referring to the speaker of the psalm, who is, according to everyone, David. Then, who is the second "lord"? By Jesus' time this "lord" was understood to be the messiah by many people, including the Christians. The messiah, then, is lord of David, according to David's own witness. This profession, however, seems to contradict the scribes' interpretation that the messiah is Son of David. How do the scribes contradict David's words? The contradiction seems to lie in the inconsistency between "being one's lord" and "being one's son." Usually, a father is not servant of his son, nor is the son thought to be lord of his father. To the degree that one cannot be both, the scribes contradict David's own profession; and to the degree that their interpretation fails to reflect the full truth of the messiah, the scribes fail to interpret reality fully.

Mark notes that the crowd, often conceived of as "simple" people, catches the inconsistency Jesus points out and recognizes as well that Jesus is a better interpreter of the scriptures than the acknowledged professionals; they take pleasure in Jesus' performance. But Mark wants Christians to take equal pleasure in the revelation Jesus has provided

here: that he, though a descendant of David and thus in some
sense inferior to him, is really the master of David and superior to him. Mark is clearly trying to establish the supe-
riority of Jesus as Jesus' life comes to its humiliating
conclusion.

Again, pictured in his role as teacher, Jesus continues
to make the scribes his principal target. In this second scene,
Jesus is teaching the people not to act like the scribes who,
from Jesus' own bitter description, are deeply hypocritical
(and the opposite of the scribe Jesus only recently thought
to be not far from the kingdom of God). The subject matter
of their hypocrisy centers on love of neighbor (or lack of
real love of neighbor) and on pretending love of God while
hurting the most defenseless of their neighbors. That a
scribe could earlier profess that real and total love of God
and love of neighbor is more valuable than "prayers" looms
as its own commentary on the lives of his fellow scribes in
general.

Perhaps it is because Jesus' last words mentioned widows that Mark now turns our attention to a scene involving
a widow. Jesus sits in view of the treasury of the temple,
where, apart from other stored wealth, donations and tem-
ple-taxes (for upkeep) were received and kept. Mark describes how Jesus took note of the fact that the Passover
crowds were donating pieces of bronze, worth a good deal,
and that the rich were giving a lot of money. But against
this background a widow gave two small coins, almost
worthless.

It is time now for Jesus' last lesson in the temple area.
Calling his disciples around him, he points out this case of
the widow. She has given more than anyone, though giving
only two pitiful coins, for she has given all she has, and the
others, from this point of view, less.

Some interpreters see that this lesson is meant by Mark

to introduce the suffering and death of Jesus, the one who gave all he had (perhaps in contrast with the leaders of Israel who gave much less for their people). But the lesson looks backward as well as forward, for the disciples have placed before them the degree to which discipleship and love spend themselves: they give their all, not less.

Chapter 13

Chapter 13 begins with the notation that Jesus and his disciples were leaving the temple. Since this "leaving" usually means that they were returning to Bethany for the evening, we can calculate that they were now finishing day two of their stay in Jerusalem. (Day one consisted of the cleansing of the temple; day two consisted of dialogues and teaching.) Two full days in the temple area after the public entry into Jerusalem seems to be all the time Jesus spent there before the day of his last supper. Some scholars think two days is too short for the reality, that Mark telescoped episodes into two days to give a certain dynamic tightness to his story. Such a literary maneuver is certainly within rights of an author of the first century A.D., but it remains hypothetical whether or not Mark actually is telescoping time here.

Before Jesus and the twelve leave the temple area for a night's stay in Bethany, the disciples, Mark tells us, exclaimed in awe to Jesus, "Teacher, look at the immense blocks of stone and the huge buildings here!" To appreciate how impressed these men must have been with the temple and its adjacent buildings, one need only recall that their own houses at Capernaum were extremely small with little rooms and roofs of tree/leaf/dirt composition. The blocks they noted, beautifully dressed and each one weighing tons,

13And as he came out of the temple, one of his disciples said to him, "Look, Teacher, what wonderful stones and what wonderful buildings!" ²And Jesus said to him, "Do you see these great buildings? There will not be left here one stone upon another, that will not be thrown down."

3 And as he sat on the Mount of Olives opposite the temple, Peter and James and John and Andrew asked him privately, ⁴"Tell us, when will this be, and what will be the sign when these things are all to be accomplished?" ⁵And Jesus began to say to them, "Take heed that no one leads you astray. ⁶Many will come in my name, saying, 'I am he!' and they will lead many astray. ⁷And when you hear of wars and rumors of wars, do not be alarmed; this must take place, but the end is not yet. ⁸For nation will rise against nation, and kingdom against kingdom; there will be earthquakes in various places, there will be famines; this is but the beginning of the birth-pangs.

9 "But take heed to yourselves; for they will deliver you up to councils; and you will be beaten in synagogues; and you will stand before governors and kings for my sake, to bear testimony before them. ¹⁰And the gospel must first be preached to all nations. ¹¹And when they bring you to trial and deliver you up, do not be anxious beforehand what you are to say; but say whatever is given you in that hour, for it is not you who speak, but the Holy Spirit. ¹²And brother will deliver up brother to death, and the father his child, and children will rise against parents and have them put to death; ¹³and you

will be hated by all for my name's sake. But he who endures to the end will be saved.

14 "But when you see the desolating sacrilege set up where it ought not to be (let the reader understand), then let those who are in Judea flee to the mountains; [15]let him who is on the housetop not go down, nor enter his house, to take anything away; [16]and let him who is in the field not turn back to take his mantle. [17]And alas for those who are with child and for those who give suck in those days! [18]Pray that it may not happen in winter. [19]For in those days there will be such tribulation as has not been from the beginning of the creation which God created until now, and never will be. [20]And if the Lord had not shortened the days, no human being would be saved; but for the sake of the elect, whom he chose, he shortened the days. [21]And then if any one says to you, 'Look, here is the Christ!' or 'Look, there he is!' do not believe it. [22]False Christs and false prophets will arise and show signs and wonders, to lead astray, if possible, the elect. [23]But take heed; I have told you all things beforehand.

24 "But in those days, after that tribulation, the sun will be darkened, and the moon will not give its light, [25]and the stars will be falling from heaven, and the powers in the heavens will be shaken. [26]And then they will see the Son of man coming in clouds with great power and glory. [27]And then he will send out the angels, and gather his elect from the four winds, from the ends of the earth to the ends of heaven.

28 "From the fig tree learn its lesson: as soon as its branch becomes tender and puts forth its leaves, you know that summer is near. [29]So also, when you see these things taking place, you know that he is near, at the very gates. [30]Truly, I say to you, this generation will not pass

away before all these things take place. [31]Heaven and earth will pass away, but my words will not pass away.

32 "But of that day or that hour no one knows, not even the angels in heaven, nor the Son, but only the Father. [33]Take heed, watch; for you do not know when the time will come. [34]It is like a man going on a journey, when he leaves home and puts his servants in charge, each with his work, and commands the doorkeeper to be on the watch. [35]Watch therefore—for you do not know when the master of the house will come, in the evening, or at midnight, or at cockcrow, or in the morning— [36]lest he come suddenly and find you asleep. [37]And what I say to you I say to all: Watch."

reached a height of 150 feet, according to some scholars, to form the walls of the temple building. Added to the immensity of the temple structure is the beauty of its architecture, with gold, silver, bronze, precious woods and marble materials. Such a sight caused the exclamation of the disciples; perhaps their exclamation meant that they could see no end to this structure, especially as it served the almighty God of Israel—it must last forever.

Whatever meaning besides just awe their exclamation signaled, Mark has Jesus take this opportunity to speak about the future of the temple. In short, within a recognizable amount of time, this grandiose and stunning building will be so ruined that not one stone will be left on another. This is Jesus' last word in the temple area, a somber word and a comment to conclude his disappointment shown in his earlier cleansing of the temple area.

Somewhere along the route back over the Mount of Olives to Bethany, the disciples ask Jesus for certain information about the destruction of the temple. In particular four of the disciples ask for two details: they would like to know just *when* the temple will be destroyed and they would like to know *signs* by which they might recognize the horror in advance, before it is too late to avoid being caught up in this terrible destruction.

Jesus, having seated himself near the top of the Mount of Olives so that he could oversee the city of Jerusalem and its temple, now gives his reply to the disciples' double question. As we will see, Jesus gives one sign which anticipates the destruction of Jerusalem; as regards the "when" of the actual destruction of Jerusalem, we will see that he cannot say just when this terrible event will take place. In this manner Jesus at least partially, and only partially, satisfactorily answers the disciples' question.

Jesus' discourse, however, covers much more ground

than what the disciples expected. Specifically, against a background of things which might be thought to be signs of the destruction of Jerusalem, but are not, Jesus begins to outline for the disciples some of the trials and tribulations they will likely have to face. His major theme becomes, not revelation of the signs of the time of the destruction of the holy city, but a general notice to be on one's guard against anything, trial or deception, which can draw one away from Christianity. Moreover, Jesus goes on beyond the destruction of Jerusalem to talk about a mysterious period which will occur after the destruction of Jerusalem, a period which seems to herald the end of this world, a period which finally serves to make him repeat his warning: "Be on your guard!" From just this brief description of the highlights of Jesus' discourse, we see that he used the disciples' question as an occasion to talk about more than what interested them at the moment. Indeed, to speak of the destruction of Jerusalem raised in Jesus a whole host of thoughts, which we should now reflect on briefly.

First of all, in the first section of his discourse Jesus describes a number of trials and sufferings the disciples can expect to undergo within the foreseeable future. Looking back from 65 A.D., Mark and his contemporaries can see how true these expectations turned out to be, for their forebears as well as for themselves. But we have here not just a prediction of calamities for those who believe in Jesus. Jesus presents these sufferings in such a way that the disciples should not think that they will inaugurate the destruction of Jerusalem (after all, they are asking for signs of the sufferings which will afflict Jerusalem). Thus, the sufferings about which the disciples are assured are not to be interpreted as the signs of "the end."

The great sufferings—wars, famines, plagues—which will afflict nations, though not the signs of Jerusalem's destruction, are signs in the sense that they are "the beginning of the birthpangs." What birth is Jesus referring to? This we will see in a moment. What is clear here is that, while Jesus denies that certain future events are signs of the destruction of Jerusalem, there will be signs which point to another event, an event which is like a birth preceded by suffering.

Among the personal sufferings of the disciples will be an attempt to deceive them on the part of false messiahs, some of whom will try to interpret the times and hope to win over the allegiance of many; against these, all that Jesus counsels now is: "Do not be deceived!" Another of the personal sufferings of Jesus' followers will be the challenging task of defending themselves before kings and great rulers; Jesus can only assure his disciples with the words, "The Holy Spirit of God will inspire you what to say at this moment." Indeed, Luke's second volume, the Acts of the Apostles, does recount the numerous times in which Christians, brought before rulers, do benefit from the inspiration of the Holy Spirit in defense of their beliefs.

That this entire period of sufferings, personal as well as universal, will not be short is suggested by Jesus' words that "first the gospel must be preached to all the nations." To the extent that the Acts of the Apostles notes that the gospel has been brought to Rome, which is essentially for this book "the ends of the earth" (cf Acts 1:8)—to this extent Jesus is predicting a lengthy period of at least some thirty-five years.

Finally, as at earlier points in his discourse, Jesus exhorts his disciples to fidelity in all these trials, for it is through perseverance to the end that one reaches that final moment of complete salvation for which Jesus, the Savior, works.

Having finished the first part of his discourse, in which he separated imminent personal and worldwide sufferings from the particular agonies of Jerusalem, Jesus now addresses himself, in the second part of his discourse, to the question of Jerusalem.

The words of Jesus about the doom to fall on Jerusalem reveal his concerns. First, Jesus gives a sign—the only sign which answers the disciples' request for "signs": it is the abomination of desolation seen to be in a place it should not be. ("Abomination of desolation" is better translated: the abominable or sacrilegious entity which makes everything around it desolate.) Both in the book of Daniel (9:27; 11:31; 12:11) and in the first book of Maccabees (1:54), enemies of the Jewish people had been depicted by this gruesome description. Now Jesus, to heighten the terribleness of this "abomination," uses the images of Daniel and Maccabees and thus communicates well the tragedy to come upon his audience. What he seems to be pointing to here is the appearance of the Roman armies in places they should not be; where they will be, however, will be places of desolation and sacrilege. When one sees them approaching, it is time to flee to the mountains for refuge outside Jerusalem.

Second, there will be no time for dallying when the abomination approaches; safety will depend on fearful haste. Moreover, Jesus sees woes for those carrying or nursing children—a particularly terrible characteristic of war and a cause for great alarm and flight.

As is typical of prophetic speech, Jesus' words describe the destruction of Jerusalem as the greatest suffering yet, or ever to be, experienced by human beings. Indeed, so great will it be that if God had not, out of love for his chosen ones, shortened the length of the destructive period, no life would be spared.

Finally, as in times of earlier sufferings, Jesus is preoccupied with the possibility that, with the emergence of "saviors" in this desperate period, his disciples might abandon

him for those offering a false hope of salvation. There is only
one wisdom to follow to eternal happiness, and, Jesus insists,
it is his. Perhaps the most beguiling aspect of these pseudo-
messiahs and pseudo-prophets is their ability to work "signs
and wonders," a special terminology used to describe the
miracles worked by Moses himself for the salvation of the
Jewish people. (The ability of others than Jesus to work miracles was a growing reason for the Christian judgment that
something more than power characterizes the true messiah.)
Jesus is very concerned that his disciples not yield their
fidelity to him, whether because of sufferings imposed on
them for their faith or because of deceptions which suggest
that another person, and not Jesus, is the true good for them.

Jesus concludes this fearsome description of Jerusalem's
fate with the warning characteristic of every prophet: "You
watch, I've told it all to you beforehand!" Indeed, Jesus has
given a valuable sign to his disciples which will help them
someday to escape the horror to come: that "abomination
which desolates everything in its wake." Will he also tell
them the day and hour of this desolation?

Jesus' next words speak of the time after the sorrow of
Jerusalem, about which, it is true, the disciples had not
asked. On the one hand, his describing this time as "in those
days after the tragedy of Jerusalem" suggests that what he
is about to describe will occur shortly after the destruction
of Jerusalem. On the other hand, it is almost axiomatic that
certain kinds of prophets—and Jesus seems to model himself on them here—will, after speaking of a terrible and imminent national disaster, purposely shorten the time that
remains between this tragedy and the end of the world; in
particular, they do this by using imagery suggesting a destruction of the rest of the entire universe. The purpose
behind this "shortening of the time" seems to be this, that
one sees, on the one hand, that only universal destruction

remains after the nation has been desolated, so great was the desolation, and, on the other hand, that the national destruction was a major step on a trajectory which ends with the destruction of the entire world.

At this point, with the mention of "trajectory," we enter into a particular characteristic and philosophy of the centuries which precede, include and follow Jesus'. For a long time, and particularly among people who had to suffer, there was a perception that the only "reality" in the world was a profound and all-embracing struggle between good and evil. Whatever else may appear to be "real," this is the only reality. Good has always, they say, tried to destroy evil by making all things good; evil, on the other hand, has always tried to destroy good by making all things evil. In Jewish thinking, God can never be destroyed by evil, for God alone is supreme. In this way of thinking, evil does its best when it destroys what God loves. Eventually, the contest between good and evil will come to a head; a great battle will be fought, as the imagery has it, and so vicious will it be that evil will take on the appearances of good so as to deceive and thus destroy those belonging to the good. Those who conceived reality this way were always optimistic: good would win the final battle with evil, even though human beings, caught up in this great struggle, might doubt the positive outcome. Once the good had won, however, all would change and there would follow a new life, a new heaven and a new earth, where there would be evil no more. Philosophy, then, and imagery combined to offer people a guide to the truth about the underlying current of the world, about its direction, about ultimate hopes. The bottom line of all this is the effort to encourage those who are suffering or about to suffer to see the truth of their sufferings: their anguish is not just happenstance or chance, nor is it reason to doubt their adherence to what they know to be the truth, to which they had earlier committed themselves. In fact, their grief is revealed to be part of the great struggle which will eventually end in success and happiness for those who remain faithful.

This philosophy of life and the imagery used to depict it was very common within and without Judaism. Jesus used it here in his discourse about Jerusalem in order to reveal to the disciples something they had not asked about, that the various trials which they will undergo, and particularly the destruction of the holy city, are parts of this greater struggle between God and Satan which will end in glory for those who remain faithful. Thus, their individual sufferings, and the national sorrow, are on the trajectory which leads ultimately to that final cataclysm which ends this age—and to that new heaven and new earth which is the time of glory for those who deserve it. One does not always understand that one's personal trial of the moment is actually part of this great struggle toward a perfect world; thus, this teaching is called a "revelation," or, in Greek, an "apocalypse." The philosophy and its attendant imagery (symbolic numbers, colors, animals, and visions of this great struggle and of the realms of God and of Satan) are summed up in the term apocalyptic. Israel had for long interpreted itself in terms of apocalyptic (as had other nations in suffering). It is not surprising, then, that Jesus spoke to his audience in language and philosophy with which they were familiar.

As with all apocalyptic so here Jesus is rather precise about the impending doom of a particular event (here a national disaster of immense proportion) and purely poetic about the time thereafter till the cataclysmic end of this age. True to the apocalyptic genre, however, he foreshortens the time between the national disaster and the cosmic disaster, so that, as mentioned earlier, one can see the clear relationship of the one to the other. Psychologically speaking, with our Jerusalem destroyed, the universal destruction cannot be far behind!

Jesus, then, has elaborated on the questions of the disciples by placing their trials and that of the entire nation within the framework of apocalyptic. The language of apocalyptic is particularly notable in the description of the cataclysmic ending of this world, but it is visible earlier in Jesus' remarks, for example, when he speaks of "the beginning of the birth pangs" (v 8), or "not yet the end" (v 7). Indeed, the language by which Jesus describes the end of the world is drawn from ancient Jewish writings, such as Isaiah 33:10; 34:4; Ezekiel 32:7–9; Joel 2:10.31; 3:15; Daniel 7:33–34; Deuteronomy 30:4; Zechariah 2:6.10. All this imagery drawn from earlier Jewish literature was integrated into the Jewish form of apocalyptic used by Jesus here in his discourse (and also later by the book of the Apocalypse or Revelation, in the Christian New Testament).

Jesus gives a particularly Christian presentation of the end of this age by noting that, with the destruction of sun and moon, stars and heavenly powers, the great Danielic figure of the Son of Man will appear on the clouds, in great power and glory. It is the time of the glorification of those who had suffered over those who had caused their sufferings. At the word of the Son of Man, the angels or messengers will gather from all the world the chosen ones; it is, for them, the time of supreme salvation, of supreme joy. As usual, for the faithful the outcome is optimistic, the fulfillment of all hopes, the reward of fidelity.

Though Jesus, here and elsewhere in the Gospel, uses certain elements of the common apocalyptic of his time, he often prefers to teach by means of parables. Now he reverts to two of these, taken from agricultural and human life. The first parable calls attention to the fact that nature gives signs of an approaching season—and all learn from them. So, too, one should look attentively for the signs that will herald the destruction of Jerusalem. (Important note: I understand that the remarks of vv 28–37, which key on the words "these things" (v 29) and "all these things" (v 30), refer to what Jesus predicted *prior* to v 24. He had concluded v 23 with a reference to "everything"; it is to this "everything" that the later words "these things" and "all these things" refer.) Jesus notes that, indeed, some of his listeners' generation will be alive to see the horror of Jerusalem. Let them be ready for it. What he has predicted is surer than heaven and earth itself.

Jesus' second parable turns on the answer he finally gives regarding the second element of the disciples' question which had occasioned this discourse. When will Jerusalem be destroyed? No one, except the Father, knows this hour or day, this "moment"—not even Jesus will admit to having this knowledge, an ignorance which must be taken into account in any explanation of the divinity of Jesus. The best Jesus can do is encourage his listeners to watch, to be alert. The parable, the second of his discourse, is a clear presentation of the situation facing the disciples. No one knows, except the master, when he will return to his house; the best, most prudent course of action is: Watch!

Jesus' final discourse to his disciples, then, touches on a number of aspects regarding the future. He is most sure and rather precise about the destruction of Jerusalem. He is poetic about the relationship of this destruction to the destruction of the whole world and about the manner of this universal destruction, not necessarily giving an actual description of the end of this age, but falling back on language and philosophy used by his audiences to convey his point. Most of all, he is anxious that at every stage of the future his disciples remain faithful, alert, on guard. The disciples had asked about the time and signs of the destruction of

Jerusalem. When Jesus finished his response, this has shown itself to be the abiding teaching: now, then and always, WATCH!

Chapter 14

We are ready for Mark's account of the last hours of Jesus' life. Ever since the fateful sequence, "Who am I? ... You are the Messiah... The Son of Man must be handed over and put to death" (8:27–31), the gospel has pointed unremittingly to this time. Whatever impression Jesus had made on his audiences in Galilee by his powers and wisdom, another side of Jesus is to be presented, one that the believer must incorporate into his understanding of Jesus and of his own discipleship.

Mark begins his narrative here with attention, not on Jesus who will become more and more passive, but on the major antagonists, those who will move the current of these hours along. The chief priests (who number about eight and are responsible for the operation of the entire temple complex) and a number of scribes (those specialists in the interpretation of the Mosaic law) carefully search for a way to so entrap Jesus that he cannot escape. No doubt their destructive motivation is a response to the challenge Jesus had given to each of these groups (in Chapters 11 and 12) as he outwitted and humiliated them in the temple area. They are no longer in the mood for dialogue; they look for a successful mechanism to take him—always, however, in such a way that the Passover crowds will not have a chance,

14 It was now two days before the Passover and the feast of Unleavened Bread. And the chief priests and the scribes were seeking how to arrest him by stealth, and kill him; ²for they said, "Not during the feast, lest there be a tumult of the people."

3 And while he was at Bethany in the house of Simon the leper, as he sat at table, a woman came with an alabaster flask of ointment of pure nard, very costly, and she broke the flask and poured it over his head. ⁴But there were some who said to themselves indignantly, "Why was the ointment thus wasted? ⁵For this ointment might have been sold for more than three hundred denarii, and given to the poor." And they reproached her. ⁶But Jesus said, "Let her alone; why do you trouble her? She has done a beautiful thing to me. ⁷For you always have the poor with you, and whenever you will, you can do good to them; but you will not always have me. ⁸She has done what she could; she has anointed my body beforehand for burying. ⁹And truly, I say to you, wherever the gospel is preached in the whole world, what she has done will be told in memory of her."

10 Then Judas Iscariot, who was one of the twelve, went to the chief priests in order to betray him to them. ¹¹And when they heard it they were glad, and promised to give him money. And he sought an opportunity to betray him.

12 And on the first day of Unleavened Bread, when they sacrificed the passover lamb, his disciples said to him, "Where will you have us go and prepare for you to eat the passover?" ¹³And he sent two of his disciples, and

said to them, "Go into the city, and a man carrying a jar of water will meet you; follow him, [14]and wherever he enters, say to the householder, 'The Teacher says, Where is my guest room, where I am to eat the passover with my disciples?' [15]And he will show you a large upper room furnished and ready; there prepare for us." [16]And the disciples set out and went to the city, and found it as he had told them; and they prepared the passover.

17 And when it was evening he came with the twelve. [18]And as they were at table eating, Jesus said, "Truly, I say to you, one of you will betray me, one who is eating with me." [19]They began to be sorrowful, and to say to him one after another, "Is it I?" [20]He said to them, "It is one of the twelve, one who is dipping bread into the dish with me. [21]For the Son of man goes as it is written of him, but woe to that man by whom the Son of man is betrayed! It would have been better for that man if he had not been born."

22 And as they were eating, he took bread, and blessed, and broke it, and gave it to them, and said, "Take; this is my body." [23]And he took a cup, and when he had given thanks he gave it to them, and they all drank of it. [24]And he said to them, "This is my blood of the covenant, which is poured out for many. [25]Truly, I say to you, I shall not drink again of the fruit of the vine until that day when I drink it new in the kingdom of God."

26 And when they had sung a hymn, they went out to the Mount of Olives. [27]And Jesus said to them, "You will all fall away; for it is written, 'I will strike the shepherd, and the sheep will be scattered.' [28]But after I am raised up, I will go before you to Galilee." [29]Peter said to him, "Even though they all fall away, I will not." [30]And Jesus said to him, "Truly, I say to you, this very night, before the cock crows twice, you will deny me three

times." ³¹But he said vehemently, "If I must die with you, I will not deny you." And they all said the same.

32 And they went to a place which was called Gethsemane; and he said to his disciples, "Sit here, while I pray." ³³And he took with him Peter and James and John, and began to be greatly distressed and troubled. ³⁴And he said to them, "My soul is very sorrowful, even to death; remain here, and watch." ³⁵And going a little farther, he fell on the ground and prayed that, if it were possible, the hour might pass from him. ³⁶And he said, "Abba, Father, all things are possible to thee; remove this cup from me; yet not what I will, but what thou wilt." ³⁷And he came and found them sleeping, and he said to Peter, "Simon, are you asleep? Could you not watch one hour? ³⁸Watch and pray that you may not enter into temptation; the spirit indeed is willing, but the flesh is weak." ³⁹And again he went away and prayed, saying the same words. ⁴⁰And again he came and found them sleeping, for their eyes were very heavy; and they did not know what to answer him. ⁴¹And he came the third time, and said to them, "Are you still sleeping and taking your rest? It is enough; the hour has come; the Son of man is betrayed into the hands of sinners. ⁴²Rise, let us be going; see, my betrayer is at hand."

43 And immediately, while he was still speaking, Judas came, one of the twelve, and with him a crowd with swords and clubs, from the chief priests and the scribes and the elders. ⁴⁴Now the betrayer had given them a sign, saying, "The one I shall kiss is the man; seize him and lead him away under guard." ⁴⁵And when he came, he went up to him at once, and said, "Master!" And he kissed him. ⁴⁶And they laid hands on him and seized him. ⁴⁷But one of those who stood by drew his sword, and struck the slave of the high priest and cut off his ear.

[48]And Jesus said to them, "Have you come out as against a robber, with swords and clubs to capture me? [49]Day after day I was with you in the temple teaching, and you did not seize me. But let the scriptures be fulfilled." [50]And they all forsook him, and fled.

51 And a young man followed him, with nothing but a linen cloth about his body; and they seized him, [52]but he left the linen cloth and ran away naked.

53 And they led Jesus to the high priest; and all the chief priests and the elders and the scribes were assembled. [54]And Peter had followed him at a distance, right into the courtyard of the high priest; and he was sitting with the guards, and warming himself at the fire. [55]Now the chief priests and the whole council sought testimony against Jesus to put him to death; but they found none. [56]For many bore false witness against him, and their witness did not agree. [57]And some stood up and bore false witness against him, saying, [58]"We heard him say, 'I will destroy this temple that is made with hands, and in three days I will build another, not made with hands.'" [59]Yet not even so did their testimony agree. [60]And the high priest stood up in the midst, and asked Jesus, "Have you no answer to make? What is it that these men testify against you?" [61]But he was silent and made no answer. Again the high priest asked him, "Are you the Christ, the Son of the Blessed?" [62]And Jesus said, "I am; and you will see the Son of man seated at the right hand of Power, and coming with the clouds of heaven." [63]And the high priest tore his garments, and said, "Why do we still need witnesses? [64]You have heard his blasphemy. What is your decision?" And they all condemned him as deserving death. [65]And some began to spit on him, and to cover his face, and to strike him, saying to him, "Prophesy!" And the guards received him with blows.

66 And as Peter was below in the courtyard, one of the maids of the high priest came; [67]and seeing Peter warming himself, she looked at him, and said, "You also were with the Nazarene, Jesus." [68]But he denied it, saying, "I neither know nor understand what you mean." And he went out into the gateway. [69]And the maid saw him, and began again to say to the bystanders, "This man is one of them." [70]But again he denied it. And after a little while again the bystanders said to Peter, "Certainly you are one of them; for you are a Galilean." [71]But he began to invoke a curse on himself and to swear, "I do not know this man of whom you speak." [72]And immediately the cock crowed a second time. And Peter remembered how Jesus had said to him, "Before the cock crows twice, you will deny me three times." And he broke down and wept.

through aroused sympathy, to react in favor of Jesus. Secrecy is the key.

With these catalysts in place, Mark introduces a story of foreboding. A number of the story's details are, historically speaking, perplexing, for they do not agree with this story as it is told by John. The unnamed woman of Mark's story is clearly identified as Mary, sister of Lazarus in John's story; the anointing takes place, according to Mark, in the house of a certain Simon, a healed leper, whereas, for John, the event took place in Lazarus' house. Since there would not have been two such anointings like this, and since both gospels agree on the curious point that the woman's perfumed material had a worth of three hundred pieces of silver, it seems that, by the time Mark and John each received this story (neither evangelist, as far as we can tell, had any contact with the other), only certain details of each version are historically founded and other details were developed by the gospel-writers.

The major points Mark makes with his story, however, are independent of the historical trustworthiness of certain details. This story is above all else a prophecy in the classical sense, a speaking through action about an event God knows will happen. The disciples fail to grasp what is being done. Jesus does not so fail and his responses underline the reality prophesied. What this woman has done is so significant that her action will be spoken of wherever the story of Jesus is recounted. Moreover, such a conclusion that the ointment would be better used for the poor simply reveals an unawareness of the death which is so imminent and which merits the dignity of a precious gift; Jesus must underline the contrast between the uniqueness of his death with the perennial human problem of care of the poor.

(Some people have regretted the saying of Jesus, "The poor you will have always with you," as though he meant that he cared little for their plight. The point at issue is not what should be done for the poor, but what should be done in this unique moment which prophesies Jesus' death. Indeed, the poor can be (and, according to Jesus, should be) cared for every day, as can Jesus. But this pouring of ointment is not just a passing event; it is the moment of death which is being prophetically announced.)

Indeed, the great value of the ointment should have been a signal to the disciples that something extraordinary was happening here, something which merited reflection and not immediate criticism. Jesus did not ask for any ointment, much less an ointment of great value. It is the sorrowful love of the woman which dictates how precious the ointment should be that prophesies the inestimable death of the Lord, and in this giving is a further lesson taught.

Mark begins then with dark plottings and sorrowful foreboding. Now a third agent is heard from, another who will pull Jesus along the way to his death. It is Judas, long ago described by Mark as the one who would betray Jesus. Whatever Judas' dark reasons for his actions, his decision to betray, coming as it does from within the most intimate circle of Jesus' disciples, casts its own black pallor over the hours to come. The forces of evil are now in place, particularly with the deal sealed with payment and one of the twelve now on the lookout for the precise moment for betrayal.

The moment of Passover and the first day of Unleavened Bread have arrived. The origin of Passover was quite different from that of Unleavened Bread, though even before Jesus' time the two feasts were celebrated simultaneously. Passover was the remembrance of a particular historical and saving event of the people of Israel, when the angel of death "passed over" those Israelite houses marked by the blood of a lamb (ever after called the Passover lamb whose blood saved Israel from death), while killing the firstborn in all the Egyptian houses not marked by lamb's blood. Unleavened Bread, on the other hand, was a yearly agricultural feast, which thanked God for the annual spring harvest by offering to him immediately, without yeast or leaven, the first wheat harvested; this offering also professed the fact that all the harvest really belonged to God and was given to human beings by God for their nourishment. Because the one-time event of the Passover and the annual event of harvest occurred in the spring, the two feasts were eventually celebrated at the same time, equivalent to our March-April. One should recall that unleavened bread, which characterizes the harvest feast of Unleavened Bread, is also an element of the celebration of Passover; it was unleavened bread which the Israelites ate at their sudden departure (or exodus) from Egypt, for there was no time to make bread with yeast.

A word should be said about the concept of "day" in the world of Jesus. For us, day begins with midnight and ends at the successive midnight. For the Jews of Jesus' time in Palestine, a "day" began at sundown or, more securely, at 6:00 P.M., and ran for twenty-four hours to finish by the following sundown. What does this difference in computing a "day" mean practically? Mark says (v 12) that Jesus will eat his Passover dinner on the *day* when he sent his disciples to secure a room for the dinner. According to our time this makes sense, for the sending of the disciples, in the late morning or early afternoon, and the eating of the Passover supper after sundown occur before midnight, the end of the day. But in the Jewish computation of time, sundown began a new day, and so Jesus would have eaten his Passover supper (eaten after sundown) on the *day after* the disciples arranged for the room for this meal. Similarly, using the Jewish computation again, Jesus died on the *same day* he ate his last supper, because the last supper and the death of Jesus occurred within the twenty-four hours between a sunset and its successor. We, on the other hand, always think that Jesus ate his last supper on one day (Thursday) and then died on the next day (Friday), because for us midnight is the divider between one day and the next. In particular, if Mark, in verse 12, indicates that Jesus sent his disciples (before sundown) to arrange for the upper room *on the same day* on which the Passover was to be eaten (and it was to be eaten after sundown), he must be using a computation of time different from that used in the Palestine of Jesus' time.

Mark notes, again in verse 12, that what he narrates now occurred on the *first* day of Unleavened Bread. By this "first" he means to recognize that the feast of Unleavened Bread, by Mosaic prescript, lasted eight days; Passover, however, was celebrated on one evening. Finally, it is this day, finishing before sundown, when the lambs for the Passover meal (to be eaten after sundown) are slaughtered and distributed to the many people come to celebrate Passover. Perhaps we are to think of this slaughter of the lambs, whose blood recalls the saving of Israel, while Jesus prepares himself for his saving death of the next day.

Jesus, reminding us of his lordly command whereby he commandeered a mule for riding into Jerusalem, now shows his command over the situation of obtaining an upper room. The point here seems to be that, though it was almost impossible to find any free space in Jerusalem at this Passover moment, Jesus knows not only where he can find a room, but the most desirable spaciousness and privacy of an upper room. To what is this favor owed? The best answer seems to be that it was a disciple of the Lord who owned this room, a disciple of whom we have never heard before. If this be the correct suggestion, it in turn serves to remind us of the many disciples Jesus must have had, of whom we now know little or nothing. Moreover, scholars, aware that the area in which the upper room was found was an area of the Essenes (an offshoot of whom were the people of Qumran at the Dead Sea), hypothesize that there may have been a link between Jesus and the Essenes, strict Jews who differed on many points with the religious authorities of Jerusalem, which we have now practically lost. The sending of the disciples into this southwestern portion of Jerusalem, however, serves again to underline the calmness and lordship of Jesus, who knew where the room would be for his last supper, though the disciples with him did not.

Mark shifts scenes rapidly: we are already in the upper room and some of the ritual of the Passover supper has already taken place. Indeed, Mark concentrates on only two moments of this supper which must have lasted for quite some time. Mark underlines two moments: the announcement of betrayal and the identification of the bread and wine with his body and blood. Both moments, but certainly the latter, go beyond just the narration of causes which brought about the death of Jesus; Mark is interested here in making clear the meaning of the eucharist which his own contemporaries were by now in the habit of celebrating each Sunday.

The first thing Jesus notes, with the meal underway, is that "one of you, eating with me, will betray me." Mark indicates the mood which results from this: sadness on the part of the disciples, corresponding to the darkness that has fallen outside. To their bewildered questions, Jesus makes the point again that it is "one of the twelve" who will betray him. Mark never has Jesus actually identify the betrayer in his story; it is to his purpose simply to underline the fact that even "one of the twelve, even one who eats with me," can be the cause of Jesus' death—bitter lesson for Mark's readers to comprehend.

Jesus then expresses the horror of the deed the betrayer

is about to do. Jesus will suffer, as the scriptures had indicated, and nothing will stand in the way of this perfidy. But the man who betrays will also suffer—woe to him! It would have been better for the man if he had not been born! Some people have drawn the conclusion that the great suffering of Judas was hell forever. The Catholic Church has never concluded this; we know of no one who is for certain in hell, nor do we, left to our own judgment, want to say someone is in hell. Mark here, rather than hinting that Judas is in eternal punishment, intends to underline the heinousness of his crime.

The lengthy supper's only other moment that Mark reports is the opposite of the previous moment he described: the earlier moment was the anguished facing up to betrayal by an intimate friend, the latter moment is the revelation of a most loving gift of self-sacrifice. The words and gestures which introduce the famous sayings of Jesus about his body and his blood are themselves so renowned that interpreters are prone to attach eucharistic symbolism to any passage in any New Testament work where they appear.

The disciples are asked to "receive" this which is now Jesus' body. The precise significance of this reception, which must have been an eating, is not expressed in Mark's gospel; evidently, it was enough for his readers to hear Jesus say this to his twelve to recall for themselves the meaning of their weekly eucharist. It seems right to say, however, that the reception of the Lord's body represents a desire of the Lord to be one with the disciple and a source of strength to the disciple. As well, one cannot forget that this body is the body which will go to the cross, as Jesus had said earlier, for the redemption of the multitudes.

While they drink of the one cup, Jesus identifies the wine therein as his blood which is both "blood of the covenant" and "blood to be poured out for the multitudes." The latter phrase is another way of saying what Jesus had said earlier, that he would give his life for the redemption of the multitudes. Thus, one meaning of this drinking is that one shares in the very life blood of the one who redeems. (For long, the Jewish view of blood was that it contained life—to lose blood was to lose life itself. Thus, to drink Jesus' blood in this mysterious form is to draw his life, his redeeming life, into oneself.) Again, there is visible the Lord's intention that he become one with the disciple through this mode of eating; at the same time the symbol of wine, as with bread, suggests that Jesus comes to his disciple as one who strengthens.

This blood of Jesus is the blood of the covenant. By this identification Jesus means to recall the earlier covenant (not those covenants made with Abraham, David, Noah, Adam) in which Israel formally became God's people and Yahweh formally became Israel's God. This covenant, made with Moses after the giving of the law at Mount Sinai, involved an exchange of promises and culminated in a sprinkling of Yahweh's altar and the people of Israel with blood drawn from one cup. With an eye to this historic moment in Israel's past, Jesus now identifies his blood as the blood by which God and human beings, redeemed, can once again belong to each other. The blood this time is not that of animals, but the blood of the messiah, of the Son of God. Participation in the drinking of this blood is a sign that one wants to be again in union with God who, on his part, has shown his willingness for union by the life-giving death of his Son.

The Marcan narrative of this last supper ends with a bittersweet saying of Jesus. On the one hand, this is the last time in this age when Jesus will drink wine with his friends. Such is this moment's genteel way of alluding to the harsh cross of tomorrow. It seems as though Mark is having Jesus end where he began in this dinner: his first act was to refer to the sorrow of tomorrow, and now the supper ends with another referral to the same imminent suffering of tomorrow.

But intertwined with this sorrowful statement of Jesus is the look ahead to another time, another age, when Jesus and his disciples will drink anew together: it will happen in the kingdom of God. Thus, though all now points somberly to the grievous event upon us, there is reserved at the last a final gesture toward that time when all will be healed, when there will be what was for the Jews of this time a symbol of great joy, the banquet in the kingdom of God.

The meal ends with the singing of hymns, a traditional act of gratitude in the Passover celebration—and perhaps a further encouragement to the disciple to look on all that has been given, against the backdrop of plotting and betrayal, with acts of gratitude.

Jesus now moves with his (presumably at this point) eleven from the southwest corner of Jerusalem eastward, then northward till they cross the low point of the Kedron Valley, which lines Jerusalem's eastern border, and enters the garden called Gethsemani. While on this walk away from the upper room, Jesus predicts the dispersal of his most intimate friends. He cites words of the old prophet Zechariah, who talked of another shepherd or leader of Israel in Zechariah's time, whose being punished for the sins of Israel led to the dispersal of the Israelites. Now, indeed, the innocent leader will be struck and the sheep will indeed scatter. Peter refuses to accept this somber prediction of cowardice. There is nothing he can see in the future which will make him "stumble," as the Greek has it. Jesus replies to this with a special stinging prediction for Peter: "Today, this night, you will deny me three times before the cock crows even twice." Jesus has turned the screw another turn and increased the tension with this more precise prediction, and Peter's self-confidence throws him into a bitter oath: even if he has to suffer with Jesus, he will not deny him. The others, Mark now says, said the same. Mark clearly sets the stage for tragedy here, with ignorance and pride challenging the unchallengeable word. Mark lets Peter have the final word here, reinforcing the lesson that the reader is asked to absorb.

A particular sentence in Jesus' remarks here is noteworthy. In v 28 Jesus indicates that after his resurrection (to follow upon "the striking of the shepherd") he will go ahead of his disciples to Galilee. Indeed, the disciples are to be reminded of this statement through the first witnesses of the empty tomb. This statement seems to confirm what was said earlier, that Jesus always considered his mission to be centered in Galilee, and not in Jerusalem, that his visit to Jerusalem—eventuating in his death—was merely a momentary diversion out of reverence for the Jewish law which obliged Jewish males to celebrate Passover in the holy city. Other gospels (Luke's notably contrary) seem to support this understanding of Jesus' intentions.

Jesus now arrives in Gethsemani, which probably means "olive press," and signifies that we are in a grove of olive trees. This olive grove, at the foot of the Mount of Olives, is across the shallow Kedron Valley and just opposite Jerusalem's northeast corner. Jesus leaves the majority of the disciples at one spot and takes Peter, James and John further along with himself. At a second point he leaves them with the words which govern a great deal of this passage of Mark: "Stay here and watch."

Mark notes, quite contrary to gospel writing in general, Jesus' interior suffering. He is perplexed and anxious, distressed and in great sorrow. In contrast to his mastery of all other situations, Jesus is now the passive element; a sign of his grief and impotence is his throwing himself to the ground. He knows now that he is soon to die, and he does not want to die. His immediate recourse is to his Father, to whom he expresses his desire to live. (The word by which Jesus addresses God here is difficult to translate. It is based on the Hebrew word for "father," but includes an ending which reveals an intimacy and love which only a son or daughter has the right to express.) What is remembered for later generations to ponder is the willingness of Jesus, who did not want to die, to do what his Father wishes. Mark has underlined well enough the abhorrence Jesus felt for death, so as to make clear just what degree of selflessness was involved in his decisive preference to do the will of his Father. One cannot fail to note, as well, that this prayer is founded on a profound intimacy and trust in the one who can do everything, even change the divinely appointed events of life. It is ultimately this trust which moves Jesus to commit himself to the will of the Father, even if it still means death.

The agony and victory of Jesus is not the sole purpose of this story, however. This is clear from the fact that at least half of the story's drama takes place between Jesus and his disciples. As in earlier stories of this gospel, the disciples are again seen as uncomprehending, not knowing what to answer. They are too weak to let the suffering and praying of Jesus keep them awake. Jesus at one point addresses Peter in particular, thereby underlining his expectations for the leader of the disciples and his disappointment as well. What makes it all the more painful is the fact that Jesus had specifically asked his chosen three, before anything had happened, to "watch!" The conclusion to be drawn from all this is that Mark is as concerned to present to the reader the obedience of Jesus as to present the disappointing performance of the disciples, who never did find strength at any point to "watch."

But Mark is not interested in simply criticizing the disciples for their lack of sympathy for the Lord. Jesus had told his disciples that they, too, should "pray so that they may not enter into trial." Jesus is concerned that the disciples pray for themselves, as well as sympathize with him. What is about to happen will in some sense dramatically touch the disciples as well as Jesus. They should pray that they not have to face this trial, and pray as he is praying. But underneath this exhortation to Peter and the others to pray about their own imminent trial is the subtle exhortation from Jesus, through the pen of Mark, to all future disciples who must face tribulation on account of their faith. Ultimately, the lesson of Jesus' prayer and of the weakness of the disciples is meant for the reader's spiritual benefit. Again, Mark uses the past in order to influence the present.

The words of Jesus to his disciples end, because the hour has come and the betrayer is at hand. Not one to wait, Jesus, with his eleven, steps forward to meet the adversaries.

The initial words of this new scene are a good example of Mark's artistry in this chapter. Contemporaneity is an artistic element: while one thing is happening, the new element is woven into it. Moreover, Judas, though clearly now known as the traitor, is still explicitly titled "one of the twelve," a title one would rather not read anymore. Finally, the description of the people with Judas pictures such violence that one easily feels the brash evil eager to swallow up Jesus and his disciples. Mark notes that the men who have come with Judas are from the "chief priests, scribes and elders"; as noted before, the naming of these groups is another way of saying "the Sanhedrin," the highest Jewish juridical and judicial body in Israel. In particular, the chief priests, because of their responsibilities for the temple in all its aspects, were allowed by the Romans to have their own police force for this sacred temple area, forbidden to the hated pagan Roman masters. It is this police force, a bit out of its area of jurisdiction, which secretly and forcefully arrests Jesus now.

Bitter are the kiss of Judas and the title "rabbi" (= "my great one," or "teacher"); all the more are these reverential gestures out of all proportion against the swords and clubs of the night. More important, perhaps, to Mark's purpose is Jesus' response to the violence that breaks out at his being taken. Jesus was in the open, in their presence, during a number of days; why did they not arrest him then? Why now, as though he were a thief? There is no answer to this charge, and the reader is once again brought to understand the extreme questionableness of the procedures which dogged Jesus till his last breath. Jesus points to the scriptures as offering some reason and intelligibility to all that is happening. At least these things make sense in that they were foreseen and predicted. Thus, a greater power is overseeing all this, and it is to this greater power that Jesus acquiesces.

Unique among the evangelists, Mark notes the presence of an unnamed young man who escaped the clutches of the police only because of his loose-fitting garment. Since this story has little meaning for the events going on here, scholars have wondered about the purpose behind the telling of this story. Many have concluded with the hypothesis that the reason this story is here is that the young man was Mark himself.

Mark now brings us to the last scenes of this frightful night. Jesus is brought to the high priest (Caiaphas was high priest this year, whereas Annas, his father-in-law, had been high priest for other years and thus still carried the title), who in turn gathers together the Sanhedrin. It is the high priest who, apart from being ultimately responsible for all that happened in the temple (and the only one who could enter the holy of holies), was by virtue of his office president of the Sanhedrin and sole representative of the entire Jewish people, in and outside Palestine, to the Roman emperor. At the same time as this gathering takes place, Mark has Peter in position for his eventual denial of Jesus.

What is purported to be a trial is described briefly by Mark. Actually, no witnesses were found who could accuse Jesus of anything, a fact which serves Mark's general thesis that the death of Jesus was absolutely unmerited. In particular, false witnesses claimed to have heard Jesus say, "I will destroy this temple made by human hands and in three days build another not made by human hands." Though the witnesses who reported this evidently differed in their versions and thus could not be considered trustworthy, their words do reveal a preoccupation that Jewish leaders had ever since Jesus entered the temple area as though it were his own and, later, took to cleansing it. Indeed, such a statement of force, such as the witnesses falsely create, may have been an interpretation of Jesus' prophetic action of purification that he was somehow claiming to be the messiah, a messiah authorized to renew the place of worship. (But there is the further possibility that Mark cited this particular accusation also because, unknown to the witnesses, it serves as an unexpected but sure prophecy of what is going to happen, not to the temple, but to Jesus.)

Whatever prompts the high priest to end this already very schematically told trial, he rises to ask Jesus to respond to the accusations, then, at his silence, asks him the all-important question of the gospel, "Are you the messiah, the Son of the Blessed One?"

One cannot help note that it is here, in the moment of Jesus' falling prey to forces which are now more powerful than he, that Mark brings us the words which match the opening words of the gospel, the words of Mark's own confession: Jesus "messiah, Son of God." It is as though Mark wants these words tightly associated with the person who must suffer, and not just with the person who appeared all-powerful and all-wise in Galilee. Similarly, it is only here, only in the midst of this dark trial, that Jesus, finally, admits he is the messiah, Son of God; only in this moment, it seems, did Mark let this affirmation appear on Jesus' lips.

Upon admitting that he is the messiah, Son of God, Jesus immediately switches images and subject and time. The "I" becomes "you" and the present tense of "am" becomes the future tense of "will see" and the title "messiah, Son of God" becomes the "Son of Man, judge of the world." Attention is turned from the present confession to the future threat when the Son of Man, known for his glorification after suffering, will come in power from the right hand of God on the clouds of heaven to judge those who had judged him. Jesus is claiming this title for himself and thereby promising his judges that he will someday be theirs. Again, Mark is making clear to his reader the proper understanding of a Jesus who, on the face of it, seemed impotent and, perhaps to some later generations, justly condemned by the Sanhedrin.

The words of Jesus drew a proper response in that they were interpreted as a claim to sonship with God himself. The high priest, in a gesture that was usual for many people in times of great stress and sorrow and sinfulness, tore his garments. Everyone else who heard Jesus claim for himself the position at the right hand of God and the power of judge of the world called Jesus a blasphemer and thus worthy of death, for in Jewish law blasphemy was to be punished by death. And so, in a very summary but direct fashion, Mark has explained how it happened that Jesus was given the extreme penalty of death. At the same time, he hopes he has shown how unjust such a condemnation was, for, in the last analysis, is not Jesus the messiah, Son of God, Son of Man?

Mark has professed him to be so, and has done his best for the length of his gospel to let the facts of Jesus' life show him to be so.

The anger and frustration of the Sanhedrin members spills over now to a crude and cruel mistreatment of Jesus; ultimately, it was aimed at ridiculing the prophetic image Jesus had created in public, particularly in Jerusalem. The police who had served the Sanhedrin in capturing Jesus take to beating him.

It is against this image of Jesus suffering and on the brink of death that Mark brings forward the final figure of this chapter. Peter, who had said that even if he must suffer with Jesus, he would never deny him, is three times asked by various people about his relationship to Jesus. Three times he denies any such relationship with him, even to denying he even knows who Jesus is, even though Peter's speech does indicate that he is, like Jesus, a Galilean. And sure enough, by the end of the third, vociferous denial a cock crows for a second time, as Jesus had predicted. It all comes clear to Peter in a moment, and he bursts out in tears. As with so many other stories in Mark's gospel, the lesson is clear enough, but it should be said again that the lesson is for the reader, the disciple, who will have his opportunity to admit (or deny) knowing Jesus, admit (or deny) being with Jesus, being "one of them."

The events of our Chapter 14 have brought us to the end of a terrible night. Part of the effect of this chapter on the reader is due to the painful material itself. But part of the effect results from Mark's ability to place stories properly in relation to one another. Jesus' passivity is stressed by opening the chapter with the plotting and betrayal and anointing; "they" are setting the pace now, "he" is just going about his business, but against the sinister backdrop which will control him to his death. Plotting and betrayal are soon brought to bitter fruition, but not until, between the plotting and the execution, Jesus reveals the scheme of betrayal and at the same time offers himself as food and drink for his disciples. On the way to his capture he predicts denial by his most intimate companions, only to be assured that such a prediction is absurd. His capture fulfills the plot and betrayal, against a background of violence. The immediate trial shows the absolute contradiction between judgments about Jesus; they say he is a blasphemer, witnessed against by all, even though unjustly, while he says that he is the messiah, Son of God and Son of Man, judge of his enemies. He is reduced again to being the object of violence, and in this atmosphere the one who promised to suffer with Jesus denies even knowing Jesus exists.

It is a time of violence and contradictions, charges and counter-charges, promises and betrayals and denials—and of extreme self-giving for the redemption of the multitudes. Mark's ability to anticipate here and fulfill anticipations there makes the entire writing tight and forceful, as tight and forceful as the charged atmosphere of the black night which culminated the career of Jesus and brings him now, battered and alone, to face the only one who actually and legally controls his life and death.

Chapter 15

It is now early morning light. The chief priests head a group which organizes a meeting of all those associated with the Sanhedrin; presumably this meeting formalizes what decisions had resulted from the earlier, late-night trial Jesus had before the high priest and other Sanhedrin members. (Luke's gospel reports only this early morning meeting of the entire Sanhedrin, with no reference to a previous judgment of Jesus by the high priest, though Luke does have Jesus, once arrested, pass the night in the house of the high priest and, like Mark, does have Jesus beaten and struck there.)

Before the Sanhedrin, usually thought to be housed in a quarters just south of the temple building, bring Jesus to Pilate, they have him whipped. Presumably, this whipping is in some sense a formal punishment, given for something like disturbance of civic order—the chief priests have not forgotten, as their taking over the leadership of this present violent movement suggests, that the main anger against Jesus now flares from his bitter criticism of the temple complex, expressed primarily in Jesus' prophet-like cleansing of the temple area and in his subsequent parable which condemns the temple leadership. Having done all they could on their own, the Sanhedrin now go to Pontius Pilate, governor of Judea, to win from him the order to have Jesus killed, for

15 And as soon as it was morning the chief priests, with the elders and scribes, and the whole council held a consultation; and they bound Jesus and led him away and delivered him to Pilate. [2]And Pilate asked him, "Are you the King of the Jews?" And he answered him, "You have said so." [3]And the chief priests accused him of many things. [4]And Pilate again asked him, "Have you no answer to make? See how many charges they bring against you." [5]But Jesus made no further answer, so that Pilate wondered.

6 Now at the feast he used to release for them one prisoner for whom they asked. [7]And among the rebels in prison, who had committed murder in the insurrection, there was a man called Barabbas. [8]And the crowd came up and began to ask Pilate to do as he was wont to do for them. [9]And he answered them, "Do you want me to release for you the King of the Jews?" [10]For he perceived that it was out of envy that the chief priests had delivered him up. [11]But the chief priests stirred up the crowd to have him release for them Barabbas instead. [12]And Pilate again said to them, "Then what shall I do with the man whom you call the King of the Jews?" [13]And they cried out again, "Crucify him." [14]And Pilate said to them, "Why, what evil has he done?" But they shouted all the more, "Crucify him." [15]So Pilate, wishing to satisfy the crowd, released for them Barabbas; and having scourged Jesus, he delivered him to be crucified.

16 And the soldiers led him away inside the palace (that is, the praetorium); and they called together the whole battalion. [17]And they clothed him in a purple

cloak, and plaiting a crown of thorns they put it on him. [18]And they began to salute him, "Hail, King of the Jews!" [19]And they struck his head with a reed, and spat upon him, and they knelt down in homage to him. [20]And when they had mocked him, they stripped him of the purple cloak, and put his own clothes on him. And they led him out to crucify him.

21 And they compelled a passer-by, Simon of Cyrene, who was coming in from the country, the father of Alexander and Rufus, to carry his cross. [22]And they brought him to the place called Golgotha (which means the place of a skull). [23]And they offered him wine mingled with myrrh; but he did not take it. [24]And they crucified him, and divided his garments among them, casting lots for them, to decide what each should take. [25]And it was the third hour, when they crucified him. [26]And the inscription of the charge against him read, "The King of the Jews." [27]And with him they crucified two robbers, one on his right and one on his left. [29]And those who passed by derided him, wagging their heads, and saying, "Aha! You who would destroy the temple and build it in three days, [30]save yourself, and come down from the cross!" [31]So also the chief priests mocked him to one another with the scribes, saying, "He saved others; he cannot save himself. [32]Let the Christ, the King of Israel, come down now from the cross, that we may see and believe." Those who were crucified with him also reviled him.

33 And when the sixth hour had come, there was darkness over the whole land until the ninth hour. [34]And at the ninth hour Jesus cried with a loud voice, "Elo-i, Elo-i, lama sabach-thani?" which means, "My God, my God, why hast thou forsaken me?" [35]And some of the bystanders hearing it said, "Behold, he is calling Elijah."

³⁶And one ran and, filling a sponge full of vinegar, put it on a reed and gave it to him to drink, saying, "Wait, let us see whether Elijah will come to take him down." ³⁷And Jesus uttered a loud cry, and breathed his last. ³⁸And the curtain of the temple was torn in two, from top to bottom. ³⁹And when the centurion, who stood facing him, saw that he thus breathed his last, he said, "Truly this man was the Son of God!"

40 There were also women looking on from afar, among whom were Mary Magdalene, and Mary the mother of James the younger and of Joses, and Salome, ⁴¹who, when he was in Galilee, followed him, and ministered to him; and also many other women who came up with him to Jerusalem.

42 And when evening had come, since it was the day of Preparation, that is, the day before the sabbath, ⁴³Joseph of Arimathea, a respected member of the council, who was also himself looking for the kingdom of God, took courage and went to Pilate, and asked for the body of Jesus. ⁴⁴And Pilate wondered if he were already dead; and summoning the centurion, he asked him whether he was already dead. ⁴⁵And when he learned from the centurion that he was dead, he granted the body to Joseph. ⁴⁶And he bought a linen shroud, and taking him down, wrapped him in the linen shroud, and laid him in a tomb which had been hewn out of the rock; and he rolled a stone against the door of the tomb. ⁴⁷Mary Magdalene and Mary the mother of Joses saw where he was laid.

Rome at this time refused to let the local authority put a person to death.

Pilate, according to long-held tradition going back at least to the twelfth century A.D., had his quarters at this time of Passover in the Fortress Antonia, a building located at the northwest corner of the temple area, in such a strategic position that Roman soldiers could watch through fortress windows the activity in the temple quadrangle and, if intervention there were necessary, hurry down stairs connecting the fortress directly with the temple area. (This fortress was first heard of in the time of Nehemiah, about 450 B.C., mentioned as rebuilt by the Hasmonean kings of Jerusalem about 100 B.C., described as enlarged and newly fortified by Herod the Great and named to honor Marc Antony, for a time partial successor to Julius Caesar, and finally destroyed about 70 A.D. by Titus, future emperor of Rome.)

Pontius Pilate ruled the southern two-thirds of Palestine (and thus not Galilee); this territory was made up of Samaria and Judea, which is south of Samaria. Unlike other procurators of this territory, Pilate ruled for a good ten years, 26– 36 A.D., under the emperor Tiberius, though it was Rome which called an end to Pilate's career when he senselessly killed a gathering of Samaritans; Pilate was exiled to Gaul or present-day France. From descriptions of Pilate by non-Christian, non-biblical authors of his time, Pilate seems to have been an insensitive person who was quick to take extreme measures to preserve the civic peace. His decision about Jesus seems to fit this pattern.

Pilate fits into a series of procurators, begun by Rome after the failure of Herod the Great's son, Archelaus, to rule successfully the areas of Judea and Samaria. Not trusting another Herod with these territories, Rome consistently assigned procurators from 9 A.D. onward, right up to the Jewish war of rebellion with Rome begun in 67 A.D.; only for a few years' time, 41–44 A.D., did a Herodian (Agrippa I) and not a procurator rule Judea and Samaria.

As with the trial of Jesus before the Sanhedrin, Mark gives only the essential recollection of Jesus' trial before Pilate. Without preliminary and expecting the reader to supply the details, Mark has Pilate ask Jesus, "Are you the king of the Jews?" Presumably this title is a translation of "messiah," made to antagonize the Romans, who care little about messiahs but a lot about people who claim to be kings. Jesus' answer is viewed variously by scholars; some think it means "yes," some think it is evasive, some think it means that Pilate, influenced by the accusers, has already decided the issue, some think that, though Jesus was willing finally to admit to the high priest that he is the messiah, he is unwilling to translate this title into "king of the Jews" and thus equivalently says, "That is your term for what I am and I refuse to discuss myself on your terms."

Mark, always alert to the influence on the reader of backgrounds to a scene, describes the accusers of Jesus charging him with "many things." Pilate picks this up and seeks answers to these "many things of which Jesus is being accused." No answer is forthcoming and Pilate is perplexed. Why Pilate is confused is clear enough. Why Jesus refuses to answer is not so clear. Perhaps the most likely answer is that Jesus sees the whole matter as a religious, Jewish case and refuses to cooperate actively in the whole affair before Romans. Certainly, whatever his motive, he does nothing to harm his case and, apparently, everything to help it, since Pilate will soon announce that he finds no charge against Jesus to be valid or true; indeed, Pilate clearly sees that it is, as he judges it, jealousy, not broken laws, which has brought Jesus to this trial. Thus the silence of Jesus can be said to have had a salutary effect on the judgment of Pilate, and perhaps Jesus, sensing silence as the right tack, held to it.

All gospels record that a possible escape route for Jesus was cut off by those around Pilate's judgment place when they chose for pardon of offenses a man called Barabbas over Jesus. Though historically not found in documents, the general record states that Pilate, at the time of this Jewish feast of Passover, a feast which underlined freedom, let go free a prisoner for whom the crowds asked. Pilate, according to Mark, began this moment with the suggestion that he set free the "king of the Jews." As far as Pilate could tell, presenting Jesus as king of the Jews might stir up enough of the national spirit in the crowd to have them take him off his hands. Pilate was convinced that only jealousy on the part of the chief priests had created this situation; national admiration for a king of the Jews might counter that jealousy and free Jesus. The chief priests, however, shook up the crowd to shout for the freedom of another patriot who had participated in uprisings against the Romans to the point of killing. Thus, the chief priests countered well the political plan of Pilate with their own political cry, "Give us our revolutionary, Barabbas!" Pilate, still playing on the nationalist sentiments of the people, hopes to get a merciful judgment for their "king," but the cry is simply, "Crucify him." The dialogue takes the final step; instead of approaching the Jesus problem from his appeal as a national figure, Pilate reverts to the original point that Jesus is simply innocent. The only reply is the steady reply, "Crucify him."

Pilate chooses to please the crowd and agrees to the drastic call for crucifixion. Why the crowd fixed on crucifixion, as opposed to other forms of death, is hard to say. It certainly would satisfy anyone's hatred and jealousy, for it was both a terrible physical and psychological punishment.

On the one hand, the Romans were willing to eventually kill crucified prisoners in order to bring the whole affair to a premature end. On the other hand, the punishment by crucifixion was meant to leave an indelible and humiliating social stigma on the prisoner's family; in this way, punishment was sure to outlast even death.

Pilate has Jesus taken away and prepared for crucifixion. This preparation formally included a whipping, meant to reduce the strength and life of the prisoner; thus again, undiluted crucifixion is acknowledged to be simply intolerable.

It is said that Jesus was led out of Pilate's hall or praetorium (a word which indicates where the praetor or, more generally, the military or civil ruler has his "ruler's chair," or his tent or his domicile). Traditionally, this hall is considered to be in the Fortress Antonia. It should be noted, however, that a number of scholars prefer to think Pilate's residence at Passover and his praetorium to be located, not adjacent to the temple area in the northeastern part of Jerusalem, but against the western wall of Jerusalem, about halfway between the north and south boundaries. Indeed, there was here a Herodian palace, where the Herodian family would stay at Passover time, and there is another set of quarters here for the Roman procurator. Of course, one's route of the cross depends on where one puts the procurator, for it is from him that the walk begins. Traditionally, the way of the cross runs from the Fortress Antonia westward till one passes through a gate to enter the place of crucifixion. Scholars who put Pilate's quarters at the western wall of Jerusalem and south of the garden will say that Jesus walked in a northerly line from Pilate to enter through the same gate to the place of crucifixion.

The final decision against Jesus has proved to be unjustified; it included release of a murderous revolutionary preferred to Jesus and an incessant cry for brutal crucifixion.

By now Jesus, who, since the Passover time, has often been the passive element in this culminating tragedy, is completely silent and at the mercy of his taunters. After his scourging to prepare for his crucifixion, he is further made the passive toy as he is the butt of "unofficial" punishment. Mark is here content to describe the story.

Under the influence of the one charge the reader has heard explicitly spoken in the trial before Pilate, the military now in charge of Jesus decide to ridicule him under title of "king of the Jews." To this they dedicate themselves with a violence peculiar to them. The pain of a crown of thorns was, of course, part of the pleasure in bestowing on Jesus the symbol of kingship. He was dressed in purple, because purple was a color reserved really only for royalty or for people of very high political status. The reed used for beating Jesus about the head was, of course, another symbol of his royal authority. And bending the knee with spitting upon him added a final touch to his humiliation. When they had finished "playing" with him, as Mark says, they changed Jesus back into his own clothing and again took up the official duties of crucifixion. Just a few moments of jest.

We are already on the narrow street that leads to the place of crucifixion, outside the city. (It should be remembered that our way of the cross, comprised of fourteen stations, is something in part taken from the gospels, in part imagined by reverent Christians, but practically all of it arranged to suit the needs of pilgrims who, after having been given vivid descriptions of these events by early teaching and preaching Franciscans, asked in Jerusalem where exactly did these biblical and non-biblical events take place.) Actually, Mark tells us of only one occurrence along the three quarters of a mile route from Pilate to the place of crucifixion. He mentions a certain Simon come for Passover from Cyrene on the coast of north Africa. (Cyrene was a Roman colony with many Jewish inhabitants [one of them, Jason, wrote five books about the revolt of the Maccabees against the Romans in the 150's B.C.] and gave both believers [for instance, Lucius, who moved eventually to Antioch of Syria and was a Christian prophet and teacher there] and preachers [recall those Cyrenians who brought the message about Jesus to Antioch of Syria] to the Christian movement. Presumably, Simon's sons are mentioned in Mark's gospel because they, too, were Christians and well-known to Mark's Roman readers: indeed, Paul, in his letter to the Romans, sends greetings to a "Rufus, chosen of the Lord," and son of a mother whom Paul calls "his own mother.")

Along the route of Jesus' cross-carrying, this Simon was dragooned into carrying Jesus' cross, i.e., the cross-beam which would hang horizontal to the ground, for the vertical beam of the cross was already in place at the site of the crucifixion. Simon's being forced to carry the cross-beam is a perfect example of the situation Jesus uses in his sermon on the mount to teach love of neighbor. In this sermon, Jesus urges in exaggeration that one who is asked by an enemy to go a mile should go two miles. He is referring to the fact that a Roman soldier, provided he was on duty, could legally force anyone to help him carry an official burden for a mile. Obviously, such a dragooning, whatever its legality, was a humiliation and a concrete sign of the subjugation of a people to Rome. Simon of Cyrene's carrying of Jesus' cross-beam was done at the behest of this law.

Mark tells us that they brought Jesus to the place of crucifixion, called, he says, Golgotha or "place of the skull." Evidently the spot got its strange name because the rocky ground there rose up to form a small roundish hill, thus creating the impression of a skull coming out of the ground. Actually, this small rise, near a garden and near a Jewish burial site as well, was the remains of a stone quarry which had been exhausted except for this one surge of rock which was thought useless because it had been damaged by an earthquake. It was into this rock, at its top, that the vertical beam of Jesus' cross had been jammed.

Before the actual crucifying took place, it was the custom to give the prisoner a drugged wine, an effort to lessen the resistance of the crucified. Jesus rejects this wine and so, as Mark so simply and tightly reports, "they crucified him."

Mark describes some of the circumstances of Jesus' long hours on the cross; evidently, by his own preference he avoids a description of the suffering itself. One circumstance of these hours is the dividing of Jesus' clothes by the soldiers, noteworthy because the way the soldiers did the divvying was a stark reminder of just what Psalm 22:19 said about a mysterious person, "They divide my clothing among them, and cast lots for my garment." How strange that in the smallest details the life of Jesus corresponds to sayings of the Old Testament!

Mark says again that Jesus was crucified when he reports that it happened at the "third hour." Since a Jewish day began at sunrise, or 6:00 A.M., the "third hour" would indicate 9:00 A.M. All other witnesses speak of Jesus being crucified at noon. There seems to be no satisfactory way of explaining Mark's computation so as to make it equivalent to what the other witnesses report. The best suggestion would offer the translation of Mark's text, "They began the crucifixion process at 9:00 A.M.," and understand the other witnesses to mean that Jesus was actually raised up, the crucifixion completely finished, in the area of noon.

The bulk of Mark's description of Jesus' hours on the cross, however, is given over to a ridicule of Jesus which is centered on the now old complaint: he said that he was "the king of the Jews." It is not clear just why Pilate had this title hung above the head of Jesus for all to read. Perhaps it was a warning to deter anyone from even thinking of claiming this title; perhaps it is the expression of Pilate's frustration with the case of Jesus and his subtle way of antagonizing the Jewish leaders who pushed him into this crucifixion. In any event, this writing sets the stage for the taunts against Jesus; also as part of the scene are two thieves, crucified, we learn for the first time, with Jesus in the area of crucifixion.

Though the taunting of Jesus has its obvious personal suffering, it also has its main thrust as a challenge to the belief that Jesus is the messiah, or, as the title has been translated for the Romans, the king of the Jews. Mark notes that a first, generalized group of bystanders wags its heads as a sign of reproach at a false claim and "blasphemes." Clearly, it is Mark the believer who calls their action a blasphemy. These bystanders seem to have knowledge of what went on in the trial of Jesus before the high priest, for they bring up the same "recollection," but now as a ridicule: if he has the power to destroy the temple and rebuild it in three days, let him use this power and authority to take himself down from the cross. These words have a significance beyond the comprehension of those speaking them, for they sum up the mystery of a Jesus who is believed to be the one who brings the kingdom of God and is yet not bringing the kingdom's most visible and very significant characteristics. At the same time, these bystanders raise the suggestion of a temple rebuilt in three days, certainly by Mark's time an image translated into the death and resurrection of the holy person of Jesus himself. Thus, what appears to be a failure, Mark reminds his reader, will in fact be a success, if one only waits for God's intervention in the death situation of Jesus.

Now, once again, the chief priests are singled out, together with the experts in the knowledge of the law of God, to ridicule Jesus from a slightly different angle. Here the

chief priests go at the power of Jesus which was so visible
in the cures he worked throughout Galilee, cures of which
the chief priests had only second-hand knowledge. Surely,
if he cured others, he can cure himself? These priests raise
an objection which many later generations, not actual par-
ticipants in Jesus' miracles, will raise; indeed, the effect of
their taunt and its apparent truth suggests that Jesus' healings were really doubtful: he has no power now, and so he
had no power then. Again, the taunt goes very deep into
the meaning of Jesus, who did work miracles for others
but—for what possible reasons?—will not save himself.

Finally, the chief priests attack the core of Jesus' messianic meaning which Mark has very patiently developed
throughout his gospel: if Jesus is the messiah, the king of
Israel, how can he possibly make sense by staying on the
cross? Indeed, were he to come down, the chief priests go
on record as saying, they will "see and believe." A third time
Mark uses the taunts of Jesus' enemies to bring home what
he considers extremely important lessons. Why is being the
messiah inconsistent with, contradictory to, remaining on
the cross till death? Moreover, why should a disciple of this
Jesus expect to be saved from the cross of death? Is there
something inconsistent about a disciple of Jesus suffering, as
did the master? Second, even if it be questionable that the
chief priests would have believed in Jesus had he come
down from the cross, the question remains: Why is belief in
Jesus only reasonable if one has seen a miracle, an expression of divine power? Can one believe without seeing a miracle, without seeing Jesus coming down from the cross?

The crucifixion of Jesus, then, in the skewered words
of Jesus' taunters, brings up again the challenge to belief in
a messiah who does not bring the messianic age, but who
instead dies ridiculously and impotently. It is the Christian
who can piece together things so that they show Jesus to

be really a messiah in wisdom and power; it has been Mark's
goal to help the Christian to gain the proper perspective
about Jesus, and about the following of this kind of Jesus as
well.

This scene of taunting ends with the recollection that
the crucified thieves join in ridiculing Jesus. Such is the
depth of humiliation and even irony in this terrible scene.
Jesus remains the passive element in Mark's telling, which
has for some time now been carried forward by the enemies
who are now in the ascendancy.

In one sentence Mark now colors the story dark—in
the brightest part of the day, a great darkness covers "the
whole earth." At the last of it, Jesus cries out what can be
recognized as the beginning of a psalm (22) (which, in fact,
has many points of contact with the description of Jesus' last
suffering and perhaps has influenced the telling of this suffering). Having given the words of the psalm in Aramaic,
Mark gives a translation for his reader's sake. The translation,
of course, suggests Jesus' state of soul, a sense of abandonment by his Father, but Psalm 22 itself, though beginning
with this sense of abandonment, ends on a note of trust in
God's wisdom; thus, many interpreters think that what is
given us is only the beginning of a psalm, the whole of which
Jesus means to use as a prayer, intending to end up with the
same confidence in his Father that the psalmist had expressed in God. It is also possible, however, to see in this
psalm quotation not so much a sense of abandonment as a
sense of perplexity; in this one would emphasize the first
words of the citation: "To what" have you abandoned me?

It soon becomes clear what particularized function the
semitic wording of Jesus' cry serves. The Hebrew word for
God is Elohim (or "El" for short); "my God" is written "Eloi."
This word, heard from a dying man, could well be confused
with the name of Elijah, and so the crowd misunderstood

Jesus. Thinking that he really might be able to call the greatest of Israel's prophets to his aid, the prophet who was to
prepare the people for the kingdom of God, some of the
crowd tried to get Jesus to drink something which would
shock him into a greater consciousness and aliveness. But
Jesus, giving a great cry (some interpreters think Mark is
here describing Jesus as a warrior whose cry is a shout of
victory), "breathes his last," as Mark carefully puts it.

Mark records two valuable moments. First, the veil of
the temple was torn in two, from top to bottom. The veil
Mark speaks of here is the veil which separates the holy of
holies (which is the holiest room, the holiest place on earth,
the private room of God himself) from the rest of the temple
and, indeed, from the rest of the world. This total tearing
of the veil is a symbol by which God reveals that by the
death of Jesus God's room, traditionally looked upon as the
room of mercy, is no longer separated from human beings,
but very readily accessible to them all. Thus, immediately
following the death "of a criminal" is the sign of his death's
true worth.

Second, the centurion (literally, "one in charge of a
hundred soldiers"), posted to watch over the waning hours
of the crucified, for whatever reason is heard to say that this
man "is truly a son of God." As is often the case, what a
person says has much more meaning to it than he himself
gives it; here, a pagan soldier, meaning to contradict the
message conveyed to passers-by that this Jesus on a cross
had been a criminal, expresses his conviction, based on what
he has seen, that Jesus is innocent and indeed an instrument
of God. For Mark, these words, all the more precious because they come from an independent source, suggest further that a pagan was able to see in the death of Jesus a sign
of his relationship with God and thus confirm in its own
limited way the opening statement of the gospel, that Jesus

is Son of God. The insight of the soldier opens a path which the soldier might or might not have followed to its deepest mysteriousness, but Mark has long followed the path into Jesus' most profound meaning and thus welcomes the witness of another which puts one's foot firmly onto the same path.

Perhaps, too, there is a subtle suggestion here that the pagan should be contrasted with the Jewish chief priests, that the pagan stands as a symbol for what eventually and unpredictably occurred: the Christian community Mark knew consisted of many more Gentiles than Jews; and, one cannot forget, it was the death of Jesus, and not his wisdom or power, which moved the centurion to his assessment. Finally, the judgment of the centurion had to include in its evidence the manner of Jesus' death. Thus, the centurion's words witness, in part, to the piety of Jesus' death, a piety which Mark wants to recommend to his readers, should they have to face a death, physical or moral, similar to Jesus'.

Mark closes the scene of the death of Jesus with a note that many women were looking on from a distance at everything that was happening here. From among these women Mark names three, who in particular were followers of Jesus in Galilee and who served his needs. Mary of Magdala had come from a town (Magdala) which is located on the western shore of the Sea of Galilee. A tradition has drawn the conclusion (not from Mark, but from other gospels) that Mary was a sinner, mainly because she had been possessed by seven devils. Demonic possession, however, does not mean that a person possessed is a sinner, and so Mary, if this possession be the sole evidence, was not a sinner.

A second Mary, rather obviously not the mother of Jesus, is named by Mark; this is a Mary who is mother of a James and Joses (= Joseph), the men who had been referred to earlier in Mark's story as the "brothers" of Jesus (6:3).

Thus, in part Jesus was followed by relatives, though we recall how unreceptive to him his own home area finally became.

(It is interesting that already in Mark's time there had developed a "titular" distinction of the two men named James who were part of the twelve. James the "Less," because he was called later than the other James, is often considered to be the son of Clopas to whom Jesus appeared on the way to Emmaus and is the person who guided the Christian community of Jerusalem after Peter's departure [and after James the Greater had been decapitated by Herod Agrippa I] and who wrote the letter of James which is part of our New Testament.)

Salome was the wife of Zebedee and thus mother of James (the Greater, beheaded in 44 A.D. by the grandson of Herod the Great) and John, famous for his gospel.

These three women are named for a particular reason. The first two serve as precise witnesses as to just where Jesus had been buried, and the three together are the ones who will return to this precise place for more proper anointing of the body. Thus, they are the living continuity between the death and resurrection of Jesus; through their witness there can be no doubt that the tomb they saw filled was the tomb they saw empty a short time later.

Mark had noted that these three women were just some of the women who stood watching these death events from afar; he returns to this larger number of women with the description which explains their presence: they had come up with Jesus from Galilee to Jerusalem. This note, so late in the gospel and quite singular, can show how difficult it is to go beyond the written text of Mark to describe the "history" of Jesus' life. Should one by some quirk of fate not know this one-half verse at the end of the gospel, one would never be able even to suggest that women, and "many" at that, followed Jesus from Galilee to Jerusalem. Indeed, to take a step further, who would know from all the descriptions given us of Jesus' work in Galilee that he had two Marys and a Salome following him and caring for him? So treacherous and hypothetical is the effort to reconstruct what happened in Jesus' time, that so much more is it justifiable to say that the gospel writers use history only to their own ends—and do not use it otherwise.

Finally, Mark brings us to the moment of burial. Darkness is again the backdrop to this grim work. A new name appears, Joseph of a town called Arimathea, located to the northwest of Jerusalem, near the Mediterranean coast. He is a member of the Sanhedrin and thus able to have access to a man of Pilate's importance, though he must also, as Mark says, have a certain degree of boldness. Described as a man who was looking for the kingdom of God, Joseph may be presumed to be, or become, a disciple of Jesus. It is worthwhile to underline here that the Sanhedrin, which seemed to a man against Jesus, is now seen as fractured in its opinion. It is difficult to explain how "all the Sanhedrin" appeared to be against Jesus and at the same time there were Sanhedrinists sympathetic to Jesus. Whatever the truth of the matter, one learns to be very careful in ascribing the responsibility for Jesus' death to people who, one learns only later or indirectly, may have had little or nothing to do with it.

Pilate should have been surprised that Jesus was so quickly dead; crucifixion was made to make a person suffer terribly for a very long time. Given the centurion's witness (and thus one cannot say that Christians pretended that Jesus was dead), Pilate consigns the dead body to Joseph for burial; at least here Pilate shows a bit of sympathy which rulers often did not show to the corpses of criminals.

As mentioned earlier, the place of crucifixion was an

abandoned stone quarry which served as a burial place for Jews. (Jews always wanted to be buried as close to the temple as possible, and so Jewish graves are often found, even today, just outside the ancient walls of the inhabited Jerusalem. Similarly, Christians for many centuries had themselves buried as close to the altar of a church as possible—if not in the church, at least just outside its walls.) The body of Jesus was wrapped in a linen cloth and placed in a stone burial chamber (a room, not a grave). This chamber was cut into a hill so that one could walk into the hill by walking into the burial chamber; separating the chamber from the "world outside the hill" was an ante-chamber or little "waiting room." It was across the front of this waiting room that the great, heavy rollable stone disk was positioned, so as to keep vagrants, animals and people, out of the tomb.

All this was done as the day was drawing to its close (our 6:00 P.M.). The next day, beginning at sundown, was a sabbath, Mark says, so the day of death and burial was Friday, a day of the week used to prepare for the weekly sabbath celebration. One notes the absence of the anointing of the body of Jesus before its entombment. This is absent simply because Jesus did not die soon enough to allow for an anointing to be done before the sabbath began—and there could be no "work" of burial on the sabbath. Thus, the women note well where the body is, because they intend to come back for a proper anointing, once the sabbath has passed.

Mark has brought these terrible hours to a close. One can see through his account a defense of Jesus and an argument that what happened to Jesus was unjustified. One can also see included in his story other material which served other purposes than just defense of Jesus. At times, Mark wants to offer piety to be followed, at times he wants to suggest the deeper mystery to the person of Jesus, at times he wants to defend the Christian record of facts. Over all, the story here, as elsewhere, has a number of lessons of various types to be drawn by the attentive reader. Above all, what is communicated is a sense of the true meaning of what happened in these hours, of the person to whom all this was done. It is through Mark's marshaling and interpretation of facts that we reach back to the reality of these world-saving events.

Chapter 16

It was just before sunset, the end of a day, that Jesus died and was buried. The new day, lasting from this sunset to the next, was a sabbath, not a day for burial "work." The Sabbath ended at sunset and a new, third day began, but since it began in darkness one would not go to the tomb but wait till it was light. And so it was that the two Marys and Salome came to anoint Jesus after the sabbath was over, and in the first good light of the next, the third day. Since the sabbath was traditionally the day of rest after the week's work, the day after the sabbath was the "first day of the new week."

The women's quoted remark is not simply here to show their quandary about the size of the stone covering the entrance to the tomb, or to justify their surprise that it was already rolled aside. More profoundly, they reflect the general state of things in all the gospels: no one expected Jesus to rise from the dead, and here, in particular, the women's thoughts were purely on the anointing of a corpse. It is against this mentality that one must measure the intensity of their response to the angelic words which greet them.

The women entered the tomb to find a young man seated to the right (presumably of the slab on which the body was laid in the inner chamber). That he was dressed in a white robe was a sign which was finally interpreted

16And when the sabbath was past, Mary Magdalene, and Mary the mother of James, and Salome, bought spices, so that they might go and anoint him. [2]And very early on the first day of the week they went to the tomb when the sun had risen. [3]And they were saying to one another, "Who will roll away the stone for us from the door of the tomb?" [4]And looking up, they saw that the stone was rolled back—it was very large. [5]And entering the tomb, they saw a young man sitting on the right side, dressed in a white robe; and they were amazed. [6]And he said to them, "Do not be amazed; you seek Jesus of Nazareth, who was crucified. He has risen, he is not here; see the place where they laid him. [7]But go, tell his disciples and Peter that he is going before you to Galilee; there you will see him, as he told you." [8]And they went out and fled from the tomb; for trembling and astonishment had come upon them; and they said nothing to any one, for they were afraid.

9 Now when he rose early on the first day of the week, he appeared first to Mary Magdalene, from whom he had cast out seven demons. [10]She went out and told those who had been with him, as they mourned and wept. [11]But when they heard that he was alive and had been seen by her, they would not believe it.

12 After this he appeared in another form to two of them, as they were walking into the country. [13]And they went back and told the rest, but they did not believe them.

14 Afterward he appeared to the eleven themselves

as they sat at table; and he upbraided them for their unbelief and hardness of heart, because they had not believed those who saw him after he had risen. [15]And he said to them, "Go into all the world and preach the gospel to the whole creation. [16]He who believes and is baptized will be saved; but he who does not believe will be condemned. [17]And these signs will accompany those who believe: in my name they will cast out demons; they will speak in new tongues; [18]they will pick up serpents, and if they drink any deadly thing, it will not hurt them; they will lay their hands on the sick, and they will recover."

19 So then the Lord Jesus, after he had spoken to them, was taken up into heaven, and sat down at the right hand of God. [20]And they went forth and preached everywhere, while the Lord worked with them and confirmed the message by the signs that attended it. Amen.

correctly: he is a messenger from God sent to deliver the divine explanation of things. As is usual in biblical narratives, fear is the first response to being in the presence of the divine.

The message of the young man has two main points. First, it makes clear that it is Jesus of Nazareth who is sought, it is he about whom it is said, "He has been raised up." Moreover, that this Jesus is not here is known from the inescapable fact that the tomb is visibly empty. Thus, it is the Jesus of the past fifteen chapters who is raised, and there is no other adequate way to identify the risen person. Thus, his resurrection is tied intimately to the fact that the tomb is empty, as seen by eye-witnesses: how else can the emptiness of the tomb be plausibly explained—for Jesus of Nazareth was truly dead and buried in it?

The second half of the young man's message is a command that the women go to tell the disciples and Peter that Jesus is going ahead of them back to Galilee, where they will see him "just as he told" them. "Just as he told" them is a reference back to Jesus' remark after the Passover supper along the route from the upper room to the Garden of Olives; at a certain moment, Jesus told his disciples that they would scatter when he had been struck, but that, after his being raised up, he would "see them in Galilee." Mark obviously used this remark as a literary "looking beyond" to recall to the reader both the long-term outcome of the crucifixion of Jesus and the certitude of this outcome, no matter what domination men might think they would have over Jesus by killing him. Now, after the crucifixion, this "chip" regarding a reunion in Galilee of the living Jesus and his disciples is about to be called in.

It is a curious point, especially when one considers the contradictory gospel of Luke, that Jesus will see his disciples again "only in Galilee." One draws the conclusion that Mark,

looking back on the Jesus event, saw only Galilee as Jesus'
immediate place of mission, that Mark considered Jesus' visit
to Jerusalem to be only a short stay to which the feast of
Passover had obligated him. Some scholars go further to suggest an anti-Jerusalem sentiment grown up because of the
rejection of Jesus implicit in his being crucified and thus the
word of salvation was withdrawn from there and offered
only, in the first years, in Galilee. Other scholars, using a
less theologically oriented hypothesis, suggest that the safety
of the renewed Christian mission could be more assured in
Galilee than in the Jerusalem which so easily killed Jesus.
Whatever the reason, Mark has no appearance of Jesus in
Jerusalem, but has the disciples return to where the mission
had begun for them, in Galilee. This return to Galilee is, to
be sure, the divine will.

The reaction of the women to this experience must be
interpreted carefully, for things are not quite what they appear. Their two main reactions are flight and silence, the
former a reflection of their bewilderment and trembling and
the latter a result of their fear. One needs to remind oneself
that the women are in a middle period, cut off from Jesus
dead and not yet in the presence of Jesus risen. They receive
a heavenly message from a heavenly messenger, yes, but we
know how often in biblical literature such an encounter
produces a variety of reactions short of joy and peace. One
cannot assume that the women will quickly and smoothly
make the connection between what this young man has just
said and the prophecies Jesus had made earlier about his
resurrection; even when Jesus did predict his resurrection
as the outcome of the crucifixion, attention fixed on his
death and no one understood at all what he meant by "resurrection from the dead." The message, then, is still as mysterious and baffling as it was months ago. Nor is the presence
of the messenger a comfort in all biblical passages; rather

the initial reaction to the messenger is fear, fear owed to a human being's being in the presence of the divine. Finally, if one cannot explain to oneself the empty tomb, the empty tomb becomes a further bewilderment and source of fear; the reaction of the women is one drawn from the facing of elements which suggest another world.

The contrast to the reactions of the women is the reaction of those who actually meet Jesus risen. In practically all cases, the reaction is one of reverence, awe, joy and peace. But the women are not "there" yet; they only hear of something which in itself brings one beyond human experience and up to the edge of that chasm which yawns to the other world which, experienced in darkness and confusion, elicits not joy, but fear. Short of experiencing the reality of the young man's message, the women react only in fear—fear induced by bewilderment and by their knowing that they are in the presence of a divine work which shatters human existence. Like most biblical reactions to the divine presence and action, their reaction is fear and haste to escape. The women's reaction is, in the last analysis, not much different from that, for instance, of the Israelites in the desert who begged Moses to speak with God on their behalf, but who did not want to go themselves "lest they come into God's presence and die." Such was the traditional depiction of the human entering the sphere of the divine.

Does Mark hurt his story by reporting that the women told "no one"? He seems to make them disobedient and their disobedience to result in failure to deliver the message to the disciples. Against the realities of what happened after Jesus' resurrection the silence of the women was no doubt not for long, nor was it injurious to the plan that the disciples meet Jesus in Galilee. What justifies Mark's reporting the way the women reacted is, above all, the fact that they are reacting to a mind-boggling empty tomb and message of resurrection, neither of which they were prepared for, as Mark clearly signaled by the women's words, "Who will roll back the stone for us?" And, as mentioned earlier, their un-preparedness for such an outcome to the death of Jesus goes far back into the gospel where no one had the slightest comprehension (not to mention hope or expectation) of any future resurrection of Jesus once dead.

In the last analysis, Mark is here presenting an experience which is in that limbo between death and resurrection, between knowing the end has occurred and being told by God's messenger that there is a new beginning. Obviously the reader, already a Christian, has gone beyond the stage of the women to experience of and belief in the risen, living Jesus. But it is salutary for a believer to relive that moment between the death and resurrection of Jesus, for one senses like the women the awesomeness of what is about to occur. What is to occur is totally beyond expectation, and, for Mark, totally beyond description. The new life of Jesus can only be talked about or entered into personally; even the experience of Jesus alive for the believer cannot substitute for the actual, personal experience of life after death. Mark, then, has brought the reader to that point, that edge; he looks into the final element of the mystery of Jesus, with fear and bewilderment and trembling. What is this life? Who is this who has gone beyond the limits of human beings, beyond the expectations of his disciples?

Most of all the gospel of Mark is written from the viewpoint of Jesus' contemporaries; all kinds of assessments are made of him, especially in regard to his function on behalf of human beings. Now, disciples, the women, those with him since Galilee, are in the presence of signs which can shatter their human Jesus and which place them before the purest action of God himself. The gospel, then, ends with a story whose tone of fear and confusion and trembling corresponds to and fleshes out the opening line of the gospel: the good news of Jesus messiah, Son of God. Yes, Son of God. It is this which the story reveals about Jesus; it is to this that the women react—without the presence of Jesus, and so with fear and trembling.

It has long been a debate among scholars whether or not Mark ended his gospel at verse 8. Perhaps, the literary style here and the difficulty in understanding such an ending argue that Mark did not intend to end his gospel here, but that he wrote on—only we have lost the rest. This is a possibility, certainly, but two observations are in order. First, practically speaking, whatever is missing cannot be interpreted, nor can even what we have be interpreted properly, for the proper interpretation depends very much on what has been lost. So, it is more profitable to interpret what we have as if it were the true ending of the gospel—if, of course, this kind of ending does make sense. Second, this kind of ending does make sense, as I hope has been made clear above. In its own way, this one story having to do with the resurrection of Jesus is a very good introduction to the mystery and awe of the resurrection; the reactions of the women go far to enhance the sense of being in the presence of an act of God which simply terrifies a person—until one is comforted by the risen Jesus himself.

However, in the history of the gospel's being handed on to Christians, dissatisfaction with the ending of Mark's gospel at v 8 produced a number of tries at writing a more satisfactory ending. One of these, simply put in our Bibles under the title of The Longer Ending and given the verse numbering 9–20, is accepted as canonical, i.e., as having the same status as the rest of Mark's gospel—inspired and deserving the name of sacred scripture. Thus, it is only right

that we explain these verses 9–20, as we have all the previous verses.

Verses 9–20 date from the first century A.D.; thus they
were composed during the period of gospel writing. In the
judgment of most scholars, however, they were not written
by the person who wrote the first sixteen chapters (up to
16:8) of the gospel. How do these scholars know this? The
judgment is based on two sets of comparisons, in which the
Greek language plays a major part. First, one compares the
thought or theology of vv 9–20 with all the previous material of the gospel with the question in mind: How likely
is it that the person who wrote the first sixteen chapters
wrote vv 9–20? Is the thought so different between the two
texts that it is impossible/improbable/unlikely that they were
both written by the same person? Second, one compares the
vocabulary and style of vv 9–20 with the vocabulary and
style of the previous material, again with the question in
mind: How likely is it that the person who wrote the first
sixteen chapters wrote vv 9–20? Is the vocabulary and style
so different between the two texts that it is impossible/im-
probable/unlikely that they were both written by the same
person? Such then is the basic formula for a literary judgment regarding authorship of vv 9–20. The overwhelming
judgment of scholars is that vv 9–20 did not come from the
person who wrote the first sixteen chapters of Mark's gospel.

One can add, in this particular case, two other observations. From a careful look at vv 9–20 one can see how
they could have been composed out of the traditions which
gave birth to the gospels of John and Luke. Moreover, it
would have been likely that, had a person been dissatisfied
with the ending of Mark's gospel at 16:8, he would have
looked to other gospel traditions for information for a better
ending. Thus, one begins to support a thesis that Luke and

John had an influence in the writing of vv 9–20—and it is most unlikely that either Luke or John had influenced the writing of the first sixteen chapters of Mark's gospel. Further, one can see how vv 9–20 answer questions that the gospel raises about the continuation of the mission of the disciples and how they add other valuable teaching as well, and so it appears that it is a remedy to something missing, rather than a part of the original text which was, for some inexplicable reason, removed to reduce the gospel text back to an ending at 16:8. Such, then, is the way of thinking used by scholars to answer the question of the relationship between vv 9–20 and the rest of the gospel of Mark.

Jesus is named in vv 9–20 only in v 19; this means that one is to draw meaning for all the pronouns from the mention of Jesus' name in v 6. Given that v 9 starts from a different perspective than the perspective visible in the story of 16:1–8, it is awkward that Jesus' name is missing for so long.

Verse 9 seems to intend to clarify certain points that the earlier account had left obscure or unspoken. For instance, earlier the young man at the tomb had said, "He has been raised up." Now, the writer indicates that Jesus "rose," thus losing the emphasis that the resurrection is worked by God. Also, the writer indicates that Jesus appeared first "to Mary Magdalene," and thus passes over the mention of the other two women; are they to be assumed as present because they had only recently been mentioned? Mary is here described for the first and only time in Mark's gospel as one "from whom seven demons had been driven." It seems that this information may have come from Luke's sources (cf Lk 8:2). Finally, Mary here is recorded as actually seeing Jesus (with no mention made of the young man at the tomb) and as reporting this to those associated with Jesus and now grieving and weeping. All this is a clear advancement on the text of 16:1–8.

The major statement of these verses 9–11 is a shift from concentration on the three women and their tomb experience to a report, the first of three, which indicates that no one believed Mary's attestation that "he lives and was seen by her." In v 8, the women had reacted with fear and trembling and confusion, but only here is emphasis begun on not believing the report of one who knows the truth from eyewitness that he lives.

This theme of contrast between an eye-witness report and unbelief continues with a second example, the basis of which reminds one of the fuller story of the two disciples who met Jesus, at first unrecognizable, on the way to Emmaus (Lk 24). In Mark's gospel the two disciples report their encounter with the living Jesus, only to have their witness rejected by "the rest."

A third situation is described: it is the meeting at a dinner between the living Jesus and the eleven, a meeting which is notable for its two major elements. First, Jesus chastises the eleven for their lack of faith in the words of witnesses. The writer often is not sparing of the reputation the eleven gained in the early church, if, through them, he can highlight a major difficulty in the Christian experience. Here he underlines the difficulty of accepting truths from God, even for the most intimate disciples of Jesus who had been given, according to the gospel, ample warning of the events now brought to completion. Through their example, the writer hopes that the reader *can* bridge by faith the kind of gap they failed to bridge because they could not believe. The writer explicitly notes that the basis of the eleven's reaction to the resurrection witnesses is "lack of faith" and "hardheartedness." It is against these two evils that he has aimed his account so far, and one must admit that his theme corresponds to what Mark had underlined in his gospel, when, on many occasions, he has Jesus criticize his disciples, if not for hardness of heart, certainly for lack of faith and understanding. The gospel concern, to shake the reader into a greater faith and trust and awareness of the full meaning of the Lord he serves, has dictated a great portion of the way in which the Jesus story has been told.

The second part of Jesus' appearance to his eleven at dinner (should we assume that this dinner is being held in Galilee?) is dedicated to a missioning of the eleven to continue the work of Jesus. Thus, we can say immediately that the subsequent Christian movement had its origin only in Jesus; it was the idea or plan of no other person. The essence of the work of the eleven is to be announcing the good news, the content of which "good news" is clear from the gospel. Unlike Jesus, who himself had preached the good news that the kingdom of God was at hand, the eleven are to go through the entire world, and to every creature; again, we are faced with the apparent intention of God that Jesus preach in Palestine (indeed, to Galilee of Palestine) and others to the rest of the world. The immediate impression is that Jesus is talking here about geography, but eventually it became clear that he was talking also about "all time, as long as this age lasts." Thus, the preaching is to go everywhere, and to go on always, as well.

Belief and baptism, which is the formal and public profession of one's belief, result in salvation—nothing less— from the destruction that will destroy this age. Not to believe (and this seems to be a person who has heard and not believed) is to remain a part of this age which is meant to be destroyed. Jesus then cites certain wondrous things which will accompany those who believe, each of which, we learn from other books of the New Testament, was witnessed to in later Christian life. Driving out demons, by the authority of the name of Jesus, is mentioned first. As noted much earlier, there is little else that can be seen at this period of history to entail greater power and authority than domination over the evil spirits from which no man could free himself. It is Satan himself who is being checked by this power, a checking which is carefully ascribed to Jesus himself, though the apparent exorcist is the disciple. To exorcise "in the name of Jesus" is not just to recall a past person to the demons; it is a call upon the living Jesus to work the exorcism himself, again.

The speaking in new tongues may well be a wonder, not because new languages were difficult to learn, but because they signaled the success of the movement of Christianity through the whole world. But perhaps "new tongues" is here a reference not to new human languages, but to the gift of speaking in tongues enjoyed, for instance, in Paul's earlier communities like that at Corinth and preeminently by the twelve at Pentecost.

Other wonders, too, are testified as happening to believers: safety from poisonous snakes, drinking poisoned liquids without harm, and finally healing the sick. Wonders, then, of various orders of creation are consequent upon union with creation's God. This harmony, so obviously missing in a world created for human beings by God and at odds with human beings even to death, is now for a time restored: signs of God's oneness with his world again and to the world, at least the believing world, of its oneness with him, again.

Once the words Jesus spoke to his disciples are recorded, the writer moves swiftly to his conclusion. Jesus, now identified as Lord, is described as "taken up to heaven," a description common to a number of early Christian traditions. Our writer adds that Jesus was seated at God's right

hand, the position of power assigned to that "lord" of whom
David sang (as Jesus himself had reminded us):

> The Lord (Yahweh) said to my lord:
> "Sit at my right hand,
> till I put your enemies as your footstool."

This lord of David was, by Jesus' time, recognized as the
messiah, and so Jesus, the messiah of the gospel, has reached
the place reserved for him by the plan of God himself. Indeed, using another imagery, the Son of Man, having undergone the expected humiliation and suffering that God
foresaw, now lives in glory and power and awaits the judgment on those who unjustly condemned him. Those who
hear of Jesus and refuse to believe in him will share in this
condemnation.

While Jesus is taken up, the disciples move out to their
assignment "everywhere," always accompanied by the Lord
who works with them and supports their preaching by great
signs.

The vista which is left open to the reader at the end of
v 20 is strikingly different from that left open to the reader
at the end of v 8. Each ending, however, has its contribution
to make to the reader as he puts down the gospel of Mark.
With the one, he has been led to the brink of that greatest
evidence for the identity of Jesus, his Lord; with the other,
he has been shown the beginnings of that great and powerful
movement, the power of which he has himself felt and been
moved to join. Both endings bring one to see that the plan
of God for human beings was to bring all people into union
with the Son, who is the good news Mark wants his story
to proclaim. It is a story, then, which is ultimately aimed at

encouraging one to believe ever more firmly and to seek ever more diligently for the ultimate truth about Jesus, the messiah and Son of God.

Conclusion

We must take a moment here to underline for a last time what has been stressed, I hope not beyond limit, throughout this commentary. If we are brought to the events of Jesus' life, we are brought to them only through Mark's story-telling. We cannot get to these events any other way. This means also that we can get to events only if Mark tells us about them and only to the degree that he tells us about them. In a sense, we can say that we are at the author's mercy. This does not mean that the events, once we relive them even though through Mark's story-telling, cannot tell us more than Mark intends to tell us. The meaning that an author intends to convey and the meaning of a narrated event are not always identical. Yet we must recognize how dependent we are on the author, who, in his turn, is constantly telling stories in such a way as to influence his reader according to his own intentions and purposes. To forget that stories are structured to influence the reader in some way is to lose awareness of the nature of the material in which the reader has let himself become engaged. Thus, though I was reluctant to keep repeating the point through the commentary, I underline here the fact that one cannot forget: when the text says "Jesus did . . ." one must always remember that he is being told by an author, for his own intentions, "Jesus did . . ."

At various stages of the commentary time was taken to show how this or that story or saying exemplified one or more of the five purposes for which the gospel was written. These five purposes are described in the Introduction and are only repeated summarily here: to show that Jesus was not executed justly, to suggest that a different interpretation of Jesus' life is called for, to bring forward the question as to why Jesus had to suffer and die, to make clear that discipleship entailed cross-carrying, and to explain why Christianity of Mark's time differed on certain fundamental questions from traditional Judaism. The bulk of the Marcan gospel, however, centers on the person of Jesus and his identity and this centering is looked at from the perspective of those who met Jesus. He is the mystery and he is their mystery to solve. In particular, however, there seems to be one concern in Mark's story-telling which derives, not from the search of Jesus' contemporaries for his meaning, but from the needs of Jesus' disciples of 65 A.D. to handle a peculiarity of their lives.

For many scholars, the gospel of Mark intends to strengthen Christians of Rome and its environs against persecution. Mark means to achieve this goal by telling of the story of Jesus; it is through a diligent vicarious participation in various moments of Jesus' life, particularly when he was under persecution, that this strength is to be found. In various ways the gospel offers help to the persecuted. Jesus is a model of the just man treated unjustly, yet responding only with patience and trust in God. Jesus' words indicate that suffering is only to be expected for his disciple, but that this suffering is a premier way to the fullness of life. Jesus has entered this fullness of life as the first of us; thus, what was only a forecast in earlier generations is now accomplished for Jesus and assured to his followers.

Most particularly, the Jesus whom the disciple follows

is revealed to be the mighty and wise Lord who dominates all creation, including demons and nature's wind and sea. He is the one who by far knows best the mind and intentions of God. No one is his equal in power and wisdom, for there was never a power too great for him or a problem too difficult for him. Indeed, on more than one occasion God himself witnessed to Jesus as his Son, and finally performed a work for Jesus before which human beings stand in awe and fear.

The gospel of Mark, then, offers strength and encouragement to the disciple through a careful telling of what happened to Jesus, through the words and deeds of Jesus, and through his fate.

Behind the reality of suffering being faced, whether of the disciple or of Jesus himself, is the question as to why one, especially one dear to God, must suffer. The gospel does not raise this question explicitly, yet deals with it constantly. The reason that this question permeates the gospel comes from the fact that the Christians follow a Jesus they call the messiah. To call Jesus the messiah, or Christ, and to call oneself Christian, suggests, at first blush, that one has identified Jesus as that one who by definition is to bring this pain-ridden age to an end and inaugurate the eternally joyous new age, the "new heavens and new earth." Yet, this is just what Jesus did not do; this definition of messiah Jesus did not fulfill. Indeed, how could Jesus, granted he did some things which made one think he might be the messiah— how could Jesus be finally called the messiah when he died so impotently and humiliatingly and, when all is said and done, so foolishly?

The reader of Mark's gospel, unlike the disciples within the book, knows that Jesus rose from the dead, and through this means has come to believe that the events of Calvary do not tell the whole story. But the real significance of Calvary is not always grasped, even by those who believe in Jesus and particularly by those who, for the first time, must face their own Calvary. Thus, Mark rehearses for his own contemporaries the life of Jesus as it unfolded before Jesus' own first disciples.

In his own time, though not all had the same perception of the identity of Jesus, most recognized "God in him." The few who did not are shown to deny "God in him" for no legitimate reason, but because of jealousy or some unworthy motive. The few particularly attached to Jesus after a while called him the messiah, for this is what his words and actions throughout Galilee meant to them. But it is right here that Jesus himself takes exception. He finds the title a good description—provided that those who call him this understand properly the limited place of power and wisdom in this title. It is his life and person which must give definition to the term messiah; it is not he who must fit pre-developed definition. In fact, the New Testament never came to one satisfactory title which did total justice to the person its constituency embraced. His power and wisdom is that of the messiah—and of someone even greater; but to define as the messiah one who will always overcome all evil by his power and wisdom is to misunderstand the definition God has given to his messiah.

Thus, after a number of stories which do reveal the immense power of Jesus, Mark tells many more stories which underline the suffering aspect of the messiah's life. Indeed, to such an extent is this suffering dominant in the life of the messiah that he does not do the one thing most expected of him, the changing of this age into the age to come. Yes, he has entered the age to come, but only through death. He has not removed the most significant element of this age, for all must still die, and there are many other painful characteristics of this age which he has not removed or lessened; indeed, in terms of human happiness, one might say that Jesus changed nothing, that whatever improvements have occurred are due to human invention. Why then call him the messiah?

It is Mark's contention that Jesus will return someday to save his followers from the destruction of this age, to lead them into the age to come. Thus, the work traditionally assigned to the messiah will be done; it simply must be admitted that it was not done the first time he came to earth. But how explain this "first time" that the messiah came among human beings? What purpose did he serve then?

First of all, out of his suffering came redemption, the "buying back" of the multitudes; once this act was understood as a primary step toward assuring human beings of a happiness they would never have by their own merits, one saw this as truly a messianic work. But underneath this is a second consideration. Though Jesus came with messianic power and wisdom, he defined his own role as calling people to repentance. It is in this appeal to a free conversion or return to God that Jesus' total mission, except for the death which redeemed the multitudes, consisted. It is this freely accepted repentance that God seeks whether the messianic power and wisdom be manifested or not. It is the will of human beings that God wants, that human will which lies at the heart of all the ills of this age, including death. The human solution to suffering is that God change the circumstances of this world so that people can be safe and free and happy. The divine solution begins elsewhere. God wants human beings to change their hearts as the prelude to that reunion with him from which will flow in time all the good gifts that will make up happiness.

The messiah came, then, to reverse the evil of this world in its cause; as Adam had brought death and corruption through sin, so human beings must begin the elimination of them through love of God and neighbor. The peculiarity of God's plan is that the messiah himself must live this life of love; not only must he preach it, but he must live it—to the end. Thus, the lesson of life is not only in words, but in the very life of God's messiah.

A great mystery of life lies in the fact that though one has repented, one still must live out this age to the bitter end, which is death; there is no other way to enter the age to come. One must face temptations, attempt victories, and thus suffer through to life everlasting. The messiah, the most beloved of all, must live life this way as well, and it is Mark's intention to write the life of Jesus so that one can find therein how life is to be lived, as well as comprehend why life is the way it is and why Jesus' view of suffering is the truth.

Finally, and perhaps most fundamentally, it is the person of Jesus which must be plumbed and understood, for it soon becomes apparent that beyond his analysis of life is his own mysterious person which not only legitimates his message but calls for a total devotion. Prophet, John the Baptist, Elijah—these were some of the estimates about the identity of Jesus. The closest disciples, on the basis of the first half of Mark's book, called Jesus the messiah. It is Mark, however, who, as author, has the last word, or, perhaps it is best to say, the last suggestion. Mark begins his work with his own profession that Jesus is the messiah and Son of God. From the increasing penetration into the facets of Jesus' person, one gets the impression that something more than the one who is to begin the new age is here. The conclusion of the gospel is not a word, but an event: we are placed beyond death, at the entrance to the greatest of mysteries about Jesus. Everyone looked forward to messianic power and wisdom, and many eventually sensed and recognized it, but no one was ready for the revelation of Jesus drawn from the

twin truths, that his life could be a ransom for the multitudes
and that he was raised up and "will go ahead of you to Galilee where he will meet you." Mark began his work with a
double profession, that Jesus was the messiah and Son of
God. Power and wisdom revealed his messiahship; the resurrection made clear what pulses through the events of Jesus' life, that he is Son of God. It is this title that finally does
the best justice to the mystery of Jesus, for it brings the
reader to realize that here inexpressibly is the divine presence itself. It is this person whom Mark gives to his reader,
particularly for his consolation and his model.

Suggested Further Reading

Achtemeier, Paul. *Mark* (2nd ed). Philadelphia: Fortress Press, 1986 (Proclamation Commentaries).

Donahue, John. *The Theology and Setting of Discipleship in the Gospel of Mark*. Milwaukee, Marquette University, 1981.

Lane, William. *The Gospel According to Mark*. Grand Rapids, Eerdmans, 1974.

Matera, Frank. *What Are They Saying About Mark?* Mahwah, Paulist Press, 1987.

Rhoades, David and Michie, Donald. *Mark as Story: An Introduction to the Narrative of a Gospel*. Philadelphia, Fortress Press, 1982.

Schenke, Ludger. *Glory and the Way of the Cross: The Gospel of Mark*. Chicago, Franciscan Herald Press, 1982.

Stock, Augustine. *Call to Discipleship: A Literary Study of Mark's Gospel*. Wilmington, Michael Glazier, 1982.

Taylor, Vincent. *The Gospel According to Mark: The Greek Text with Introduction, Notes and Indexes* (2nd ed). New York, St. Martin's Press, 1966.